DOING SENSORY ETHNOGRAPHY

SAGE
50
YEARS

SARAH PINK

DOING SENSORY ETHNOGRAPHY

2ND EDITION

Los Angeles | London | New Delhi
Singapore | Washington DC

Los Angeles | London | New Delhi
Singapore | Washington DC

SAGE Publications Ltd
1 Oliver's Yard
55 City Road
London EC1Y 1SP

SAGE Publications Inc.
2455 Teller Road
Thousand Oaks, California 91320

SAGE Publications India Pvt Ltd
B 1/I 1 Mohan Cooperative Industrial Area
Mathura Road
New Delhi 110 044

SAGE Publications Asia-Pacific Pte Ltd
3 Church Street
#10-04 Samsung Hub
Singapore 049483

Editor: Jai Seaman
Assistant editor: Lily Mehrbod
Production editor: Ian Antcliff
Copyeditor: Andy Baxter
Proofreader: Sharon Cawood
Indexer: David Rudeforth
Marketing manager: Sally Ransom
Cover design: Francis Kenney
Typeset by: C&M Digitals (P) Ltd, Chennai, India
Printed in Great Britain by
CPI Group (UK) Ltd, Croydon, CR0 4YY

First published 2009

Library of Congress Control Number: 2014943844

British Library Cataloguing in Publication data

A catalogue record for this book is available from the British Library

ISBN 978-1-4739-0595-5
ISBN 978-1-4462-8759-0 (pbk)

Contents

Acknowledgements

Doing Sensory Ethnography is the outcome of several years of research projects, reflections, discussions and readings and experiences of the work of other academics and artists. Without the people who have participated in my research projects, institutions, audiences, authors and practitioners who have supported my work, commented on presentations and articles, and worked as scholars and practitioners in this field, this book would have been impossible to write. Some research participants are mentioned in this book, others have chosen to remain anonymous, but to all I am enormously grateful for their enthusiasm to be involved in my work.

My sensory ethnography research emerged from two projects developed with Unilever Research in 1999–2000, a collaboration that led to my book *Home Truths* (2004) which outlines the notion of the sensory home. My *The Future of Visual Anthropology* (2006) consolidated some of my ideas about the senses in anthropology and began to shape some of the ideas expanded on here. My subsequent publications about Slow Cities in the UK, Spain and Australia all engage (with) the senses for thinking through questions relating to research environments and participants *and* to understanding the approach of the movement itself. This research was during different stages of its development funded by the Faculty of Social Sciences and Humanities at Loughborough University, a Nuffield Foundation small grant and RMIT University in Australia and hosted by the IN3 at the Open University of Catalonia in Barcelona. Other research discussed in this book has been undertaken with colleagues through my CI roles in the 'Lower Effort Energy Demand Reduction' project (LEEDR), based at Loughborough University, funded by the Engineering and Physical Sciences Research Council (UK) through the UK Research Councils' Digital Economy and Energy programmes (grant number EP/I000267/1), and the 'Management of OSH in Networked Systems of Production or Service Delivery: Comparisons between Healthcare, Construction and Logistic' project funded by the Institution of Occupational Safety and Health (IOSH), UK. For further information about the LEEDR project, collaborating research groups and industrial partners, please visit www.leedr-project.co.uk.

I have collaborated, talked and corresponded with many colleagues and co-researchers and corresponded with people about sensory ethnography. I thank everyone who has engaged with me in this field and am especially grateful to colleagues and co-authors who have joined me in projects, including: LEEDR colleagues, in particular Kerstin Leder Mackley, Roxana Morosanu, Val Mitchell, Tracy Bhamra and Richard Buswell; IOSH colleagues, in particular Jennie Morgan, Andrew Dainty and Alistair Gibb; Yolande Strengers with whom I have developed our standby consumption research at RMIT; and Lisa Servon and Tania Lewis who have respectively joined me in two Slow City projects in Spain and Australia. I am also especially grateful to the colleagues with whom it has been fantastic to think and work over the last years, and who have definitely helped to shape my thinking about the senses and to affirm that thinking about the senses is a good idea, especially: Elisenda Ardevol and Debora Lanzeni at the IN3 in Barcelona; my colleagues based in Sweden – Vaike Fors, Tom O'Dell, Martin Berg, Robert Willim and Asa Backstrom – for the work we have done together and all the ideas we have discussed over the last years. This second edition of *Doing Sensory Ethnography* has also been influenced by my research focus on design and futures which has grown since I moved to Australia in 2012, and has been nurtured by my collaborations with Yoko Akama and Juan Francisco Salazar.

While this book is independently written, some of the ideas and examples have been introduced in earlier articles. Earlier versions of the idea of ethnography as place-making have been developed in 'Walking with video' published in *Visual Studies* (Pink, 2007d) and 'An urban tour: the sensory sociality of ethnographic place-making' published in *Ethnography* (Pink, 2008b); selected examples from these articles are also discussed here.

About the author

Sarah Pink is Professor of Design and Media Ethnography at RMIT University, Australia. She has Visiting Professorships in Applied Cultural Analysis at Halmstad University, Sweden, and in Social Sciences, in the Schools of Civil and Building Engineering and Design at Loughborough University, UK. She is known internationally for her work relating to sensory, visual and digital methodology. Her most recent works in this area include the *Energy and Digital Living* website (2014) and the books *Doing Visual Ethnography* (2013), *Ethnographic Research in the Construction Industry* (co-ed., 2013), *Situating Everyday Life* (2012) and *Advances in Visual Methodology* (ed. 2012). Her research is usually interdisciplinary and is both funded by research councils, and developed collaboratively with research partners.

Introduction

About *Doing Sensory Ethnography*

In *Doing Sensory Ethnography* I outline a way of thinking about and doing ethnography that takes as its starting point the multisensoriality of experience, perception, knowing and practice. Sensory ethnography is used across scholarly, practice-based and applied disciplines. It develops an approach to the world and to research that accounts for how sensory ways of experiencing and knowing are integral both to the lives of people who participate in our research *and* to how we ethnographers practise our craft.

Ethnographers, from a range of different disciplines, are increasingly accounting for and commenting on the multisensoriality of the ethnographic process. As I wrote the first edition of this book in the first decade of the twenty-first century, interdisciplinary academic conferences, seminars and arts events were simultaneously building on other recent explorations of the senses in relation to a plethora of different aspects of individual social and cultural experiences. These and other explorations are now being materialised into a new literature that accounts for the senses across the social sciences and humanities. In the half decade between the publication of that first edition of *Doing Sensory Ethnography* and this second edition there has been an explosion in scholarship and practice around the senses, across social science, humanities and arts disciplines including human geography, design, film and photography, anthropology, sociology and a range of interdisciplinary fields including cultural and media studies, education studies and health studies. Indeed, a sensory approach can be applied to most projects that involve human experience and practical activity. That does not mean that all ethnography should be done explicitly through the senses, but that to be theoretically and methodologically equipped to engage with the world sensorially is a key skill to own.

This book responds to the discussions and proposals that emerge from existing literature and practice, and draws on examples from my own and other scholars' and practitioners' experiences of doing ethnography with attention to the senses across domestic, urban and organisational environments. The central theme and task of the book is to establish a methodology for *Doing Sensory Ethnography*. It differs from other books that account for the senses in ethnography, in a number of ways, notably because it is interdisciplinary. It moreover goes beyond simply playing the role of advocate for a sensory approach, demonstrating how we can learn through attending to the senses or showing how we might study the senses. *Doing Sensory Ethnography* instead offers an approach to doing and representing research. It proposes a way of thinking about doing ethnography through the senses.

A focus on methodology leads to the question of what 'bigger picture' is emerging that takes sensory ethnography beyond just studying the senses or using our own senses to study other people's worlds. It is important that we understand how knowledge and ways of knowing are produced, what particular qualities and types of knowledge are currently emerging and the implications of this for how researchers, artists, designers or policy makers comprehend the world and intervene in it, and how futures are imagined and made. To do this we need to understand the implications of particular research methodologies for how we research, account for and potentially participate in change-making. By drawing together contemporary scholarship and practice concerned with the senses in ethnography I show how what has been called the 'sensory turn' is part of a wider shift in how we might understand the world, and that this has implications for how we might intervene in the world – as designers, artists, activists, by influencing policy, as educators or through other forms of action. These turns are also increasingly orienting scholarship towards the future, in impulses towards the development of ethnography that along with design is change-making.

While most of the earlier 'sensory ethnographies', as well as much of my own work, were rooted in social anthropology, the reach and relevance of *Doing Sensory Ethnography* reflects the growing interest in the senses across disciplines. Its theoretical commitments to concepts of place, memory, imagination, improvisation and intervention reach out to ideas and practices developed across the social sciences and humanities. Moreover, these theoretical themes consistently resonate though the work of researchers concerned with the senses across scholarly and practice-based disciplines. Indeed, my research for this book has traversed diverse 'ethnographic' scholarly and practice-based disciplines and interdisciplinary areas of study. It has also introduced me to new academic, applied and arts practices. The work of some scholars has emerged as outstanding illustrations of how sensory ethnography might be done, and I return to their examples across the chapters. In writing the second edition of this book I encountered a much deeper wealth of literature and practice around the senses than was available for its 2009 edition. Yet, still many ethnographers (whose work demonstrates so well the significance of the senses in culture and society) have neglected to write about the processes through which they came to these understandings. In this vein I would urge contemporary ethnographers, artists and designers who engage with the senses to be more explicit about the ways of experiencing and knowing that become central to their ethnographies, to share with others the senses of place they felt as they sought to occupy similar places to those of their research participants, and to acknowledge the processes through which their sensory knowing has become part of their scholarship or practice. This is not a call for an excess of reflexivity above the need for ethnographers to represent the findings of their research. Rather, in a context where interest in the senses is increasing across disciplines, it is more a question of sharing knowledge about practice.

When preparing this book I was faced with a choice. I could either approach sensory ethnography through an exploration of practical activity conceived as multisensorial and emplaced, or I could examine in turn how different sensory modalities might be engaged and/or attended to in the ethnographic process. The book is structured through a series of chapters that each address issues and questions relating to ethnographic approaches, practices and methods, rather than by discussing sensory categories chapter by chapter. The decision to develop the narrative in this way is based on both a theoretical commitment to understanding the senses as interconnected and not always possible to understand as if separate categories, and a methodological focus on the role of subjectivity and experience in ethnography. This is in contrast to many recent ethnographic discussions of sensory experience (including my own – Pink, 2004), the use of the senses in ethnography (Atkinson et al., 2007) and even a book series (*Sensory Formations*, Berg Publishers), where discussions are structured through reference to different sensory modalities or categories.

Because researchers often focus on one or another sensory modality or category in their analyses, I discuss plenty of examples of sensory ethnography practice concerned with mainly smell, taste, touch or vision. Indeed, in particular research contexts one sensory modality might be verbalised or otherwise referred to more frequently than others, and might serve as a prism through which to understand multisensory experiences (Fors et al., 2013). Nevertheless, this does not mean that the experience the ethnographer is attending to is only related to that one category or to just one sense organ. Rather, the idea of a sensory ethnography advanced here is based on an understanding of the senses as interconnected and interrelated.

Doing Sensory Ethnography is presented through this Introduction, eight chapters and an Afterword. Chapter 1 both defines sensory ethnography, situates it in relation to debates about how ethnography 'should' be done, and sets the interdisciplinary scene for the book. I explore the historical development of the focus on the senses in the key academic and applied disciplines where it is represented. This discussion identifies key debates, themes and convergences within and across these areas, providing a necessary backdrop against which to understand the developments discussed in later chapters, and in particular through which to situate ethnographic examples in relation to historical and disciplinary trajectories.

Chapter 2 establishes the principles of a sensory ethnography and the theoretical commitments of the book. It examines a set of key concepts that inform the idea of a sensory ethnography though a consideration of existing thought and debates concerning sensory experience, perception and knowing. These fundamental questions, which are embedded in debates that are themselves not totally resolved, inform not only how ethnographers comprehend the lives of others, but also how they understand their own research practices. Here I also propose understanding sensory ethnography through a theory of place and place-making, and outline the significance of memory and imagination in the ethnographic process. The conceptual tools presented in Chapter 2 inform the analytical strand of the following chapters.

Chapter 3 takes a necessarily more practical approach to the doing of sensory ethnography. Here I identify and discuss how ethnographers might prepare for and anticipate some of the issues and practices that are particular to an approach to ethnography that both seeks out knowledge about the senses and uses the senses as a route to knowledge. In doing so I explore the reflexivity demanded by this approach and argue for an appreciation of the subjectivity and intersubjectivity of the sensory ethnography process.

Chapters 4 and 5 follow conventional ethnographic methodology texts in that they are dedicated to 'ethnographic interviewing' and 'participant observation' respectively. However, the purpose of these chapters is to challenge, revise and rethink both of these established ethnographic practices through the senses. In doing so I draw from my own work and a series of examples from the work of other ethnographers who attend to the senses to both review the theoretical and practical concerns that have grown around these methods and to suggest re-conceptualising them through sensory methodologies. Chapter 6 continues in this revisionary vein. Here I examine the role digital technologies might play in a multisensory approach to ethnography. First, I outline how we might go about understanding the sensory affordances and qualities of digital media as part of the very digital–material–sensory worlds in which we research. I then discuss how we might harness them for sensory ethnography practice. I discuss how digital visual and audio methods and media are being used to research sensory experience, knowledge and practice across the social sciences and humanities, as well as potential uses of locative and body-monitoring technologies in ethnography. Chapters 4, 5 and 6 also respond to and develop further the understanding of the relationship between ethnography and place introduced in Chapter 2.

Chapter 7 approaches the issue of analysis in sensory ethnography. This is a question that (given the messiness of the ethnographic process and the frequent impossibility of distinguishing analysis as a separate stage from research or representation) some would be forgiven for thinking might be redundant. Accounting for this problem I suggest thinking of analysis as a way of making ethnographic places. Analysis might be variously situated in the ethnographic process and not always distinguishable from other activities. It is indeed as sensorial a process as the research itself: a context where sensory memories and imaginaries are at their full force as the ethnographer draws relationships between the experiential field of the research and the scholarly practices of academia.

Chapter 8 discusses how the multisensory realities of ethnographers' and research participants' lives might be represented. Here I explore how representations might be developed to communicate something of both the ethnographer's own experiences and those of the people participating in the research, to their audiences, while simultaneously making a contribution to scholarship. This investigation both reviews existing sensory representation within academic contexts and goes beyond academia to explore sensory arts practice.

This edition of the book ends with a brief Afterword, where I draw together some of the themes of *Doing Sensory Ethnography* to reflect on the implications of design, intervention and future-focused research and practice for sensory ethnography.

This book is programmatic in that it argues for, and indeed undertakes, a systematic thinking through of the theoretical, methodological and practical elements that a sensory approach to ethnography might engage. Nevertheless, *Doing Sensory Ethnography* is not intended to be prescriptive. Rather, I suggest how a sensory ethnographic process might be understood and how it might be achieved and in doing so discuss a wide range of examples of existing practice. I do not propose a 'how to' account of doing ethnography with the senses in mind, but a framework for a sensory ethnography that can serve as a reference point for future developments and creativity. Like any 'type' of ethnography, ultimately a sensory approach cannot simply be learnt from a book, but will be developed through the ethnographer's engagement with her or his environment. Therefore, at the end of this journey through the chapters the reader should not expect to have learnt *how to* do sensory ethnography. Rather, I hope that she or he will feel inspired to build on the exciting and innovative practice of others. The existing literature now offers a strong basis from which to reflect on the possibilities and opportunities afforded by an ethnographic methodology that attends to the senses in its epistemology and its practices of research, analysis and representation.

1

Rethinking ethnography through the senses

ONE

Situating sensory ethnography

From academia to intervention

In this chapter I situate sensory ethnography as a field of scholarship and practice. I first outline the characteristics of sensory ethnography. I discuss its relationship to and growth out of other inflections in ethnographic practice, and identify its continuities and departures from existing ethnographic methodologies. I then locate it in relation to the intellectual and practical trajectories of discipline-specific scholarship and applied research. I focus on the disciplines of anthropology, human geography and sociology and on the practice of applied ethnography, art and design. Finally, I consider the potential of sensory ethnography in interdisciplinary scholarship and practice.

INTRODUCTION: SENSORIALITY

Doing Sensory Ethnography investigates the possibilities afforded by attending to the senses in ethnographic research and representation. An acknowledgement that sensoriality is fundamental to how we learn about, understand and represent other people's lives is increasingly central to academic and applied practice in the social sciences and humanities. It is part of how we understand our past, how we engage with our present and how we imagine our futures. This appreciation, which David Howes has referred to as a 'sensorial turn' (2003: xii), has been couched in terms of an anthropology of the senses (Howes, 1991a), sensuous scholarship (Stoller, 1997), sensuous geography (Rodaway, 1994), sociology of the senses (Simmel, 1997 [1907]; Low, 2005; Back, 2009; Lyon and Back, 2012; Vannini et al., 2012), the senses in communication and interaction (Finnegan, 2002), the sensorium and arts practice (Jones, 2006a; Zardini, 2005), the sensoriality of film (MacDougall, 1998, 2005; Marks, 2000), a cultural history of the senses (Classen, 1993, 1998), the sensuous nature of the 'tourist encounter' (Crouch and Desforges, 2003) or of medical practice (Edvardsson and Street, 2007; Hindmarsh and Pilnick, 2007; Lammer, 2007), sensory design and architecture (Malnar and Vodvarka, 2004; Pallasmaa, 2005 [1999]), attention to the senses in material culture studies (e.g. Tilley, 2006) and in performance studies (Hahn, 2007), in branding (Lindstrom, 2005), the 'multi-modality' paradigm (Kress and Van Leeuwen, 2001), archaeology (e.g. Levy et al., 2004; Witmore, 2004), history (Classen, 1998; Cowan and Steward, 2007) and within the notion of 'complex ethnography' (Atkinson et al., 2007).

The approach to sensory ethnography advocated here does not need to be owned by any one academic discipline. Instead, across these fields of study scholars are creating new paths in academic debate through the theoretical exploration of sensory experience, perception, sociality, knowing, knowledge, practice and culture (e.g. Ingold, 2000; Thrift, 2004; Howes, 2005a; Pink and Howes, 2010; Ingold and Howes, 2011). The debates and arguments inspired by these literatures are shaping academic scholarship, empirical studies, interventions and futures across a broad range of substantive areas. They inform how researchers represent their findings in conventional written and audiovisual texts and in innovative forms designed to communicate about sensory experience. They also have implications for ethnographic methodology.

WHAT IS SENSORY ETHNOGRAPHY?

Uses of the term 'ethnography' refer to a range of qualitative research practices, employed, with varying levels of theoretical engagement, in academic and applied research contexts. Ethnographic practice tends to include participant observation, ethnographic interviewing and a range of other collaborative research techniques that are often developed and adapted in context and as appropriate to the needs and possibilities afforded by specific research projects. There is now no standard way of doing ethnography that is universally practised. In this context Paul Atkinson, Sara Delamont and William Housley have suggested that there has been a shift from the 'classic' emphasis on 'holism, context and similar ideas' to the increasing fragmentation of ethnographic research. They moreover claim this has led to a situation where 'different authors adopt and promote specific approaches to the collection and analysis of data' and 'particular kinds of data become celebrated in the process' (2007: 33).

Sensory ethnography as proposed in this book is certainly not just another route in an increasingly fragmented map of approaches to ethnographic practice. Rather, it is a critical methodology which, like my existing work on visual ethnography (Pink, 2013), departs from the classic observational approach promoted by Atkinson et al. (2007) to insist that ethnography is a reflexive and experiential process through which academic and applied understanding, knowing and knowledge are produced. Indeed, as Regina Bendix argued, to research 'sensory perception and reception' requires methods that 'are capable of grasping "the most profound type of knowledge [which] is not spoken of at all and thus inaccessible to ethnographic observation or interview" (Bloch, 1998: 46)' (Bendix, 2000: 41). Thus sensory ethnography discussed in this book does not privilege any one type of data or research method. Rather, it is open to multiple ways of knowing and to the exploration of and reflection on new routes to knowledge. Indeed, it would be erroneous to see sensory ethnography as a method for data collection at all: in this book I do not use the term 'data' to refer to the ways of knowing and understanding that are produced through ethnographic practice.

To reiterate the definition of ethnography I have suggested elsewhere:

> as a process of creating and representing knowledge or ways of knowing that are based on ethnographers' own experiences and the ways these intersect with the persons, places and things encountered during that process. Therefore visual ethnography, as I interpret it, does not claim to produce an objective or truthful account of reality, but should aim to offer versions of ethnographers' experiences of reality that are as loyal as possible to the context, the embodied, sensory and affective experiences, and the negotiations and intersubjectivities through which the knowledge was produced. (Pink, 2013: 35)

Atkinson et al. have suggested that what they term 'post-modern' approaches to ethnography have 'devalued systematic analysis of action and representations, while privileging rather vague ideas of experience, evocation and personal engagement' (2007: 35). In my view, an acknowledgment of the importance of these experiential and evocative elements of ethnography is in fact essential, but a lack of attention to the practices and material cultures of research participants is not its automatic corollary. Moreover, while the concept of experience has unquestionably become central to ethnographic practice, recent methodological approaches to experience in ethnography are far from vague. Rather, they have begun to interrogate this concept (see Throop, 2003; Pink, 2006; Pickering, 2008; Pink, 2008c) to consider its relevance in social anthropology and cultural studies. These points are taken further in Chapter 2.

What ethnography actually entails in a more practical sense is best discerned by asking what ethnographers do. This means defining ethnography through its very practice rather than in prescriptive terms. For example, Karen O'Reilly, reviewing definitions of ethnography across different disciplines, has suggested a minimum definition as:

> iterative-inductive research (that evolves in design through the study), drawing on a family of methods, involving direct and sustained contact with human agents, within the context of their daily lives (and cultures), watching what happens, listening to what is said, asking questions, and producing a richly written account that respects the irreducibility of human experience, that acknowledges the role of theory as well as the researcher's own role and that views humans as part object/part subject. (2005: 3)

While in this book I will go beyond this definition to re-think ethnography through the senses, the principle of O'Reilly's approach is important. Her definition provides a basic sense of what an ethnographer might do, without prescribing exactly how this has to be done. Delamont, in contrast, is more prescriptive in her definition of 'proper ethnography' as being 'participant observation during fieldwork' (2007: 206) – something that she proposes is 'done by living with the people being studied, watching them work and play, thinking carefully about what is seen, interpreting it and talking to the actors to check the emerging interpretations' (2007: 206). Delamont's interpretation reflects what might be seen as the classic approach to ethnography as developed in social anthropology in the twentieth century.

While classic observational methods certainly produce valuable in-depth and often detailed descriptions of other people's lives, this type of fieldwork is often not viable in contemporary contexts. This might be because the research is focused in environments where it would be impractical and inappropriate for researchers to go and live for long periods with research participants – for instance, in a modern western home (see Pink, 2004, 2013; Pink and Leder Mackley, 2012, 2014) or in a workplace to which the researcher has limited access (see Bust et al., 2007; Pink and Morgan, 2013). Limitations might also be related to the types of practices the researcher seeks to understand, due to constraints of time and other practical issues impacting on the working lives of ethnographers as well as those of research participants. In applied research other constraints can influence the amount of time available to spend on a project (see Pink, 2005a; Pink and Morgan, 2013). This has meant that innovative methods have been developed by ethnographers to provide routes into understanding other people's lives, experiences, values, social worlds and more that go beyond the classic observational approach. These are not short cuts to the same materials that would be produced through the classic approach (see Pink, 2007e; Pink and Morgan, 2013). Indeed, they involve 'direct and sustained contact with human agents, within the context of their daily lives' (O'Reilly, 2005: 3). Nevertheless, they are alternative, and ultimately valid, ways of seeking to understand and engage with other people's worlds through sharing activities and practices and inviting new forms of expression. It is these emergent methods that are defining the new sensory ethnography as it is practised. The mission of this book is not to argue for a single model of sensory ethnography. Rather, I understand sensory ethnography as a developing field of practice.

As the definitions discussed above indicate, a set of existing methods are already associated with ethnography, and usually covered in ethnographic methodology books. These include participant observation, interviewing and other participatory methods. Ethnography frequently involves the use of digital visual and audio technologies in the practice of such methods (Pink, 2007a; Pink et al., 2004) and might also be conducted, at least in part, virtually or online (see Hine, 2000; Kozinets, 2010; Postill and Pink, 2012), in addition to the ethnographer's physical engagements with the materiality and sensoriality of everyday and other contexts (see Pink et al., forthcoming). Whereas participatory methods often entail ethnographers participating in, observing (or sensing) and learning how to do what the people participating in their research are already engaged in (and presumably would have been doing anyway), interviewing normally involves a collaborative process of exploring specific themes and topics with an interviewee. Other less conventional methods may entail more intentional interventions on the part of the researcher. For instance, these could include collaborations such as producing a film, writing a song or inventing a new recipe with one's research participants. Moving into the design research field, it might involve co-designing prototypes of objects or services for everyday use (Halse, 2013) and usually has a future orientation that differs from the conventional focus on ethnographic writing on the ethnographic past. Doing sensory ethnography entails taking a series of conceptual and practical steps that allow the researcher to re-think both established and new participatory and collaborative ethnographic research techniques in terms of sensory perception, categories, meanings and values, ways of knowing and practices. It involves the researcher self-consciously and reflexively attending to the senses throughout the research process: that is, during the planning, reviewing, fieldwork, analysis and representational processes of a project. It also invites us, through growing connections between sensory ethnography and design ethnography (Pink, 2014; Pink et al., 2013), to re-think the temporalities of ethnography.

One might argue that sensory experience and perception has 'always' been central to the ethnographic encounter, and thus also to ethnographers' engagements with the sociality and materiality of research. This makes it all the more necessary to re-think ethnography to explicitly *account for* the senses. Indeed, when classic ethnographic examples are reinterpreted through attention to sensory experience, new understandings might be developed (see Howes, 2003). To some readers these dual arguments – that ethnography is already *necessarily* sensory and the call to re-think ethnography as sensory – may be reminiscent of earlier revisions. Around the end of the twentieth century it was proposed that all ethnographic practice should be reflexive, and is gendered (e.g. Bell et al., 1993), embodied (e.g. Coffey, 1999) and visual (e.g. Banks, 2001; Pink, 2007a). Another contemporary wave of technology and practice makes for online (e.g. Hine, 2000; Boellstorf, 2009; Kozinets, 2010) and digital ethnography (e.g. Pink et al., forthcoming). These perspectives were and are accompanied by powerful arguments for understanding ethnographic practice through new paradigms. A sensory ethnography methodology, as originally developed in the 2009 edition of this book, accounts for and expands this existing scholarship that re-thought ethnography as gendered, embodied and more. It also connects with the need to understand the experiential and sensory affordances and possibilities of digital technologies (Pink, 2015; Richardson, 2010, 2011). In doing so it draws from theories of human perception and place to propose a framework for understanding the ethnographic process and the ethnographer's practice (this is developed in Chapter 2). By connecting with recent developments in design anthropology (Gunn and

Donovan, 2012; Gunn et al., 2013) a sensory ethnography also takes a critical perspective on the temporalities of the ethnographic place, to enable researchers to develop ethnographic work with a future orientation (Pink et al., 2013; Pink, 2014). Thus the idea of a sensory ethnography involves not only attending to the senses in ethnographic research and representation, but reaches out towards an altogether more sophisticated set of ideas through which to understand what ethnography itself entails.

The proposal for a sensory ethnography presented in this book draws from and responds to a series of existing discipline-specific intellectual and practice-oriented trajectories that already attend to the senses through theoretical, empirical or applied engagements. In the remainder of this chapter I identify a set of themes and debates in the existing literature in relation to which a sensory ethnographic methodology is situated.

THE ANTHROPOLOGY OF THE SENSES AND ITS CRITICS

The history of anthropology and the senses

While there was intermittent anthropological interest in the senses earlier in the twentieth century (see Howes, 2003; Pink, 2006; Robben, 2007; Porcello et al., 2010), the subdiscipline known as 'the anthropology of the senses' became established in the 1980s and 1990s, preceded by and related to existing work on embodiment (see Howes, 2003: 29–32). Led by the work of scholars including David Howes (1991a), Paul Stoller (1989, 1997), Nadia Seremetakis (1994), Steven Feld (1982) and Feld and Keith Basso (1996a) this has involved the exploration of both the sensory experiences and classification systems of 'others' and of the ethnographer her- or himself (see also Herzfeld, 2001). These scholars played a key role in agenda-setting for anthropological studies of sensory experience, and their ideas continue to shape the work of contemporary ethnographers and theorists of the senses (e.g. Geurts, 2002: 17; Hahn, 2007: 3–4; see Porcello et al., 2010). However, at the turn of the century, Tim Ingold (2000) proposed a critical and influential departure from the anthropology of the senses developed by Howes, Classen, Stoller, Feld and others. These debates have played an important role in framing subsequent treatments of the senses in anthropology and have implications for how the senses are understood in other disciplines. For example, Howes' approach had connections to the branch of communication studies developed by Marshall McLuhan (Porcello et al., 2010) and, as I outline elsewhere (Pink, 2015), therefore has synergies to some semiotic approaches to media studies. They moreover raise critical issues for the principles of a sensory ethnography, as developed in Chapter 2.

The anthropology of the senses was to some extent a revisionary movement, calling for a re-thinking of the discipline through attention to the senses.

Howes' edited volume *The Varieties of Sensory Experience* (1991a) laid out a programme for the sub-discipline. This was a project in cross-cultural comparison that Howes described as 'primarily concerned with how the patterning of sense experience varies from one culture to the next in accordance with the meaning and emphasis attached to each of the modalities of perception' (1991a: 3). These concerns proposed an analytical route that sought to identify the role of the senses in producing different configurations across culture, as Howes put it, to trace 'the influence such variations have on forms of social organization, conceptions of self and cosmos, the regulation of the emotions, and other domains of cultural expression' (1991a: 3). This approach was focused on comparing how different cultures map out the senses. Based on the assumption that in all cultures the senses are organised hierarchically, one of the tasks of the sensory researcher would be to determine the 'sensory profile' (Howes and Classen, 1991: 257) or sensory 'order' of the culture being studied. A good example of how this approach is put into practice can be found in Howes' (2003) work concerning Melanesian peoples.

Debates over anthropology and the senses

While Howes' approach opened up new avenues of investigation and scholarship, it did not escape criticism. The ethnographic evidence certainly demonstrated that different cultures could be associated with the use of different sets of sensory categories and meanings (e.g. Geurts, 2002; Pink, 2004). Indeed, as I have argued elsewhere, the comparison of how sensory categories and moralities and practices associated with them are articulated and engaged across cultures is a viable proposition and can offer useful insights (Pink, 2004, 2006). Nevertheless, taking cultural difference as the unit of comparison can be problematic when it shifts attention away from the immediacy of sensory experience as lived, and abstracts it into representational categories. Ingold's critique of this dimension of Howes' approach was that its focus on the 'incorporeal "ideas" and "beliefs" of a culture' treated 'sensory experience as but a vehicle for the expression of extra-sensory, cultural values' (2000: 156). This, Ingold wrote, 'reduces the body to a locus of objectified and enumerable sense whose one and only role is to carry the semantic load projected onto them by a collective, supersensory subject – namely society – and whose balance or ratio may be calculated according to the load borne by each' (Ingold, 2000: 284). Instead, Ingold proposed a re-focusing of research in the anthropology of the senses, away from 'the collective sensory consciousness of society' and towards the 'creative interweaving of experience in discourse and to the ways in which the resulting discursive constructions in turn affect people's perceptions of the world around them' (2000: 285). Howes responded to the critique with a further insistence on the importance of undertaking 'an in-depth examination' of the 'social significance' of the 'sensory features of a society' (2003: 49). The disagreement between Howes and Ingold is based both in their different theoretical commitments and in their agendas for approaching the senses in culture and society. While Howes has recognised the importance of perception (2003: 40), he nevertheless seems to be calling for anthropologists of the senses to take cultural models as their starting point. This, like the classic approach to ethnography discussed above, focuses attention away from the specificity of individuals' practices and the experiential (see also Pink, 2004). In contrast Ingold places human perception at the centre of his analysis (see also Chapter 2 of this book).

A second strand in the work of Howes (1991a) and Stoller (1989) emphasised the commonly assumed dominance of vision, or occularcentrism, in modern western culture. Through cross-cultural comparison a body of work emerged that suggested how in other cultures non-visual senses may play a more dominant role. A particularly striking example is presented in Constance Classen's, Howes' and Anthony Synnott's work on smell, through their discussion of Pandaya's work on the Ongee people in the Andaman Islands. They describe how for the Ongee 'the identifying characteristic and life force of all living beings is thought to reside in their smell'. Indeed, they write: 'it is through catching a whiff of oneself, and being able to distinguish that scent from all the other odours that surround one, that one arrives at a sense of one's own identity in Ongee society' (Classen et al., 1994: 113). This and other ethnographic studies (see also Classen et al., 1994) leave little doubt that in different cultures notions of self and more might be attributed verbally and/or gesturally to different sensory categories. Yet it does not follow from this that the embodied experience of the self, for instance, is necessarily perceived simply through one sensory modality. To deconstruct the argument that in different cultures different sensory modalities are dominant we need to separate out the idea of there being a hierarchically dominant sense on the one hand, and on the other, the ethnographic evidence that in specific cultural contexts people tend to use particular sensory categories to conceptualise aspects of their lives and identities. While the latter is well supported, the former is challenged in recent literature. This argument can be expanded with reference to the status of vision in modern western societies. Ingold argues that the assumption that vision is necessarily a dominant and objectifying sense is incorrect (2000: 287). He suggests this assumption was brought about because instead of asking, 'How do we see the environment around us?' (Gibson, 1979: 1, cited by Ingold, 2000: 286), 'philosophical critics of visualism' presuppose that 'to see is to reduce the environment to objects that are to be grasped and appropriated as representations in the mind' (2000: 286). Based on theories that understand perception as multisensory, in that the senses are not separated out at the point of perception, but culturally defined, Ingold thus suggests understanding vision in terms of its interrelationship with other senses (in his own discussion through an analysis of the relationship between vision and hearing). As noted above, the debate between Ingold and Howes is ongoing, and has since been played out in the context of a written debate in four parts in the journal *Social Anthropology*. In this 2011 debate between Ingold and Howes it becomes clear how, while Howes' approach can be aligned with a culturalist and representational trajectory, Ingold's is aligned with the non-representational or more-than-representational accounts associated with human geography (Howes, 2011a, 2011b; Ingold, 2011a, 2011b; see also Howes, 2010a, 2010b and Pink, 2010a, 2010b, 2015).

Following Ingold's (2000) critiques, others took up questions related to vision and sensory experience (e.g. Grasseni, 2007a, 2007c; Willerslev, 2007). Cristina Grasseni proposed a 'rehabilitation of vision' not 'as an isolated given but within its interplay with the other senses' (2007a: 1). Grasseni argued that vision is 'not necessarily identifiable with "detached observation" and should not be opposed by definition to "the immediacy of fleeting sounds. Ineffable odours, confused emotions, and the flow of Time passing" (Fabian 1983: 108)'. Rather, she proposed the idea of '*skilled visions* [which] are embedded in multi-sensory practices, where look is coordinated with skilled movement, with rapidly changing points of view, or with other senses such as touch' (2007a: 4). Tom Rice, whose research has focused on sound, also questions the usefulness of what he calls 'anti-visualism'. Rice suggested that in the case of sound the effect of the anti-visualist argument is in '*re*-re-establishing the visual/auditory dichotomy that has pervaded anthropological thought on sensory experience' (2005: 201, original italics; and see also Rice, 2008). My own research about the modern western 'sensory home' (Pink, 2004), through a focus on categories of sound, vision, smell and touch likewise suggested that no sensory modality necessarily *dominates* how domestic environments or practices are experienced in any one culture. Rather, the home is an environment that is constituted, experienced, understood, evaluated and maintained through all the senses. For example, British and Spanish research participants decided whether or not they would clean their homes based on multisensory evaluations and knowledge that they verbalised in terms of how clothes, or sinks or floors look, smell or feel under foot. The sensory modalities research participants cited as being those that mattered when they evaluated their homes varied both culturally and individually. However, this was not because their perceptions of cleanliness were dominated by one sensory modality. Rather, they used sensory modalities as expressive categories through which to communicate about both cleanliness and self-identity (see Pink, 2004).

Reflexivity in the anthropology of the senses

The 'reflexive turn' in social and cultural anthropology is usually attributed to the 'writing culture' debate and the emergence of a dialogical anthropology (e.g. Clifford and Marcus, 1986; James et al., 1997). This highlighted amongst other things the constructedness of ethnographic texts, the importance of attending to the processes by which ethnographic knowledge is produced and the need to bring local voices into academic representations. The reflexivity that emerged from discussions in sensory anthropology was a critical response to this literature.

Howes argued that the 'verbo-centric' approach of dialogical anthropology was limited as it failed to account for the senses (1991b: 7–8) and Regina Bendix criticised 'its focus on the authorial self [which] shies away from seeking to understand the role of the senses and affect within as well as outside of the researcher-and-researched dynamic' (2000: 34). In the late 1980s reflexive accounts of the roles played by the senses in anthropological fieldwork began to emerge in connection with both the issues raised by the 'writing culture' shift and the contemporary emphasis on embodiment. These works stressed the need for reflexive engagements with how ethnographic knowledge was produced and an acknowledgement of the importance of the body in human experience and in academic practice. Paul Stoller's *The Taste of Ethnographic Things* (1989), followed almost a decade later by his *Sensuous Scholarship* (1997), pushed this 'reflexive' and 'embodied' turn in social theory further. Stoller's work shows how anthropological practice is a corporeal process that involves the ethnographer engaging not only in the ideas of others, but in learning about their understandings through her or his own physical and sensorial experiences, such as tastes (e.g. 1989) or pain and illness (e.g. 1997, 2007c). Likewise, Nadia Seremetakis (1994) and Judith Okely (1994) both used their own experiences as the basis for discussions that placed the ethnographer's sensing body at the centre of the analysis. As for any ethnographic process, reflexivity is central to sensory ethnography practice. In Chapter 3 I build on these existing works to outline how a sensory reflexivity and intersubjectivity might be understood and practised.

New approaches in the anthropology of the senses

In the first decade of the twenty-first century several book-length anthropological 'sensory ethnographies', as well as an increasing number of articles (e.g. in the journal *The Senses and Society*) and book chapters, were published. The legacy of the earlier anthropology of the senses is evident in these ethnographies with their foci on, for instance, cross-cultural comparison (Geurts, 2002; Pink, 2004), apprenticeship (e.g. Grasseni, 2004b; Downey, 2005, 2007; Marchand, 2007), memory and the senses (Sutton, 2001; Desjarlais, 2003), and commitment to reflexive interrogation. These later works also took the anthropology of the senses in important new directions. While the earlier sensory ethnographies focused almost exclusively on cultures that were strikingly different from that which the ethnographer had originated from, this group of anthropological studies also attended to the senses 'at home', or at least in modern western cultures. This has included a focus on everyday practices such as housework (Pink, 2004, 2012) and laundry (Pink, 2005b, 2012; Pink et al., 2013), gardening (Tilley, 2006), leisure practices such as walking and climbing (e.g. Lund, 2006), clinical work practices (e.g. Rice, 2008), food (see Sutton, 2010) and homelessness (Desjarlais, 2005). Such sensory ethnographies both attend to and interpret the experiential, individual, idiosyncratic and contextual nature of research participants' sensory practices *and* also seek to comprehend the culturally specific categories, conventions, moralities and knowledge that inform how people understand their experiences. Moving into the second decade of the twenty-first century, accounting for the senses is becoming increasingly connected with ethnographic practice. In my own work it has become part of an approach, rather than being the central strand of a study. This I believe is a shift that needs to happen, so that attention to the senses becomes part of ethnographic practice, rather than the object of ethnographic study. As I develop below in relation to the discussion of future-oriented design ethnography, in recent years design anthropology publications (Gunn and Donovan, 2012; Gunn et al., 2013) also make explicit connections to sensory approaches, offering ways for us to begin to consider the role of sensory ways of knowing in change-making processes and applied uses of ethnography.

To sum up, the anthropology of the senses is characterised by three main issues/debates. It explores the question of the relationship between sensory perception and culture, engages with questions concerning the status of vision and its relationship to the other senses, and demands a form of reflexivity that goes beyond the interrogation of how culture is 'written' to examine the sites of embodied knowing. Drawing from these debates, I suggest that while ethnographers need to attempt to establish sets of reference points regarding collective or shared culturally specific knowledge about sensory categories and meanings, such categories should be understood in terms of a model of culture as constantly being produced and thus as contingent. This, however, cannot be built independently of the study and analysis of actual sensory practices and experienced realities. To undertake this, a sensory ethnography must be informed by a theory of sensory perception. I expand on this in Chapter 2.

SENSUOUS GEOGRAPHIES, ETHNOGRAPHY AND SPATIAL THEORY

A history of the senses in geography

Theories of space, place and the experience of the environment are central concerns to human geographers. These theoretical strands, as well as recent ethnographic studies in human geography, are particularly relevant to a sensory ethnography that attends to both social and physical/material practices and relations.

As for social anthropology, a notable interest in sensory experience became evident in the latter part of the twentieth century. The geographer Yi-Fu Tuan stressed the role of the senses in his earlier work, proposing that 'An object or place achieves concrete reality when our experience of it is total, that is through all the senses as well as with the active and reflective mind' (1977: 18). Nevertheless, it was around the same time as the emergence of the anthropology of the senses, that geographical approaches to the senses were articulated more fully. However, in contrast to the anthropological literature, this work did not explore sensory experience ethnographically, or cross-culturally, but tended to draw from existing social science studies, philosophy or literature. Also, in common with the anthropology of the senses, in part this literature proposed a revision of dominant concepts in the discipline, through the senses. Thus in *Landscapes of the Mind* (1990) Douglas Porteous called for a rethinking of the centrality of landscape in geography through a focus on 'non-visual sensory modes' (1990: 5) resonating with contemporary work in anthropology (e.g. Howes, 1991a). Indeed, in accord with the approaches of his time, Porteous took an accusatory stance against vision. He proposed that 'vision drives out the other senses' and defined it as 'the ideal sense for an intellectualised, information-crazed species that has withdrawn from many areas of direct sensation' (1990: 5). In response he set out notions of 'smellscape' and 'soundscape' (1990: 23) to examine how these different modalities of sensory experience figure in the way people experience their environments. While Porteous' scapes tend to separate out different sensory modalities, Tuan stressed multisensoriality in his (1993) volume *Passing Strange and Wonderful*. Within his wider task of exploring 'the importance of the aesthetic in our lives' (1993: 1) Tuan suggested understanding our experience of 'natural' or built environments as multisensory.

In *Sensuous Geographies* (1994) Paul Rodaway sought to take a sensory geography in another direction. Rodaway aligned his work with a revival of humanistic geography and links between humanistic and postmodern geography that developed in the 1990s (e.g. in the work of Tuan) and phenomenological approaches (1994: 6–9). Rather than separating the 'physical, social, cultural and aesthetic dimensions of human experience' as Porteous and Tuan had, Rodaway, influenced by Gibson's ecological theory of perception (Rodaway, 1994: ix), sought 'to offer a more integrated view of the role of the senses in geographical understanding: *the sense both as a relationship to a world and the senses as themselves a kind of structuring of space and defining of place*' (Rodaway, 1994: 4, original italics). Of particular interest are the common threads his work shares with social anthropologists. Like his contemporary anthropologists Rodaway noted that 'Everyday experience is multisensual, though one or more sense may be dominant in a given situation' (1994: 5). These earlier calls for attention to the senses sought to theorise key geographical concepts in relation to the multisensoriality of human experience, focusing on space, place and landscape. However, although they have undoubtedly been inspiring texts, neither individually nor collectively do they offer a satisfactory or complete framework for sensory analysis. While Porteous took the important step of turning academic attention to the non-visual elements of landscape, by situating his work as a response to visualism he limited its scope. The critiques of the anti-visualism thesis as it developed in anthropology (e.g. by Ingold, 2000; Grasseni, 2007a, 2007c), discussed in the previous section, can equally be applied to this body of work in human geography.

New approaches to the senses in geography

More recently, geographers have continued to develop these core theoretical themes, of space, place and landscape with attention to the senses. For example, Nigel Thrift has conceptualised space through a paradigm that recognises its sensual and affective dimensions (e.g. Thrift, 2006). Other developments include theoretical discussions in the context of urban geography and future geographies. For instance, discussing collective culture and urban public space, Ash Amin discusses what he calls 'situated surplus' which is produced out of 'the entanglements of bodies in motion and the environmental conditions and physical architecture of a given space'. This, he suggests, drawing also from the work of other geographers (citing Pile, 2005; Thrift, 2005) and resonating in several ways with the work of contemporary anthropologists (e.g. Harris, 2007), is 'collectively experienced as a form of *tacit, neurological and sensory knowing*' (Amin, 2008: 11, my italics). Thrift has moreover speculated about how 'new kinds of sensorium' (2004: 582) might develop in an emergent context of 'qualculative' space, where new ways of perceiving space and time would develop and our senses of (for example) touch and direction would be transformed.

Geographers who have recently taken ethnographic approaches to the senses include Divya P. Tolia-Kelly's collaborative work concerning migrants' perceptions of the Lake District in the UK (2007), Tim Edensor's writings on industrial ruins (e.g. 2007), Justin Spinney's mobile (2008) ethnography of urban cyclists and Lisa Law's (2005) analysis of how Filipina domestic workers negotiated their identities in Hong Kong. Some of this ethnographic work examines the senses through the geographical paradigm of landscape. For instance, Law shows how, amongst other things, Filipina domestic workers produce their own sensory landscapes in public spaces of the city on their days off. Through this she suggests that they evoke 'a sense of home', which 'incorporates elements of history and memory, of past and present times and spaces, helping to create a familiar place' (2005: 236). In the context of an existing lack of 'a methodology for researching sensory landscapes' Law suggests ethnographic research can make an important contribution (2005: 227). This and other work, such as the innovative collaborative arts practice-based methodologies developed by Tolia-Kelly in her work on migrants' experiences of landscape (2007) demonstrate the potential for ethnographic methodologies in human geography. By focusing the sensory experiencing body and exploring its interdependency with landscape (see Casey, 2001) a sensory ethnography can reveal important insights into the constitution of self and the articulation of power relations.

A particularly important influence in the way the senses have been discussed in human geography has been through the notion of the 'visceral'. For the geographers Allison Hayes-Conroy and Jessica Hayes-Conroy 'visceral refers to the realm of internally-felt sensations, moods and states of being, which are born from sensory engagement with the material world' including that of 'the cognitive mind', since they stress: 'visceral refers to a fully minded-body (as used by McWhorter 1999) that is capable of judgment' (Hayes-Conroy and Hayes-Conroy, 2008: 462). In their work, which focuses on the visceral nature of food experiences, they connect the politics of everyday life to the way it is experienced, therefore seeing the study of the sensory experience of food as being a route through which to understand how power relations are embedded in everyday life. Their view of what they refer to as 'visceral politics' moves away from the idea of 'individualistic forms of being-political' and instead they profess to 'move towards a radically relational view of the world, in which structural modes of critique are brought together with an appreciation of chaotic, unstructured ways in which bodily intensities unfold in the production of everyday life' (Hayes-Conroy and Hayes-Conroy, 2008: 462). In their later work they move beyond the focus on food experiences and argue for a wider application of a visceral approach in geography; indeed, suggesting that

> geographic work demands attentiveness to the visceral realm, a realm where social structures and bodily sensations come together and exude each other, where dispositions and discourses seem to relate as organic-synthetic plasma, and where categories and incarnations defy themselves, daring to be understood. (Hayes-Conroy and Hayes-Conroy, 2010: 1281)

The interests in spatial theory, the senses and the 'visceral' that have converged in the work of human geographers create a fertile intellectual trajectory for a sensory approach to ethnography to draw from. In Chapter 2 I take these connections further to suggest how geographical theories of place and space (Massey, 2005) might, in combination with philosophical (Casey, 1996) and anthropological (Ingold, 2007, 2008) work on place and the phenomenology of perception, inform our understanding of sensory ethnography practice. The attention that human geographers tend to pay to the political and the power relations that are embedded in the everyday, the way it is experienced and the spatial relations that it is implicated in, sheds a specific light on the questions that we might ask through sensory ethnography practice.

SOCIOLOGY OF THE SENSES: INTERACTION AND CORPOREALITY

A history of the sociology of the senses

An initial impulse towards a sociology of the senses was proposed by Georg Simmel in his 1907 essay 'Sociology of the senses') (1997 [1907]). Simmel's agenda was not to establish a subdiscipline of a sociology of the senses. Rather, as part of an argument about the importance of a micro-sociology (1997 [1907]: 109) he focused on, as he puts it, 'the meanings that mutual sensory perception and influencing have for the social life of human beings, their coexistence, cooperation and opposition' (1997 [1907]: 110). He suggested that our sensory perception of others plays two key roles in human interaction. First, our 'sensory impression' of another person invokes emotional or physical responses in us. Second, 'sense impression' becomes 'a route of knowledge of the other' (1997 [1907): 111). Although Simmel concluded by proposing that 'One will no longer be able to consider as unworthy of attention the delicate, invisible threads that are spun from one person to another' (1997 [1907]: 120) it was a century later that sociologists began to engage seriously with this question. In part Simmel's legacy encouraged sociologists to focus on a sensory sociology of human interaction. When I wrote the first edition of *Doing Sensory Ethnography*, published in 2009, coinciding with my own rather frustrated search for sociological research about the senses, Kelvin Low had recently confirmed the earlier assessment of Gail Largey and Rod Watson (2006 [1972]: 39) in his observation that 'sociologists have seldom researched the senses' (Low, 2005: 399). Nevertheless, some significant sociological work on the senses has since emerged, including that of Low himself, discussed below.

Although Simmel saw the 'lower senses' to be of secondary sociological significance to vision and hearing (1997 [1907]: 117), he suggested that 'smelling a person's body odour is the most intimate perception of them' since 'they penetrate, so to speak in a gaseous form into our most sensory inner being' (1997 [1907]: 119). This interest in smell and social interaction has continued in the sociology of the senses. Largey and Watson's essay entitled 'The Sociology of Odors' (2006 [1972]) also extends the sociological interest in social interaction to propose that 'Much moral symbolism relevant to interaction is expressed in terms of olfactory imagery' (2006 [1972]: 29). They stress the 'real' consequences that might follow from this (2006 [1972]: 30). For instance, they note how 'odors are often referred to as the insurmountable barrier to close interracial and/or interclass interaction' (2006 [1972]: 32) as well as being associated with intimacy amongst an 'in-group' (2006 [1972]: 34). Also, with reference to social interaction, Largey and Watson see odour as a form of 'impression management' by which individuals try 'to avoid moral stigmatization' and present an appropriate/approved 'olfactory identity' (2006 [1972]: 35). Low (who proposes that this approach might be extended to other senses (2005: 411)) also examines the role of smell in social interaction. He argues that

> smell functions as a social medium employed by social actors towards formulating constructions/judgements of race-d, class-ed and gender-ed others, operating on polemic/categorical constructions (and also, other nuances between polarities) which may involve a process of *othering*. (2005: 405)

As such he suggests that 'the differentiation of smell stands as that which involves not only an identification of "us" vs "them" or "you" vs "me", but, also, processes of judgement and ranking of social others' (2005: 405). Building on Simmel's ideas Low's study of smell (which involved ethnographic research) 'attempts to move beyond "absolutely supra-individual total structures" (Simmel, 1997: 110) towards individual, lived experiences where smell may be utilized as a social medium in the (re) construction of social realities' (Low, 2005: 398).

Departures from the early sociology of the senses

Other sociological studies that attend to the senses have departed from Simmel's original impetus in two ways. On the one hand Michael Bull's (2000) study of personal stereo users' experiences of urban environments takes the sociology of the senses in a new direction. Noting how 'Sound has remained an invisible presence in urban and media studies', Bull sets out 'an auditory epistemology of everyday life' (2001: 180). Using a phenomenological methodology he demonstrates how this focus on sound allows us to understand not simply how urban soundscapes are experienced by personal stereo users, but also how practices and experiences of looking are produced in relation to this (2001: 191). Other developments in sociology have continued to focus on social interactions, but rather than focusing on one sensory modality or category, have stressed the multisensoriality and corporeality of these encounters. While not identified as a 'sociology of the senses', use of the multi-modality paradigm (Kress and Van Leeuwen, 2001) by sociologists has also allowed researchers undertaking observational studies of interaction to acknowledge the sensoriality of these contexts and processes (e.g. Dicks et al., 2006).

Innovative approaches to the senses in sociology

However, of most interest for the development of a sensory ethnography are projects such as the work of Christina Lammer (e.g. 2007) and of Jon Hindmarsh and Alison Pilnick (2007) in clinical contexts and Les Back's, Dawn Lyon's and John Hockey and Jacquelyn Allen-Collinson's calls for further attention to the phenomenology of corporeal and sensory experiences in the sociology of work (e.g. Hockey and Allen-Collinson, 2009; Lyon and Back, 2012) and community (Back, 2009). Hindmarsh and Pilnick's study of the interactions between members of the pre-operative anaesthetic team in a teaching hospital shows how what they call '*intercorporeal knowing* [...] underpins the team's ability to seamlessly coordinate emerging activities'. In this context they describe how 'The sights, sounds and feel of colleagues are used to sense, anticipate, appreciate and respond to emerging tasks and activities' (2007: 1413), thus indicating the importance of multisensorial embodied ways of knowing in human interaction. Lammer's research about 'how radiological personnel perceive and define "contact" as it relates to their interaction with patients' has similar implications. Lammer set out to explore the 'sensual realities ... at work in a radiology unit' (Lammer, 2007: 91), using video as part of her method of participant observation. She argued that in a context where patients tended to pass through the radiology department rapidly 'a multisensual approach would encourage empathy and create a deeper sensibility amongst health professionals at a teaching hospital' (2007: 113).

More recently, the place of the senses in sociological research has become increasingly established. Les Back and Nirmal Puwar (2012) have called for 'live methods' in sociology. This approach puts the senses at the centre of their project in that they write:

> We are arguing for the cultivation of a sociological sensibility not confined to the predominant lines of sight, the focal points of public concern. Rather, we are arguing for paying attention to the social world within a wider range of senses and placing critical evaluation and ethical judgement at the centre of research craft. (Back and Puwar, 2012: 15)

As part of this, Back proposes that 'The first principle of live sociology is *an attention to how a wider range of the senses* changes the quality of data and makes other kinds of critical imagination possible' (Back, 2012: 29, original italics). Phillip Vannini, Dennis Waskul and Simon Gottschalk (2012) have sought to write the sociology of the senses through what they describe as a focus on the social, with a commitment to the study of interaction and what they call 'somatic work'. There, taking a distinctly sociological approach, they bring together sociological attention to the body, the senses and human interaction. Again, the authors' interest in social interaction tends to define the sociological approach to the senses, making this a distinctive element of what we might think of as a sociology of the senses, which runs through the different works discussed in this section.

Collectively, these works draw our attention to the corporeality and multisensoriality of any social encounter or interaction – including not only the relationships between research participants but those between ethnographer and research participants. Building on this in Chapter 3 I suggest that understanding our interactions with others as multisensorial encounters necessitates a reflexive awareness of the sensory intersubjectivity that characterises such meetings. Thus we might see the sociology of the senses as an important reminder that social interaction is a fundamental unit of analysis for not only understanding what is happening in the world, but also for part of the research process itself.

SENSORY ETHNOGRAPHY AND APPLIED RESEARCH

The use of ethnographic methods in applied research – whether or not this is led by academic practitioners – is widespread across a range of fields of applied research, including consumer research, marketing, product development, health, education, overseas development and more. In some of these fields sensory analysis is also particularly important. In this section, by means of example, I reflect on consumer research and health studies.

In consumer research a range of methods have long since been used to analyse people's sensory perceptions of products and brands to the point where now, in a context of consumer capitalism, 'tapping the subjective sensory preferences of the consumer and creating enticing "interfaces" has come to take precedence over conventional design principles' (Howes, 2005c: 286–7). In 1999 and 2000 I developed two ethnographic studies with Unilever Research in which the multisensoriality of how people experience their homes, material cultures and domestic products and practices was essential to both the research questions and processes engaged in. Both projects were situated in the domestic sphere and involved using video and interviews to research and represent how cleaning and home decorating (Pink, 2004) and laundry (Pink, 2005b, 2007c) are part of everyday practice, identity and morality. My current and recent applied research with industry partners and with designers also always incorporates attention to the sensory elements of experience and environments. For example, my research about occupational safety and health with Jennie Morgan and Andrew Dainty involved a focus on sensory ways of knowing through the hand in health care (Pink et al., 2015) and on the way other people's homes are experienced as sites of familiarity or danger by workers in logistics and health care who have to perform home visits as part of their everyday working lives. An ethnographic approach to exploring people's multisensory relationships to the materialities and environments of their everyday lives, and to their feelings about them, offers a remarkably rich and informative source of knowledge for academic and applied researchers alike. However, in these contexts ethnography has not historically necessarily been the dominant methodology. Indeed, in consumer and marketing research a range of sensory research methods have been developed. Some of these have been qualitative, for example Howes noted the example of '"body-storming" focus groups (see Bonapace, 2002: 191)', which aimed to 'divine the most potent sensory channel, and within each channel the most potent sensory signal, through which to distinguish their products from those of their competitors and capture the attention of potential customers' (2005c: 288). Therefore, consumer researchers are interested in and attend to the senses in ways that show there is great potential for sensory ethnography in this applied field.

In health research the applied potential of sensory approaches to research is also becoming evident. Recent studies have focused on contexts of nursing (Edvardsson and Street, 2007), interventional radiology (Lammer, 2007) and anaesthesia (Hindmarsh and Pilnick, 2007). Located academically in sociology some of this research focuses on the embodied and sensory nature of social interactions and environments in clinical contexts, often using visual methods. The importance of acknowledging the sensorial dimensions of biomedical practices is evident from Hindmarsh and Pilnick's (2007) study. David Edvardsson and Annette Street's work developed this in a slightly different way by providing a reflexive and 'insider' account of health contexts. They discussed the idea of 'The nurse as embodied ethnographer' (the subtitle of their article), suggesting that researchers should account 'for the embodied illness experience' *and* 'the sensate experience of the nurse as ethnographer', and thus 'open up nursing practice to phenomenological descriptions' (2007: 30). Although their work is clearly rooted in academic debates (drawing from the work of Stoller and Emily Martin) it has practical implications and Street has 'taken this idea further into teaching neophyte nurses to attend to their senses and their embodied responses, in order to better understand the lived experiences of patients and their families' (2007: 30). Lammer (2007) was also concerned to find ways to present her findings concerning the interactions between clinicians and patients (see above) to clinical staff and as part of this produced the documentary video *Making Contact* (2004). This and her later project *CORPOrealities* (n.d.) (which also involves collaborations with artists) create innovative links between arts and biomedical practice (Lammer, 2012). As noted above, my research with Jennie Morgan and Andrew Dainty also engaged a sensory approach to attend to how community nurses and occupational therapists who perform home visits, sense their environments, and to explore their sensory ways of knowing about health and safety (Pink et al., 2014).

Together these studies and forms of social intervention show that a sensory ethnography approach has a key role to play in applied research. It draws out the everyday realities of people's experience and practice and provides insights about how to make these experiences and practices more pleasurable and effective – whether this means developing products that people will desire to use and foods they will enjoy eating or making medical procedures and care contexts more comfortable.

SENSORY ETHNOGRAPHY FOR DESIGN RESEARCH AND PRACTICE

Ethnography has long since been part of the practice of design researchers, although the ways and context in which it is used for design have tended to differ in significant ways from its development in anthropology. In part this can be explained through the applied nature of design research, and in that it has often been associated with the desire to make change through psychologically informed rational actor type behaviour change models (see Tromp and Hekkert, 2012). However, design research has been a constant strand in the 'sensory' turn since the beginning of the twenty-first century. For example, Malnar and Vodvarka (2004) led the way with their book *Sensory Design* which used examples from a range of practice-based and literary contexts to establish the importance of sensoriality in design (and see Lucas and Romice, 2008; Zomerdijk and Voss, 2010; Leder Mackley and Pink, 2013; Pink et al., 2013). This shared emphasis creates potential for theoretical and ethnographic elements of anthropological practice to connect with the concerns of designers who, like Malnar and Vodvarka (2004), are concerned with questions including those relating to sensory perception and experience. In addition, forms of user-centred design, experience design and emotional design (all of which bear some relation to the sensory) play a role in contemporary design thinking. In my work with designers at Loughborough University, UK, we explored the relationship between a sensory ethnography approach and phenomenological approaches to design (Pink et al., 2013). There we identified that there are

> clear parallels between the phenomenological sensory ethnography approach and the notion of embodied interaction that is core to 3rd Paradigm HCI [Dourish 2001a]. At the heart of both is a commitment to the idea that we encounter the world as a meaningful place within which we act [Harrison and Dourish 1996]: 'It is through our actions in the world – through the ways in which we move through the world, react to it, turn it to our needs, and engage with it to solve problems – that the meaning that the world has for us is revealed'. (Pink et al., 2013: 10–11)

There we suggest that such an approach

> provides us with both a theoretical and experiential framework for design because it allows us to on the one hand appreciate the meaning and nature of the experiential environments into which we seek to introduce design interventions. On the other it offers us a set of theoretical tools that guide us away from attempts to change 'behavior' and to instead ask how interventions might sit in relation to the existing routines, contingencies and innovations that ongoingly make and re-make the practices and places of everyday life. (Pink et al., 2013: 15)

Indeed, sensoriality is at the core of the agenda in the emergent field of design anthropology. As Wendy Gunn and Jared Donovan put it, design anthropology

> resonates with four areas of interest that are generating some of the most exciting new work in the discipline: exchange and personhood in the use of technology, the understanding of skilled practice, anthropology of the senses and the aesthetics of everyday life. (2012: 10)

In a contemporary context the relationship between design and the social sciences is growing, specifically in fields of applied research where the research orientation of the social sciences towards the present-past can grow through the orientation of design research towards the future. In the Afterword to this book I elaborate on this to suggest that sensory ethnography offers a new focus for change-making and future-oriented research.

SENSORY ETHNOGRAPHY AND ARTS PRACTICE

Attention to the senses in arts practice has developed in parallel to and sometimes overlapping or in collaboration with ethnographic work on the senses (see, for example, Zardini, 2005; Jones, 2006a, b, c). It is not within the scope of this book to undertake an art historical review of the senses. Instead, I draw out some of the most salient contemporary parallels and connections between these fields. There is already a growing literature concerning the relationship between anthropology and arts practice (Silva and Pink, 2004; Schneider and Wright, 2006, 2013; Ravetz, 2007; Schneider, 2008), some of which places some emphasis on sensoriality (Grimshaw and Ravetz, 2005) and highlights a turn to collaborative arts practice, noting how an anthropological approach can bring to the fore issues around the politics and power relations of such collaborations (Schneider and Wright, 2013).

There are some obvious crossovers between sensory ethnography and creative practice, such as the work of the ethnographic filmmaker David MacDougall (see MacDougall, 1998, 2005), the audiovisual practice of the sociologist Christina Lammer (e.g. 2007, 2012) and soundscape studies (e.g. Drever, 2002; Feld, 1991, 2003). These works are discussed in the following chapters. Specific connections tend to be less frequently made between ethnography, the senses and arts practices as developed in installation and performance art. Nevertheless, there are interesting parallels between recent developments in sensory ethnographic methods and arts practice. Perhaps the clearest example is in forms of practice in each discipline that uses walking as a method of research (e.g. the arts practice of Sissel Tolaas (see Hand, 2007) and the ethnographic practice of e.g. Katrín Lund, 2006, 2008; Jo Lee Vergunst, 2008; and Andrew Irving, 2010, 2013), representing or engaging audiences in other people's sensory experiences or in specific smell- or soundscapes (e.g. the work of Jenny Marketou, discussed by Drobnick and Fisher, 2008). These discussions of arts practice and the sensory ways of knowing that are implied through them invite a consideration of how sensory ethnography practice might develop in relation to explorations in art. Contributors to Schneider and Wright's *Anthropology and Art Practice* (2013) also bring questions around the senses to the fore. Some of these examples are discussed in Chapter 8.

AN INTERDISCIPLINARY CONTEXT FOR SENSORY ETHNOGRAPHY

Since the early twenty-first century an increasingly interdisciplinary focus on the senses has emerged. This has been promoted through a series of edited volumes including Howes' *Empire of the Senses* (2005a). These collections unite the work of academics from a range of disciplines to explore sensory aspects of culture and society (Howes, 2005a) using modern western categories of audition (Bull and Back, 2003), smell (Drobnick, 2006), taste (Korsmeyer, 2005), touch (Classen, 2005) and visual culture (Edwards and Bhaumik, 2008). According to Howes this increased focus on the senses represents a 'sensual revolution' – an ideological move that has turned 'the tables and recover(ed) a full-bodied understanding of culture and experience' as opposed to one that is modelled on linguistics (2005a: 1; see also Howes, 2003). Although some would disagree that the revolution contra linguistics (e.g. Bendix, 2006: 6) should be the central concern of a sensory approach to ethnography, Howes is correct that the senses have come to the fore in the work of many contemporary academics. Moreover, as we have seen in this chapter, the senses are becoming increasingly important to scholarship and research across social science, arts and humanities disciplines – including design, geography, anthropology, sociology and arts practice. In what is an increasingly interdisciplinary context for scholarship and practice within these fields – for instance, with the emergence of design anthropology and the connections between anthropology and arts practice – as well as between the social, technological, engineering sciences and medical sciences more generally, we can see how the theoretical, methodological and practical emphasis on the senses in the social sciences and humanities is also having impact through them in wider fields. Therefore, for example, in my own experience of working with designers, engineers and construction industry experts, a sensory ethnography approach can inform the development of strong research collaborations that bring to interdisciplinary and hard-to-address research problems, new ways of knowing that are not usually applied in those fields.

Summing up

In this chapter I have shown how an interest in the senses has extended across academic and applied ethnographic disciplines concerned with understanding and representing human experience. Each existing body of literature offers important insights that I draw on to propose a sensory ethnographic methodology in the following chapters. I have suggested that a sensory ethnography could be of use not only in discipline-specific projects and in applied research. Rather, it can additionally make an important contribution in projects that bridge the divide between applied and academic work, in projects that develop and combine perspectives and aims of different disciplines in interdisciplinary analysis.

Recommended further reading

- Hayes-Conroy, A. and Hayes-Conroy, J. (2008) 'Taking back taste: feminism, food and visceral politics', *Gender, Place & Culture: a Journal of Feminist Geography*, 15(5): 461–73.
- Howes, D. (2003) *Sensing Culture: engaging the senses in culture and social theory*. Ann Arbor: University of Michigan Press.
- Ingold, T. (2010) *Being Alive*. London: Routledge.
- Schneider, A. and C. Wright (2013) *Anthropology and Art Practice*. Oxford: Bloomsbury.
- Stoller, P. (1997) *Sensuous Scholarship*. Philadelphia: University of Pennsylvania Press.
- Vannini, P., D. Waskul and S. Gottschalk (2012) *The Senses in Self, Society, and Culture: a sociology of the senses*. Oxford: Routledge.

TWO

Principles for sensory ethnography

Perception, place, knowing, memory and imagination

In this chapter I outline a set of principles for doing sensory ethnography through a focus on questions of perception, place, knowing, memory and imagination. I propose that one of the goals of the sensory ethnographer is to seek to know places in other people's worlds that are similar to how they are known by those people. In doing so we aim to come closer to understanding how other people experience, remember and imagine. This perspective, while rooted in social anthropology, is interdisciplinary since it also draws from theoretical approaches developed in human geography and philosophy and provides a theoretical focus for design ethnography. To frame this perspective I outline a re-thinking of the ethnographic process through theories of the phenomenology of place and the politics of space. This approach recognises the emplaced ethnographer as her- or himself part of a social, sensory and material environment and acknowledges the political and ideological agendas and power relations integral to the contexts and circumstances of ethnographic processes.

INTRODUCTION: ETHNOGRAPHY, SENSORY EXPERIENCE AND THE BODY

Experience

Existing scholarship about the senses reveals a strong interest in human experience. This includes analysis of other people's sensory experiences of social interactions (e.g. Simmel, 1997 [1907]; Howes, 2003; Low, 2005; Vannini et al., 2012), their physical environments (e.g. Porteous, 1990; Ingold, 2000, 2010) and memory (Seremetakis, 1994; Sutton, 2001; Irving, 2010). Ethnographers have also been concerned with how their own sensory embodied experiences might assist them in learning about other people's worlds (e.g. Okely, 1994; Stoller, 1997; Geurts, 2003; Downey, 2005; Marchand, 2010). It has moreover been anticipated that novel forms of ethnographic writing (e.g. Stoller, 1997), filmmaking (e.g. MacDougall, 1998, 2005) and using techniques from arts practice might communicate theoretically sensitive representations of the sensory embodied experiences of one group of people and/or ethnographers themselves to (potentially diverse) target audiences (e.g. Lammer, 2012; O'Neill, 2012). Given this focus on experience, to undertake sensory ethnographies researchers need to have a clear idea of what sensory and embodied experience involves.

I first set this question in its historical context, since it has been of concern throughout the last decades and across academic disciplines. In earlier discussions sensory experience was often regarded as existing on two levels, tending to separate body and mind. Thus, for example, for the geographer Tuan this meant: 'The one [level] is experienced by the body; the other is constructed by the mind' (Tuan, 1993: 165–6). The former was 'a fact of nature or an unplanned property of the built environment' and the latter 'more or less a deliberative creation' (1993: 166). These ideas resonate with those developed contemporaneously in social anthropology. Victor Turner had argued that we should distinguish between 'mere experience' (the continuous flow of events that we passively accept) and 'an experience' (a defined and reflected on event that has a beginning and an end) (1986: 35). Turner's approach separated body and mind by allocating each distinct roles in the production of experience. The distinction between sensation and intellect implied by the idea that one might define a corporeal experience by reflecting on it and giving it meaning, however, implies a separation between body and mind and between doing (or practice) and knowing. This implies the objectification of the corporeal experience by the rational(ising) mind.

Embodiment

The notion of embodiment, which had a significant impact across the social sciences by the 1990s (see, for example, Shilling, 1991, 2003), resolved this dichotomy to some extent. An important implication of the literature that emerged on this topic was to deconstruct the notion of a mind/body divide, to understand the body not simply as a source of experience and activity that would be rationalised and/or controlled by the mind, but itself as a source of knowledge and subsequently of agency. An approach that informed subsequent sensory ethnography was set out by Thomas Csordas in his developments of the phenomenology of the philosopher Maurice Merleau-Ponty (who I discuss below) and the practice theory of the sociologist Pierre Bourdieu. Csordas argued that while 'on the level of perception it is not legitimate to distinguish between mind and body' (1990: 36), we might subsequently ask 'how our bodies may become objectified through processes of reflection' (1990: 36). This understanding enables us to think of the body as a site of knowing while recognising that we are capable of objectification through intellectual activity. However, more recently the anthropologist Greg Downey has pointed out that embodied knowledge is not simply 'stored information' but that it involves biological processes. This involves taking two further steps in understanding embodiment. Downey first cited Ingold's point that 'the body *is* the human organism, as the process of embodiment is one and the same as the development of that organism in its environment' (Ingold, 1998: 28, cited in Downey, 2007: 223), thus bringing to the fore the idea of embodiment as a *process* that is integral to the relationship between humans and their environments. Then (drawing on his ethnographic work on Brazilian Capoeira), Downey argued that to make the concept of embodiment fulfil its potential, we should re-formulate the question to ask: 'how does the body come to "know", and what kind of *biological* changes might occur when learning a skill'? (2007: 223, my italics). These points refigure the way embodiment might be understood in terms of an appreciation of the relationship with the environment and as a biological process.

Embodied ethnography

The idea that ethnographic experiences are 'embodied' – in that the researcher learns and knows through her or his whole experiencing body – has been recognised in much existing methodological literature, across the 'ethnographic disciplines'. In the 1990s the gendered nature of ethnography was highlighted by anthropologists (e.g. Bell et al., 1993) and in some of this literature physical experience became central as relationships not only between minds but between bodies were brought to the fore, through, for example, Don Kulick and Margaret Willson's (1995) exploration of how sexual encounters between anthropologist and 'informant' might be productive of ethnographic knowledge. The sociologist Amanda Coffey summed up the centrality of the body to ethnographic fieldwork, writing that:

> Our bodies and the bodies of others are central to the practical accomplishment of fieldwork. We locate our physical being alongside those of others as we negotiate the spatial context of the field. We concern ourselves with the positioning, visibility and performance of our own embodied self as we undertake participant observation. (Coffey, 1999: 59)

Coffey argued that fieldwork was 'reliant on the analyses of body and body work' and that as such it should be situated 'alongside [what was at the time] contemporary scholarly interest in the body and the nature of embodiment' (Coffey, 1999: 59). While these discussions of the embodiment of the ethnographer were pertinent at the time, the revisions to the notion of embodiment itself – to account for the situatedness of the knowing body as in biological progress as part of a total (material, sensorial and more) environment – suggest attention beyond the limits of a body–mind relationship. Howes has suggested that 'While the paradigm of "embodiment" implies an integration of mind and body, the emergent paradigm of emplacement suggests the sensuous interrelationship of body–mind–environment' (2005b: 7). Indeed, there the idea of emplacement supersedes that of embodiment. Here I use the term emplacement to foreground the idea of the 'emplaced ethnographer' in relation to theories of place discussed later in this chapter. Thus, whereas Coffey (1999) argued for an embodied ethnography, I propose an emplaced ethnography that attends to the question of experience by accounting for the relationships between bodies, minds, and the materiality and sensoriality of the environment. It is now frequently recognised that we need to investigate both the emplacement of the people who participate in our ethnographic research and ethnographers' own emplacement as individuals in and as part of specific research contexts.

The experiencing, knowing and emplaced body is therefore central to the idea of a sensory ethnography. Ethnographic practice entails our multisensorial embodied engagements with others (perhaps through participation in activities or exploring their understandings in part verbally) and with their social, material, discursive and sensory environments. It moreover requires us to reflect on these engagements, to conceptualise their meanings theoretically and to seek ways to communicate the relatedness of experiential and intellectual meanings to others. Next, I examine how theories of sensory perception can support an understanding of the sensory ethnographic process.

MULTISENSORIALITY AND THE INTERCONNECTED SENSES

Phenomenological approaches to the senses

That perception is fundamental to understanding the principles upon which a sensory approach to ethnography must depend would not be disputed. Howes has argued that 'perception' is central to 'good ethnography' (2003: 40). Rodaway suggested that a theory of perception is needed to understand our 'sensuous encounter with the environment' (1994: 19) and Steven Feld proposed that 'emplacement always implicates the intertwined nature of sensual bodily presence and perceptual engagement' (1996: 94). However, the questions of what human perception involves, the interconnections between the senses, the relationship between perception and culture and the implications of this for sensory ethnography practice, are debated issues. Before outlining the disagreements in this field I discuss how the ideas of the phenomenological philosopher Maurice Merleau-Ponty and the ecological psychologist James Gibson have influenced scholarship in this area. Although the deliberations of these theorists have been based mainly on discussions of vision, they have inspired work that stresses multisensoriality.

Although Merleau-Ponty's *The Phenomenology of Perception* was published in French in 1945 and in English in the 1960s his work has more recently become important to the social sciences. Indeed, now 'his discussions of the "intentionality" of consciousness ... and of the role of the body in perception are recognised as important contributions to the understanding of these difficult topics' (Baldwin, 2004: 6). Merleau-Ponty's ideas are relevant to the formulation of sensory ethnography because he placed sensation at the centre of human perception. For Merleau-Ponty sensation could only be realised in relation to other elements, therefore it could not be defined as 'pure impression' (2002 [1962]: 4); indeed 'pure sensation would amount to no sensation thus to not feeling at all' (2002 [1962]: 5). Thus he proposed that, for example, 'to see is to have colours or lights before one, to hear is to encounter sounds, to feel is to come up against qualities', that is, sensations are produced through our encounters with 'sense-data' or the qualities which are the properties of objects (2002 [1962]: 4). But, he argued that to be realised sensation needs to be 'overlaid by a body of knowledge' since it cannot exist in a pure form (2002 [1962]: 5). Merleau-Ponty's approach has been influential amongst both social and visual anthropologists concerned with the body (e.g. Csordas, 1990) and the senses, particularly in discussions concerning the relationships between different sensory modalities. Ingold (2000) has drawn from Merleau-Ponty's point that: '"My body", as Merleau-Ponty puts it, "is not a collection of adjacent organs but a synergic system, all of the functions of which are exercised and linked together in the general action of being in the world" (1962: 234)'. Following this Ingold argued that 'Sight and hearing, to the extent they can be distinguished at all are but facets of this action' (Ingold, 2000: 268). The anthropological filmmaker David MacDougall has similarly drawn from Merleau-Ponty's ideas to argue that 'although seeing and touching are not the same, they originate in the same body and their objects overlap', they 'share an experiential field' and 'Each refers to a more general faculty' (1998: 51). Other anthropologists of the senses have developed more ethnographic applications of Merleau-Ponty's work. For example, Geurts (2003) followed Csordas' proposal that

> If our perception 'ends in objects,' the goal of a phenomenological anthropology of perception is to capture that moment of transcendence when perception begins, and *in the midst of arbitrariness and indeterminacy*, constitutes and is constituted by culture. (Csordas, 1990: 9, emphasis added by Geurts, 2003: 74)

Applying this idea to her sensory ethnography of the Anlo Ewe people, Geurts outlined the terminology the Anlo Ewe used to categorise sensory experiences – a set of 'cultural categories or a scheme ... for organising experience'. However, she stressed that although these cultural patterns could be discerned, from a phenomenological perspective 'or from the experiential standpoint of being-in-the-world, analytic categories of language, cognition, sensation, perception, culture and embodiment exist as a complex and sticky web' (2003: 74) – the 'arbitrariness and indeterminacy' that were referred to by Csordas.

Ecological psychology and the senses

Gibson's work on 'ecological psychology' has likewise been of continuing appeal to scholars exploring the senses, initially informing Rodaway's sensuous geography in the 1990s. Departing from earlier approaches to 'perception geography', Rodaway suggested Gibson's theory of perception was particularly relevant to geography because 'it not only gives importance to the environment itself in perception but also considers perception by a mobile observer' (1994: 19). He takes two key strands from Gibson's ecological theory of perception: the idea of the senses as perceptual systems which 'emphasises the interrelationships between the different senses ... in perception and the integration of sensory bodily and mental processes' (1994: 19–20); and the idea of ecological optics which 'emphasises the role of the environment itself in structuring optical (auditory, tactile, etc.) stimulation' whereby 'the environment becomes a source of *information*, not merely raw data' (1994: 20). Ingold's more recent development of Gibson's ideas has however been more influential in subsequent 'sensory ethnographies'. Ingold also takes up Gibson's understanding that 'Perception ... is not the achievement of a mind in a body, but of the organism as whole in its environment, and is tantamount to the organism's own exploratory movement through the world'. This, he continues, makes 'mind' 'immanent in the network of sensory pathways that are set up by virtue of the perceiver's immersion in his or her environment' (Ingold, 2000: 3). Also of particular interest for understanding the senses in ethnography, Ingold draws out the relevance of Gibson's understanding of the relationship between different modalities of sensory experience, summed up in: 'the perceptual systems not only overlap in their functions, but are also subsumed under a total system of bodily orientation', therefore 'Looking, listening and touching ... are not separate activities they are just different facets of the same activity: that of the whole organism in its environment' (Ingold, 2000: 261). Gibson's ideas are increasingly influential in ethnographic work that attends to the senses. This is particularly evident in the writing of scholars in geography and anthropology who have built on Ingold's developments in this area (e.g. Grasseni, 2004b, 2011; Strang, 2005; Downey, 2007; Spinney, 2007).

Literature in neurobiology also offers interesting insights into the relationship between the senses that are broadly congruent with the ideas discussed above, and also, as discussed later in this chapter, that are coherent with theories of place. For instance, in 2001 Shinsuke Shimojo and Ladan Shams reported that 'behavioral and brain imaging studies' had challenged the conventional opinion in this field that perception was 'a modular function, with the different sensory modalities operating independently of each other'. The newer work they discussed proposed that 'cross-modal interactions are the rule and not the exception in perception, and that the cortical pathways previously thought to be sensory-specific are modulated by signals from other modalities' (Shimojo and Shams, 2001: 505). Newell and Shams also later proposed that:

> our phenomenological experience is not of disjointed sensory sensations but is instead of a coherent multisensory world, where sounds, smells, tastes, lights, and touches amalgamate. What we perceive or where we perceive it to be located in space is a product of inputs from different sensory modalities that combine, substitute, or integrate. (Newell and Shams, 2007: 1415)

In doing so they also recognised that it is not simply the immediacy of experience that informs this process, in that: 'these inputs are further modulated by learning and by more cognitive or top-down effects including previous knowledge, attention, and the task at hand' (2007: 1415).

Debates about perception

There is disagreement amongst scholars of the senses regarding how phenomenological understandings might be employed, and how they might be engaged in relation to the findings of neuroscience. One of the most significant debates concerns the utility of theories of sensory perception for understanding everyday (and research) practices. Ingold draws on the ideas of Gibson and Merleau-Ponty to suggest (amongst other things) 'that the eyes and ears should not be understood as separate keyboards for the registration of sensation but as organs of the body as a whole, in whose movement, within an environment, the activity of perception consists' (Ingold, 2000: 268). In contrast, Howes has argued that both thinkers are preoccupied with vision and oblivious 'to the senses in social context'. He suggests that researchers would be unwise to 'think they can derive grounding from the asocial contextless models of "perceptual systems" proposed by Western philosophers (e.g. Merleau-Ponty, 2002 [1962]) and psychologists (e.g. Gibson, 1966, 1979)' (2003: 49–50). Instead, Howes stresses the need for ethnographic researchers to 'elicit the sensory models of the people they are studying' (2003: 49–50). He is particularly critical of Ingold's (2000) and Rodaway's (1994) use of Gibson's (1966, 1979) view of 'the environment as a set of "affordances"' and insists that 'Without some sense of how the senses are "culturally attuned", in Feld's terms, there is no telling what information the environment affords' (Howes, 2005a: 144). More recently Howes and Classen have pursued their argument further, opening their book *Ways of Sensing* with the claim that 'The ways we use our senses, and the ways we create and understand the sensory world, are shaped by culture. Perception is informed not only by the personal meaning a particular sensation has for us, but also by the social values it carries' (Howes and Classen, 2014: 1). The 'culturalist' approach adopted by Howes and Classen offers an analytical route that connects with an intellectual trajectory, which spans across anthropology, media and cultural studies and other disciplines. Its focus is on the cultural and the representational, even though it has an interest in the senses (see Pink, 2014). This approach often (co)exists in debate with that of non-representational theorists, as outlined in Chapter 1.

The work of neurobiologists (e.g. Shimojo and Shams, 2001; Newell and Shams, 2007), combined with MacDougall's (1998) and Ingold's (2000) interpretations of the senses as interconnected and inseparable, invites ethnographic researchers to comprehend our perception of social, material and intangible elements of our environments as being dominated by no one sensory modality (see Chapter 1). These notions of the interconnectedness of the senses also permit us to understand how in different contexts similar meanings might be expressed through different sensory modalities and media. This does not mean that Howes' (Howes, 2003, 2005a; Howes and Classen, 2014) emphasis on culture and the social significance of sensory models and meanings is redundant. There are ways that an analysis that attends to the level of culture and uses representational categories as its units of analysis can offer useful understandings of the world (see Pink, 2012). Indeed, it is essential that the sensory ethnographer appreciates the cultural and (biographical) specificity of the sensory meanings and modalities people call on and the sets of discourses through which they mobilise embodied ways of knowing in social contexts. However, simultaneously, our sensory perception is inextricable from the cultural categories that we use to give meaning to sensory experiences in social and material interactions (including when doing ethnography). Indeed, perception is integral to the very production of these categories: culture itself is not fixed. Rather, human beings are continuously and actively involved in the processes through which not only culture, but rather the total environments in which they live are constituted, experienced, and change continually over time. In the next section I propose how a theory of place and space can enable us to understand both these processes and the emplacement of the ethnographer.

PLACE, SPACE AND ETHNOGRAPHY

Thinking through place and space

Concepts of space and place have long since been the concerns of geographers and have (along with theories of landscape) often framed discussions of the senses in the discipline (e.g. Porteous, 1990; Tuan, 1993; Rodaway, 1994; Thrift, 2004). Connections between understandings of place in human geography, environmental psychology and neuroscience have been discussed by Charis Lengen and Thomas Kistemann in their review of literature in this field. They conclude that 'Neuroscience has provided evidence that place constitutes a very specific, distinct dimension in neuronal processing. This reinforces the phenomenological argumentation of human geographers and environmental psychologists' (Lengen and Kistemann, 2012: 1169). Social anthropologists have also mobilised concepts of place in relation to the senses, notably demonstrating how attention to the senses in ethnography offers routes to analysing other people's place-making practices (e.g. Feld and Basso, 1996b). Place is moreover an important concept for other disciplines for which the senses are particularly relevant, including design theory and practice (e.g. Silberg, 2013).

Building on this, I suggest going beyond a focus on the affinity between the study of the senses and of place-making or place, to consider how the concepts of place and space offer a framework for rethinking the ethnographic process, and the situatedness of the ethnographer. A focus on space and place also enables us to re-think the temporality of the ethnographic process in ways that connect it more closely with the future-oriented approach of design research, which in turn invites new ways of opening up ethnographic practice to applied and change-making agendas. Below I interrogate recent critical anthropological, philosophical and geographical commentaries on existing treatments of space and place in ethnography and theory in order to develop such a framework. My starting point is the anthropological literature in which the critique of spatial assumptions is directed to a rethinking of ethnographic practice and process. I then consider how the phenomenology of place contributes to understanding how these ethnographic practices are played out, before asking how universal theories of space and place can situate ethnographic practice and process in its political context.

As Simon Coleman and Peter Collins have pointed out, 'place' has been of continuing importance in the ethnographic practice of anthropology, in part because 'the process of demonstrating the physical connection of researcher and text with place has remained of prime importance to the discipline' (2006: 1). This connection has been a conventional means of establishing the 'authority' of the ethnographer and the authenticity of her or his work. Nevertheless, the question of place in ethnography has become increasingly problematised with 'challenges to the anthropologist as producer of text, and to place as a container of culture' (2006: 2). These challenges were set out in a volume edited by Akhil Gupta and James Ferguson, known for its emphasis on the dislocation of a fixed role between culture and place. Gupta and Ferguson argued for 'a focus on social and political processes of place making' as in 'embodied practices that shape identities and enable resistances' (2001: 6). Indeed, anthropologists now normally do not consider their research as the study of closed cultures in circumscribed territorial places. This questioning of place in anthropology raises a set of theoretical and methodological issues for ethnographic researchers of any discipline. This can be expressed through two related questions: first, how can place be defined if it is something that is not fixed or enclosed, that is constituted as much through the flows that link it to other locations, persons and things, as it is through what goes on 'inside' it? And second, given that places are continually constituted, rather than fixed, then how can we understand the role of the emplaced ethnographer as a participant in and eventually author of the places she or he studies? This question requires thinking about both the politics and power relations that global flows entail and attending to the detail of our everyday embodied and sensory engagements in our environments. As such it requires that analytically we examine the politics and phenomenology of space and place. For this purpose a coherent theory of space and place is needed. In what follows I consider three theoretical developments concerning place and space. First, I discuss the philosopher Edward Casey's phenomenological theory of place (1996), which is especially relevant for considering questions about the sensoriality of ethnographic practices and processes (see Basso, 1996; Feld, 1996), the emplacement of the ethnographer and the centrality of the body. Then I draw from the geographer Doreen Massey's (2005) discussion of the relationship between place and space, which brings our attention to the politics of space. Massey's understanding of place and space as 'open' offers a way to understand the situatedness of the ethnographer in relation to social relations and power structures. Finally, I consider the anthropologist Ingold's re-thinking of place in terms of 'entanglement' (2008, 2010). This critical response to the idea of place as bounded facilitates an understanding of ethnographic places as both based in human perception and open.

The 'gathering power' of place (Edward Casey)

Casey's earlier work responded to what he refers to as 'anthropological treatments of place as something supposedly made up from space – something factitious carved out of space or superimposed on space' (1996: 43). While it would seem to be (modern western) commonsense to assume that space exists 'out there' already and that places are thus made in it, for Casey, conversely place and our emplacement would be the starting point for understanding the relationship between place and space. Because he (following Merleau-Ponty) understood perception as primary (1996: 17), and the first point in our ability to know place, through being 'in a place' (1996: 18), it follows that in Casey's argument space and time 'arise from the experience of place itself' (1996: 36). He argued that space and time are contained in place rather than *vice versa* (1996: 43–4); as such it is place rather than space that is universal (but not pre-cultural) (1996: 46). This implies that as ethnographers our primary context for any piece of research is place. Indeed, Casey's work stresses that place is central to what Merleau-Ponty has called our way of 'being in the world' in that we are always 'emplaced' (1996: 44). The 'lived body' (Casey, 1996: 21) is central to Casey's understanding of place, manifested in his argument that '*lived bodies belong to places* and help to constitute them' and '*places belong to lived bodies* and depend on them' (1996: 24, original italics), thus seeing the two as interdependent. Following Casey, we cannot escape from place, since it is simultaneously the context we inhabit and our site of investigation; it is what we are seeking to understand and it is where our sensory experiences are produced, defined and acted on. To understand the relevance of Casey's theory of place for the practice of a sensory ethnography there are two further key points: first, place is not static, rather he has conceptualised it as an 'event' that is in process, constantly changing and subject to redefinition; second, place is endowed with what he called a 'gathering power' (Casey, 1996: 44) by which 'Minimally, places gather things in their midst – where "things" connote various animate and inanimate entities. Places also gather experiences and histories, even languages and thoughts' (1996: 24). This is particularly significant for a sensory ethnography in that it allows us to conceptualise place as a domain where a set of different types of 'thing' come together. Casey presents place as a form of constantly changing event, but emphasises that it is not so contingent that it is elusive, writing that

> Places are at once elastic – for example, in regard to their outer edges and internal paths – and yet sufficiently coherent for them to be considered as the *same* (hence to be remembered, returned to, etc.) as well as to be classified as places as certain *types* (e.g., home-place, workplace, visiting place). (1996: 44)

It is these *types* of place that most often become the locations for and subjects/ objects of ethnography as researchers strive to understand how people's lives are lived out and felt, and they inhabit and move through, for instance, the home, a city or a hospital.

Place as 'open' (Doreen Massey)

While Casey redefined the relationship between space and place by suggesting that the latter is secondary to the former, Massey has critiqued common and dominant conceptualisation of space as closed and abstract. In doing so she also challenges the idea of the primacy of place represented in Casey's formulation. Her stated aim is 'to uproot "space" from that constellation of concepts in which it has so unquestioningly so often been embedded (stasis; closure; representation) and to settle it among another set of ideas (heterogeneity; relationality; coevalness' (Massey, 2005: 13). This suggests a way of understanding space as something more contingent and active. Massey proposes that it should be understood through three main principles, as: first, 'the product of interrelations'; second, 'the sphere of the possibility of multiplicity in the sense of contemporaneous plurality'; and third, 'always under construction' (2005: 9). Thus Massey invites us to re-think the idea that space might be something abstract that might be mapped out, flattened or occupied by places (2005: 13). Rather, she proposes that 'If space is ... a simultaneity of stories-so-far [rather than a 'surface'], then places are collections of those stories, articulations of the wider power-geometries of space' (2005: 130). As collections of the trajectories that run through space, places are always unique. Massey's conceptualisation of place recognises 'the specificity of place' and that places (which might range from, for example, a city, the countryside, to a family home) are '*spatio-temporal* events' (2005: 130, original italics). Indeed, for Massey the 'event of place' involves: 'the coming together of the previously unrelated, a constellation of processes rather than a thing' (2005: 141), which she conceptualises through the idea of the 'throwntogetherness of place' (2005: 140) which involves not only human but material elements.

While in making this argument Massey (2005) does not elaborate on the phenomenology of place, in terms of how we might experience place her idea is not exclusively an abstraction. She describes what it might mean to go from one place to another, using examples from her own experience, to suggest that: 'To travel between places is to move between collections of trajectories and to reinsert yourself in the ones to which you relate' (2005: 130). Massey's work offers an exciting paradigm for understanding the relationship between place and space through a focus on the politics of space. She acknowledges 'the on-going and ever-specific project of the practices through which' the '*sociability* [of space] is to be configured' (2005: 195, my italics). However, while recognising the significance of the social, her starting point is quite different from Casey's (1996) understanding of place as rooted in human perception. Yet, in a pluralistic conceptualisation of place in relation to space, is there a reason to subordinate human perception to spatial politics and/or vice versa? Are they not both implicated in the same processes?

To some extent Casey and Massey coincide. They both refer to place as 'event', and as such recognise the fluidity of place. Whereas Casey writes about place as a 'gathering' process, Massey emphasises its 'throwntogetherness' – in these formulations they both acknowledge the human and non-human elements of place and suggest how place as event is constantly changing through social and material relations and practices. Yet I do not want to construct a false sense of compatibility between these two approaches. One of the key differences between Casey's rendering of place and that developed by Massey is Casey's perspective on how places hold together. Casey understands places as having a capacity to '*gather* things in their midst' (my italics). Things include 'various animate and inanimate entities', 'experiences and histories, even languages and thoughts' (1996: 24). Part of this gathering capacity also involves having a 'hold' or 'mode of containment', which involves 'a holding *in* and a holding *out*' (1996: 25). As such Casey suggests that 'gathering gives to a place its peculiar perduringness, allowing us to return to it again and again as *the same place*' (1996: 26, original italics). Massey conversely refers to places as 'open' and 'as woven together out of ongoing stories, as a moment within power-geometries, as a particular constellation within the wider topographies of space, and as in process, as unfinished business' (2005: 131). Indeed, Massey's disagreement is with Casey's assertion: 'that "To live is to live locally, and to know is first of all to know the places one is in" (Casey 1996: 18)' (Massey, 2005: 183). Rather, Massey argues that both place *and* space are 'concrete, grounded, real, lived etc. etc.' (2005: 185) and the implication of this is that both are relevant to understanding the political, social, material and sensorial relationships and negotiations of ethnographic research. Nevertheless, if both space and place are lived, then it would follow that we need to account for human perception in the task of understanding either of them.

'Entanglement' and 'meshwork' (Tim Ingold)

Ingold (2008) has proposed an alternative way of understanding not simply 'place' but the way we live in relation to an environment that offers a route to addressing these questions. He refigures the notion of environment to propose that 'The environment ... comprises not the surroundings of the organism but a zone of entanglement' (2008: 1797). While one might conceptualise such a zone of entanglement as a 'place', we do not live *in* such places. Rather, Ingold gives primacy to movement rather than to place, thus he argues that places are produced from movement because 'there would be no places were it not for the comings and goings of human beings and other organisms to and from them, from and to places elsewhere' (2008: 1808). Significantly, in this formulation he sees places as unbounded. Ingold's work also provides a new way of conceptualising what Casey (1996) and Massey (2005) in their own ways refer to as place as event, in that he suggests that places do not exist so much as they '*occur*' (2008: 1808, original italics). In keeping with the idea of place as produced through movement he proposes that places 'occur along the lifepaths of beings' as part of a 'meshwork of paths' (2008: 1808). Following this we are always emplaced because we are always in movement. These ideas moreover invite a solution to the emphases in both Casey's (1996) notion of place as involving 'gathering' and Massey's (2005) idea of the 'throwntogetherness' of place. Whereas the former might be seen to endow places themselves with an undue degree of agency *to gather*, the latter implies both a randomness and/or the role of external (possibly spatial) forces in determining the composition of places. If we see places as 'occurring' through the intersections and proximities of pathways as they are entangled then they are events that are constituted neither internally nor externally but as varying intensities in what Ingold (2008) calls a 'meshwork'.

Place for sensory ethnography

Ingold's approach could be used to suggest that a concept of space is hardly necessary for the sensory ethnographer, since if we view the world through a notion of entanglement it may be unnecessary to distinguish between space and place. However, because an approach to understanding people's everyday realities is needed that will allow for both global power configurations and the immediacy of experience I suggest that Ingold's ideas can help us to moderate between concepts of place and space. Casey's (1996) writing on place is relevant to ethnographers because his understanding of place as event, constituted through lived bodies and things, offers a way of understanding the immediacy of perception and as such of our sensory engagements with material, social and power-imbued environments, as well as with the actual involvement of ethnographers in the production of the places they research. Indeed, place and our relationship to it cannot be understood without attention to precisely how we learn through, know and move in material and sensory environments. However, Massey's (2005) challenge to the primacy of the local, and indeed of the association of place with 'local', offers an important counterpoint that I suggest allows us to situate the sensory ethnographer further. Massey's ideas invite ethnographers to consider how the specificity of place can only be understood through recognition of its actual configurations being mutually contingent with those of space as she defines it. As such the lived immediacy of the 'local' as constituted through the making of ethnographic places is inevitably interwoven or entangled with the 'global'. This is not a relationship that contemporary anthropologists are unaware of; the complexities of the relationship between local and global have been an explicit theme in anthropological discussions since at least the 1990s, and are dealt with in the work of Gupta and Ferguson (2001) discussed above. Yet conceptualising these relations through a theory of place and space provides a useful framework through which to understand the phenomenology of everyday encounters in relation to and as co-implicated with the complexity of global processes.

The focus on place developed here works as an analytical construct to conceptualise fundamental aspects of how both ethnographers and participants in ethnographic research are emplaced in social, sensory and material contexts, characterised by and productive of particular power configurations, that they experience through their whole bodies and that are constantly changing (even if in very minor ways). In doing so it allows us to pursue the reflexive project of a sensory ethnography. The idea of place as lived but open invokes the inevitable question of how researchers themselves are entangled in, participate in the production of and are co-present in the ethnographic places they share with research participants, their materialities and power relations. These ethnographic places extend away from the intensity and immediacy of the local and are entangled with multiple trajectories.

LEARNING ABOUT OTHER PEOPLE'S EMPLACEMENT: SENSORY EMBODIED KNOWING, KNOWLEDGE AND ITS 'TRANSMISSION'

The 'transmission' of knowledge

The question of how sensory knowledge is transmitted, flows or is learned between persons and/or generations has been debated extensively in the existing literature. Moreover, the terminology used to discuss this question is contested, with some preferring to speak of transmission (Marchand, 2010) while others opt for the notion of learning, arguing that knowledge cannot as such be 'transmitted' between persons (see Fors et al., 2013). In this section I use both terms as they have been engaged in recent literatures, acknowledging the need to assess how the terms are used rather than to take for granted that specific meanings and processes are universally attributed to them. For instance, Trevor Marchand (2010) uses 'transmission' to refer to different processes in a way that makes the work of scholars who take different approaches comparable. Therefore, he comments on 'cultural transmission' in the work of Maurice Bloch (Marchand, 2010: S10), while writing of 'individual strategies of transmission and enskillment' in the work of Greg Downey (Marchand, 2010: S13) along with Ingold's idea that '"knowledge" is an ongoing activity rather than an object or definable entity' (Marchand, 2010: S14). Scholars interested in the senses seem generally agreed that the transmission or learning of knowledge should be seen as a social, participatory and embodied process (e.g. Ingold, 2000; Geurts, 2003; Downey, 2007; Grasseni, 2007b; Hahn, 2007; Marchand, 2007). As Marchand puts it, reflecting on articles included in a journal issue which explored 'anthropology's thinking about human knowledge through exploration of the interdependence of nurture with nature', although the contributors took different perspectives on this, 'there is mutual recognition that knowledge-making is a dynamic process arising directly from the indissoluble relations that exist between minds, bodies, and environment' (2010: S2).

Understanding how knowledge is transmitted or learned is important for at least two reasons – first, because it should inform our understandings of how we as ethnographers might learn through our sensory embodied and emplaced experiences, and, second, because it raises a research question: How do the people who participate in our research learn and know? In participatory methods, where the researcher learns through her or his own embodied or emplaced practices, the boundaries between these two questions can become blurred. If, as I have suggested in the previous sections, the sensory ethnographer is always emplaced and seeking to understand the emplacement of others, this raises the question of how we might understand the processes through which she or he can arrive at such an understanding. Put another way, how can we learn to occupy or imagine places and ways of perceiving and being that are similar to, parallel to or indeed interrelated with and contingent on those engaged in by research participants?

Learning and knowing

Existing theories of learning offer a starting point for thinking about these questions. Etienne Wenger outlines the ideas of 'knowing in practice' (1998: 141) and 'the experience of knowing' (1998: 142). For Wenger 'knowing is defined only in the context of specific practices, where it arises out of the combination of a regime of competence and an experience of meaning'. He conceptualises 'the experience of knowing' as one of 'participation' (1998: 142). This means that individuals themselves cannot be the source of knowing. Rather, knowing is contingent on its connectedness both historically and with others. Yet knowing is also specific, engaged, active, engaged and 'experiential' (1998: 141). As such while the 'experience of knowing' is 'one of participation' it is simultaneously unique and constantly changing. The implication of understanding knowing as situated in practice is that it implies that to 'know' as others do, we need to engage in practices with them, making participation central to this task. The idea can be extended to seeing 'knowing in practice' as being an embodied and multisensorial way of knowing that is inextricable from our sensorial and material engagements with the environment and is as such an emplaced knowing. Although it is possible to speak or write about it, such knowing might be difficult to express in words. This is one of the challenges faced by the sensory ethnographer seeking to access and represent other people's emplacement. However, this should not preclude an understanding of talking with others as itself a form of practice through which emplaced knowing might be acquired (as, for instance, in the ethnographic interview as conceptualised in Chapter 5).

The concept of knowing is engaged across academic disciplines, particularly in literatures concerned with questions of practice (e.g. Nicolini et al., 2003; Harris, 2007). The notion of knowing raises the question of the status of its companion concept of knowledge. According to Wenger, knowing might be used to emphasise the experience or competence (1998: 140) of participating in a practice. He treats knowledge as inextricable from this, by seeing practice itself as a 'form of knowledge' (1998: 141). Harris likewise emphasises the specificity of knowledge in terms of its situatedness in 'a particular place and moment' and that 'it is inhabited by individual knowers and that it is always changing and emergent' (2007: 4). Yet while knowledge is always produced and lived in situated specificity it can be interpreted as having a different relationship to the directness of experience associated with a concept of emplaced knowing. Wenger qualifies his understanding of practice as knowledge (1998: 141) by acknowledging that knowledge is not *only* specific to or within practices because it is also attached to broader discourses and as such situates practices. He thus suggests that 'knowing in practice involves an interaction between the local and the global' (1998: 141). Thus he offers a connection between the idea that our emplacement and direct relationship with a sensory, material and social environment is necessarily made meaningful in relationship with the politics of space, including the wider (global) discourses and power relations that are also entangled in the 'local' places where ethnographers know through their practice.

If one of the objectives of the ethnographer is to come to know as others do, then we need to account for the processes through which we, and the participants in our research, come to know. Wenger's 'social perspective on learning' (1998: 226–8) provides a good starting point for thinking about how we learn and establishes learning as primarily '*the ability to negotiate new meanings*' (1998: 226) and '*fundamentally experiential and fundamentally social*' (1998: 227, original italics). The experiential and social aspects of learning have been explored further through recent anthropological investigations concerning the transmission of knowledge. As a foundation for his understanding of the transmission of knowledge, Ingold calls for an ecological approach to what he calls 'skill'.

For Ingold skill is a property, not of an 'individual human body', but of 'the total field of relations constituted by the presence of the organism-person, indissolubly body and mind, in a richly structured environment' (2000: 353). He suggests that 'skilled practice cannot be reduced to a formula' and thus skills cannot be passed intergenerationally through the transmission of formulae (2000: 353). Instead, he proposes that rather than a generation passing on to the next 'a corpus of representations, or information' it introduces 'novices into contexts which afford selected opportunities for perception and action, and by providing the scaffolding that enables them to make use of these affordances'. Ingold argues that because practitioners develop an 'attentive engagement' with the material they work with 'rather than a mere mechanical coupling, that skilled activity carries its own intrinsic intentionality' (2000: 354). By requiring attention to the roles of perception and action Ingold thus invites us to understand knowledge transmission as something that occurs through our emplaced engagements with persons and things. As ethnographers we learn through/in practice but in doing so we make this knowing our own rather than simply assuming that of others.

Examples of learning, knowing and transmission

Several ethnographers of the senses have explored knowledge transmission in practice. Grasseni, like Ingold, locates the transmission of knowledge within an 'ecology of practice'. She discusses how cattle breeders' children play with toy cows which are modelled on the attributes that represent the 'ideal cow' by mimicking 'the ideal of good form that is founding cattle fair champions' (2007b: 61). Grasseni found that when the ten-year-old boy who features in her research spoke of his toy cows, he was 'reproducing the discerning knowledge that breeders have of their cattle', but also linking this expertise to his actual experience of and actions in the real world with cattle. She identifies that he 'was engaging from very early on in what Jean Lave calls "legitimate peripheral participation" (Lave and Wenger 1991)' since 'Learning to be a breeder implies an education of attention that starts at an early age, a veritable apprenticeship in skilled vision' (2007b: 60). Grasseni argues that the development of this skilled vision

> or the ways we see beauty, that we embody skill and enjoy participating in moral order … does not happen solely as a result of the individual workings of the mind, or of the brain, or of the body of each of us, but rather through highly socialised means. (2007b: 63)

Other ethnographic studies likewise demonstrate that learning through practice involves not simply mimicking others' but creating one's own emplaced skill and knowing in ways that are acceptable to others. For example, about learning Japanese dance Hahn writes:

> there is a struggle in learning. The transmission process is through physical imitation and sensory information, yet at a certain point we must embody the dance and instil our personal self through the strictures of the choreography and style. I believe this is where the body sensually situates movement to orient 'self'. (2007: 49)

Hahn understands this constitution of 'self' in the dance transmission process as being what follows from the dance student's 'enculturation of [dance] aesthetics via the body' (2007: 67); this produces an elusive state that she calls 'presence'. Presence is very different from the transmission processes in learning about dance that Hahn analyses as being visual, tactile and aural/oral processes. While, she writes, these processes involve 'an inward motion, a taking in of sensory information to train the body', presence emanates from the dancer: 'once apperception occurs, assimilation and realised embodiment, the very sensory paths that were the vehicles of transmission now enhance presence' (2007: 163).

Geurts' discussion of the Anlo Ewe people of Ghana has similar implications. Writing of the importance of learning to balance in Anlo Ewe childrearing practices, Geurts emphasises how amongst her research participants 'balancing was described as one of the ultimate symbols for being human' (2003: 105). She notes how 'children were often placed on mats in the centre of our compound and encouraged to sit up, to crawl, and to begin trying to [balance]' (2003: 102). This was a stage prior to walking at which 'a baby mastered standing and *balancing* on his own two feet while the sibling let go of his hands' (2003: 103). She notes how one of her research participants 'believed there was a fairly explicit connection between the physical practice of balancing and a temperamental quality of being level-headed and calm' (2003: 105). Guerts points out how values and ideologies are embedded in these socialisation processes. She suggests 'the sensory order is reproduced through sensory engagements in routine practices and the enactment of traditions'. But as she comments: 'these processes are neither automatic nor mechanically implanted into passive individuals. They are what constitutes the stuff of experience, the feelings that make up the micro-level of social interactions (or sensory engagements).' She sees these processes as requiring 'some kind of agency and intentionality' (2003: 107).

Transmission, knowing, learning: issues for sensory ethnography

These existing works on senses and transmission raise two key issues. The first is an emphasis on the social, material and sensorial practices and contexts of knowledge transmission, the second the question of the location of the individual, the 'self', 'intentionality' and 'agency' in the transmission process. The former suggests that to understand the relevance of sensory experiences, categories and meanings in people's lives ethnographers need to research how these are known in practice within contexts of specific socialities and materialities. However, this does not preclude established forms of practice. The practical question of how researchers might access or understand these social and material relationships is explored in the later chapters.

The second issue refers to the idea that the transmission of knowledge does not simply involve the repetitive process of learning a template for action (e.g. Ingold, 2000); rather, that self and agency, intentionality and creativity are pivotal to the transmission process. Indeed, following Wenger, learning might change 'all at once who we are' (1998: 226–8) and, as Downey points out, can lead to 'perceptual, physiological and behavioural change' (2007: 236). Thus the ethnographer who is hoping that the sensory knowing of others will be transmitted to her or him might ask how such sensory knowing, which is intimately related to the researcher's perception of her or his environment, sense of self and embodiment, might lead to academic knowledge (if this indeed is what happens). I pursue this question in Chapter 7. In the following two sections I ask how, by seeking to share a similar place through forms of co-presence with research participants, ethnographers might endeavour to use their own imaginations to generate a sense of the pasts and futures of others, thus extending the idea of 'knowing in practice' (Wenger, 1998) to one of 'imagining in practice'.

SENSORY MEMORIES

Recent literature that engages with the relationships between memory and the senses (e.g. Seremetakis, 1994; Marks, 2000; Sutton, 2001) indicates two key themes of relevance to understanding sensory ethnography practice: sensory memory as an individual practice, for example in biographical research; and collective sensory memory, for example as invoked through, and invested in, ritual. These are not mutually exclusive categories.

The work of the historian Paul Connerton (1989) has been influential in discussions of collective memory. Connerton asks 'how is the memory of groups conveyed and sustained?' and suggests we might understand this through a focus on 'recollection and bodies' (1989: 4). He thus suggests 'social memory' might be found in the performativity of 'commemorative ceremonies' to which bodies are central (1989: 4–5). Connerton's approach has been influential in the work of anthropologists of the senses, since, as David Sutton puts it, 'he draws our attention to the importance of these of types of memories that can be found sedimented in the body' (2001: 12). As Sutton's (2001) work demonstrates, this approach is relevant for understanding how, for instance, collective memories are invested in food practices. Nadia Seremetakis (1994) has taken a similar approach to the question of 'sensory memory'. Seremetakis suggests that the senses 'are a collective medium of communication' which is 'like language' but '*are not* reducible to language' (1994: 6, original italics). She argues that 'The sensory landscape and its meaning-endowed objects bear within them emotional and historical sedimentation that can provoke and ignite gestures, discourses and acts'. However, the memories and meanings that might be sensorially invoked are not fixed. Rather, Seremetakis suggests that 'sensory memory or the mediation on the historical substance of experience is not mere repetition but transformation that brings the past into the present as a natal event' (1994: 7). These understandings of sensory memory as embodied, and continually reconstituted through practice, are particularly relevant to an ethnographic methodology that attends to the body and place. They imply that sensory memory is an inextricable element of how we know in practice, and indeed part of the processes through which ways of knowing are constituted.

While individual memories are related to collective memories, it is also worth considering the relationship of the senses and memory in the context of biographical research. This involves also accounting for how individual biographical past experiences are implicated in the constitution of place in the present. Connections between these concepts have been made explicit in the work of Stoller (1994) and Feld (1996). Reflecting on Seremetakis' ideas, Stoller notes how 'The human body is not principally a text; rather, it is consumed by a world filled with smells, textures, sights, sounds and tastes, all of which trigger cultural memories' (1994: 119). However, the body is not merely constituted as Stoller describes by its sensory environment, but our embodied practices also contribute to such emplaced memory processes. For instance, Feld emphasises a relationship between memory and place, citing Casey's point that 'Moving in or through a given place, the body imports its own emplaced past into its present experience' (Casey, 1987: 194, cited by Feld, 1996: 93). Indeed, the question of embodied knowing and remembering can also be seen as part of our everyday life experiences as we go about ordinary mundane tasks. These memories (and moments of improvisation) are not necessarily things we speak about or discuss with others but ways of knowing and remembering that are embedded in our habitual physical movements as part of particular environments (Pink and Leder Mackley, 2014). Thus our experiences of place – and its social, physical and intangible components – are inextricable from the invocation, creation and re-investment of memories.

These points imply three related roles for a theory of sensory memory in ethnography. The first is to aid us in understanding the meanings and nature of the memories that research participants recount, enact, define or reflect on for researchers. The second is to help us to understand how ethnographers might generate insights into the ways other people remember through trying to share their emplacement. The third is to assist us to comprehend how ethnographers use their own memories in auto-ethnographic accounts (e.g. Seremetakis, 1994; Okely, 1996) or to reflexively reconstruct their fieldwork experiences. In the next section I suggest understanding the relationship between the senses and ways of imagining in a similar way. Ethnographers rely on both memory and imagination (and indeed the distinction between the two can become blurred) to create what we might call ethnographic places.

SENSORY IMAGINATIONS

The anthropologist Arjun Appadurai has argued that in contemporary modernity – what he calls the 'postelectronic world' – the imagination has 'a newly significant role'. He suggests that understanding the role of imagination in this contemporary context requires going beyond the idea that 'all societies' have transcended everyday life through mythologies and ritual, and that in dreams individuals 'might refigure their social lives, live out proscribed emotional states and sensations, and see things that have spilled over their sense of ordinary life' (1996: 5). In a contemporary context Appadurai proposes first that the imagination is important because it has 'become a part of the quotidian mental work of ordinary people in many societies'. Imagination can thus be seen as a practice of everyday life (1996: 5). Second, he distinguishes between fantasy and imagination in that while fantasy might be 'divorced from projects and actions', 'the imagination especially when collective, can become the fuel for action' (1996: 7). Third, Appadurai stresses the significance of 'collective imagination', through which groups of people might move from 'shared imagination to collective action' (1996: 8). This configuration of the role of imagination in contemporary social processes provides a compelling argument for our attending to the imagination in academic and applied research. Appadurai himself suggests that because imagination has come to play such a central role in a world where mass media permeates many areas of people's lives, 'These complex, partly imagined lives must now form the bedrock of ethnography that wishes to retain a special voice in a transnational, deterritorialized world' (1996: 54). This work extends an important invitation to ethnographers to attend to how other people imagine. However, here I suggest two adaptations to the proposal. First, Appadurai's focus is on the deterritorialisation that he theorises as part of processes of globalisation. Here my interest is different because rather than seeing imagination as something that becomes more prevalent or at least more significant in the context of deterritorialisation, I suggest a focus on how imagination is implicated in everyday place-making practices. This does not mean dislocating imagination from political processes and spaces (in Massey's, 2005, sense of the term). Rather, it means seeing imagination as integral to our everyday individual ways of being in the world and in some circumstances understanding imagination as a collective practice that operates in ways similar to those suggested for collective memory. Second, although Appadurai is clearly aware of the embodied and sensorial dimension of how we experience our environments (e.g. see Appadurai, 1996: 1–2), his main focus is on the relationship between (media) representations and the imagination. Here, following Ingold's definition of imagination as 'the activity of a being whose puzzle-solving is carried on within the context of involvement in the real world of persons, objects and relations' (2000: 419), I take imagining to be a more emplaced everyday practice carried out in relation to the multisensoriality of our actual social and material relations.

The anthropologist Vincent Crapanzano has argued that imagination should be re-thought, not as something that 'is dominated by the visual', but rather, he poses: 'Can we not "imagine" the beyond in musical terms? In tactile or even gustatory ones? In propriocentric ones? In varying combinations of these – and perhaps other senses' (2004: 23). Such multisensory imagining would be an embodied, rather than simply cognitive practice. Indeed, taking the question of how such everyday imagining emerges as part of the way in which people go about living in the world – as part of the way we do ethnography – opens the sensory ethnographer to the possibility that the temporality of everyday actions is often referential to possible futures and memories of the past – both of which might be thought of as ways of imagining.

Imagination is of course not simply about the future – it might concern imagining a past, another person's experience of the past or even of the present as it merges with the immediate past. Indeed, this is very much what ethnographers are in the business of doing when they engage in research practices aimed at imagining other people's immediate experiences and memories. As Crapanzano puts it, 'Ethnographies are themselves constructions of the hinterland' (2004: 23). They are as such dependent on practices of imagination. It is moreover equally important for the sensory ethnographer to attend to how others imagine as it is for her or him to understand how her or his own practices of imagination – of past and future – are implicated in the ethnographic process.

The idea of a collective imagination is itself tricky, especially if an ethnographer seeks to share it. It is impossible to directly access the imaginations of others, to know precisely if and how an imagined 'irreal' future is felt by an individual or shared by a 'collective', or to know if one has shared it oneself. A collectivity might collaborate to produce written documents, material objects and sensory environments. Nevertheless, the sameness rests not in their imaginations, but in the material realities and discourses that inspire them to action and in the outcomes of this action. As Connerton has suggested, to understand collective memories a focus on 'recollection and bodies' is required (1989: 4). A similar approach can be used to understand the idea of individual and collective imagination. This means directing the focus to how the 'irreal' (Crapanzano, 2004) of the future (i.e. the imagined) is communicated both through verbal projections and embodied practices.

If place is central to our way of being in the world and we are thus always participating in places, the task of the reflexive ethnographer would be to consider how she or he is emplaced, or entangled, and her or his role in the constitution of that place. By attending to the sensoriality and materiality of other people's ways of being in the world, we cannot directly access or share their personal, individual, biographical, shared or 'collective' memories, experiences or imaginations (see also Okely, 1994: 47; Desjarlais, 2003: 6). However, we can, by attuning our bodies, rhythms, tastes, ways of seeing and more to theirs, begin to become involved in making places that are similar to theirs and thus feel that we are similarly emplaced (or, following Massey (2005), try to insert ourselves into the trajectories to which *they* relate and thus attempt to relate similarly to them). This might enable us to do what Okely (1994) has referred to as to 'creatively construct correspondences' between our own and others' experiences. In doing so we should be better enabled to understand how others remember and imagine (in ways that might not be articulated verbally) through their own immediate emplaced experiences. Such an approach might also help us to develop ethnographies with a future orientation, for instance what have been called 'ethnographies of the possible' (Halse, 2013). A sensory ethnography approach invites us to use our own experiences to seek to imagine how other people 'feel' their futures, and imagine their futures through their bodies, as much as the ways in which they talk about them.

SCHOLARLY KNOWING AND NOT KNOWING

Above I have suggested working with the idea that sensory knowing is produced through participation in the world. Following this idea the self emerges from processes of sensory learning, being shaped through a person's engagement with the social, sensory and material environment of which she or he is a part. Similar understandings of 'ways of knowing' are current in anthropology. For instance, Mark Harris has pointed out that discussions of 'knowledge' have neglected the idea that 'knowing is always situated'. He stresses that even very abstract forms of knowing occur within specific environments, and in movement – in that a person does not '*stop* in order to know: she continues' (2007: 1, original italics). As such, knowing is continuous and processual, it is situated and it is bound up with human engagement, participation and movement (Harris, 2007: 4). Sensory knowing might be understood both as an everyday process and as continuous throughout the life course. As Desjarlais has suggested, 'what people come to sense in their lives and how they are perceived, observed and talked about by others contribute to the making of selfhood and subjectivity' (2003: 342).

However, if we locate all meaningful knowledge in processes of active participation and engagement, the conundrum we are faced with is that of how we might extract them to represent them as academic knowledge: how might we use them to contribute to academic scholarship? Ingold has pointed out that for academics 'our very activity, in thinking and writing, is underpinned by a belief in the absolute worth of disciplined, rational inquiry', itself defined through a modern western dichotomy (2000: 6). Such scholarship is indeed fundamental to the modern western academic project of intellectualising ethnographic happenings. Yet if we understand even abstract thought as an emplaced practice then to a certain extent the problem is resolved. We might abstract, isolate or rationalise embodied knowing into written description through theoretical frames. Yet we remain embodied beings interacting with environments that might include discursive, sensory, material and social strands. We do not simply retreat into our minds to write theoretical texts, but we create discourses and narratives that are themselves entangled with the materiality and sensoriality of the moment and of memories and imaginaries. Therefore, a less intellectualised form of sensory knowing in practice also has a role to play in academia and in academic representation. As Throop (2003) has pointed out, there are many ways in which we can experience and reflect on and define experience. The same applies to the ways that we represent sensory experiences and the knowledge, memories and imaginations embedded in them. I continue the discussion of this in Chapter 8.

Finally, a future orientation to sensory ethnography, which is implied by its association with imagination, opens up the possibility of also engaging with not knowing. Not knowing is important because our awareness of it enables us to acknowledge the gaps and voids and significantly the *uncertainties* that are part of the way that life is lived. For any approach to ethnography such acknowledgements are very important. Yet for a sensory ethnography they are particularly pertinent in terms of interrogating not only what is not known but the ways in which not knowing is experienced, perhaps unsaid, but felt, as a form of anxiety, uncertainty or optimism. However, the unknown and uncertain should not be seen as negative ghosts that haunt the way we live in the present, but rather as the very things that we should harness as part of the openness of a world that a future-oriented applied ethnography might engage with.

ETHNOGRAPHIC PLACES

The understanding of place that I have suggested in this chapter draws on the ideas of Casey (1996), Massey (2005) and Ingold (2008) to formulate place as a coming together and 'entanglement' of persons, things, trajectories, sensations, discourses, and more. As events or occurrences, places are constantly changing and open, moreover they do not end. The suggestion that we as ethnographers and the people who participate in ethnographic research are always emplaced, then invites the further question of how we might conceptualise the ethnographic representation of other people as emplaced persons. I propose the idea of 'ethnographic places'. Ethnographic places are thus not the same actual real experienced places ethnographers participate in when they do fieldwork. Rather, they are the places that we as ethnographers make when communicating about our research to others. Whatever medium is involved, ethnographic representation involves the combining, connecting and interweaving of theory, experience, reflection, discourse, memory and imagination. It has a material and sensorial presence, be this in the form of a book, a film, an exhibition of scents, pictures, a musical composition, or a combination of these. It moreover can never be understood without accounting for how its meanings are constituted in relation to readers and audiences through *their* participation. Indeed, the task of the sensory ethnographer is in part to invite her or his reader or audience to imagine themselves into the places of both the ethnographer and the research participants represented. Yet, as we know, these places are not static, they are not places we can 'go back to' or places that we can reconstruct; indeed they are places that we make because we are participating in them.

The idea of ethnographic representation as an ethnographic place thus employs an abstract concept of place as a way of understanding these interrelationships. However, it differs slightly from the understanding of place developed above as it involves the ethnographer *intentionally pulling together* theory, experiential knowing, discourses, and more, into a unique configuration of trajectories and then taking them with her or him as she or he moves forward and comes to know and understand in new ways. The challenge for ethnographers is to do this in such a way that also invites our audiences to imagine themselves into the places of others, while simultaneously invoking theoretical and practical points of meaning and learning, and be self-conscious about their own learning. While usually ethnographic representations become permanent texts – as in the case of written texts, films and sound compositions – they can still be understood as open to other places and to space in that their meanings will always be contingent on what is going on around them, that is, in relation to new findings, politics, theories, approaches and audiences, as they move on temporally and in the imaginations of their viewers and readers. Some more innovative multimedia texts which offer their users opportunities to re-invent narratives and reconfigure meanings offer more obvious scope for the participation and forward movement of their audiences. Thus the idea of ethnographic-place-as-event I am suggesting is one where representations are known in practice.

The notion of the ethnographic place also offers us another opportunity, that is, to connect with the future orientation that is part of the commitment of design research to make change. As I have argued elsewhere:

> By connecting this [the notion of the ethnographic place] to the future oriented approach of design we can think of an ethnographic place that will continue to move forward, and envision our role in this, thus we can see the future as *part of* rather than as *after* ethnography. (Pink, 2014: 422)

Summing up

To conceptualise a sensory ethnography process we need to account for both human perception and the political and power relations from which ethnographic research is inextricable. In this chapter I have suggested that a theory of place as experiential, open and in process – as 'event' or 'occurrence' – offers a way of thinking about the contexts

(Continued)

(Continued)

of sensory ethnographic research and the processes through which ethnographic representations become meaningful and will continue to emerge as meaningful as they become entangled in future and as yet unknown configurations. It moreover allows us to situate the emplaced ethnographer in relation to the sociality and materiality of the situations in which she or he becomes engaged and comes to know through active participation in practice. I have then proposed that if ethnographers can come to occupy similar, parallel or related places to those people whose experiences, memories and imaginations (of the past or future) they seek to understand, then this can provide a basis for the development of ways of knowing that will promote such understanding. Yet coming to know and imagine in ways similar to others involves not simply the ethnographer's imitation of other people's practices, but also a personal engagement and embodied knowing. One of the tasks of the reflexive sensory ethnographer is to develop an awareness of how she or he becomes involved not only in participating in 'other people's' practices. Rather, she or he needs to go further than this to anticipate her or his co-involvement in the constitution of places, and to as such identify the points of intervention of her or his own intentionality and subjectivity and how this might change over time.

Recommended further reading

- Connerton, P. (1989) *How Societies Remember*. Cambridge: Cambridge University Press.
- Crapanzano, V. (2004) *Imaginative Horizons*. London: University of Chicago Press.
- Harris, M. (ed.) (2007) *Ways of Knowing: new approaches in the anthropology of experience and learning*. Oxford: Berghahn.
- Ingold, T. (2010) *Being Alive*. London: Routledge.
- Massey, D. (2005) *For Space*. London: Sage.
- Pink, S. (2014) 'Digital-visual-sensory-design anthropology: ethnography, imagination and intervention', *Arts and Humanities in Higher Education*, 13(4): 412–27.

THREE

Preparing for sensory research

Practical and orientation issues

In this chapter I suggest how researchers might set about preparing themselves to be open and attentive to the sensory ways of knowing, categories, meanings, moralities and practices of others. This raises a series of questions originating in the approaches and perspectives discussed in previous chapters, concerning what kinds of self-awareness, technologies and epistemologies might equip us well for this task. It involves asking: What is the sensory ethnographer seeking to find out? What are the implications of 'researcher subjectivity'? How does one choose a method? How might media figure in sensory ethnography? And is there a particular sensory approach to ethics? Moreover, preparation to do ethnography in a way that attends to the senses includes considering how one might use one's own body and senses alongside and in combination with both more classic and contemporary innovative digital research methods and technologies.

INTRODUCTION: PREPARING IN AN UNPREDICTABLE WORLD

It is impossible to ever be completely prepared for or know precisely how an ethnographic project will be conducted before starting. Many researchers who have undertaken ethnographies that attend to the senses have done so without any special preparation: the multisensoriality of the research context is often something that emerges though one's encounter with both people and the physical environment one is participating in. It involves unanticipated smells, tastes, sounds and textures, and unexpected ways of comprehending them. These lead to similarly unanticipated moments of realisation. This point is demonstrated in one of the earliest ethnographies to bring to the fore the importance of the non-visual senses. Steven Feld has described how during his long-term anthropological research in Papua New Guinea the Kaluli man working with him had 'blurted back' to one of Feld's questions regarding 'bird taxonomy and identification' to point out to him: '"Listen – to you they are birds, to me they are voices of the forest"'. Feld realised he had been imposing 'a method of knowledge construction ... onto a domain of experience that Kaluli do not isolate or reduce'. He explains that 'Birds are "voices" because Kaluli *recognise and acknowledge their existence primarily through sound*, and because they are spirit reflections ... of deceased men and women' (1982: 45, italics added). For Feld the methodological implication of this realisation led him to rebalance 'the empirical questioning and hypothesis-making activities ... with a less direct approach' (1982: 46). Such unforeseen realisations are quite characteristic of the way ethnographers learn during fieldwork. In some cases they might occur in ways that are quite subtle and over time. For instance, David Sutton describes how when he was doing research in Kalymnos (Greece) local people repeatedly told him to 'Eat, in order to remember Kalymnos' (Sutton, 2001: 2). Over time he realised that, as he puts it: '*telling me to use the transitory and repetitive act of eating as a medium for the more enduring act of remembering, they were, in fact, telling me to act like a Kalymnian*' (2001: 2, original italics) since in this particular cultural context foods formed a fundamental part of local people's memories.

In other circumstances researchers learn in more abrupt ways. The performer and scholar Hahn writes of what she calls the 'sensually extreme' in ethnography, suggesting that 'disorienting experiences' (2006: 94) in fieldwork create a type of liminality through which researchers might come to reflexive realisations. Hahn describes her own experiences of doing fieldwork at monster truck rallies as 'sensually more intense than I could have conjured: enormous trucks, deafening sounds, thick clouds of exhaust, and visions of extreme physical force as these 10,000-pound trucks flew into the air and crushed piles of cars or performed freestyle' (2006: 87–8). She proposes that 'The extreme pushes one to reorient sensibilities and consider the thresholds of what is sensually extreme from where we stand at the moment' (2006: 95). As Hahn points out such 'disorienting' moments are unexpected (2006: 92) – and they somehow 'jolt' (Young and Goulet, 1994: 20–1, cited by Hahn 2006: 94) us into a new level of understanding. This 'jolt' may be gradual, enjoyable, perhaps disturbing if the disorientation experienced leaves the ethnographer grasping out for points of familiarly, or it might be sudden. Whatever the nature of the experience we cannot be prepared for the specificity of such jolting, disorientating or revelatory moments. However, we can do our best to be open to them, and be prepared to engage reflexively and analytically with such experiences. We should be aware that even with extensive preparation, researchers' own sensory experiences will most likely still surprise them, sometimes giving them access to a new form of knowing.

THE RESEARCH QUESTION: WHAT IS THE SENSORY ETHNOGRAPHER TRYING TO FIND OUT?

The suggestions made in this chapter are based on the assumption that the study of the senses would not normally be the sole and primary objective of research itself, but that it forms part of a methodology for understanding other people's experiences, values, identities and ways of life. A methodology based in and a commitment to understanding the senses provides a route to forms of knowledge and knowing not accounted for in conventional forms of ethnography. It often leads us to the normally not spoken, the invisible and the unexpected – those things that people do not perhaps necessarily think it would be worth mentioning, or those things that tend to be felt or sensed rather than spoken about. For example, in my own experience, in studying how self-identity is constituted in the home (Pink, 2004) I found the concept of the 'sensory home' to be an important route to understanding people's everyday practices and decision making about domestic work; this led me to understand tacit sensory and normally never spoken-about ways that people knew their houses were clean or dirty. The concept of the sensory home was also used again in my later work as a way in which to think about how laundry was implicated as part of everyday sensory environments (Pink, 2012). For example, we found that laundry was part of the texture of home in ways that would go beyond a focus simply on what participants would have said it looked, smelled and felt like (Pink et al., 2013). I took a similar approach in my research about the Cittàslow (Slow City) movement in Britain. There I used an analysis of the sensoriality of urban experience to develop the idea of the 'sensory city' (Pink, 2007b) and to explore the role of sensorial experience in sustainable development in England (Pink, 2008a) and in Spain (Pink and Servon, 2013. In later research in Australia I was careful to attend to how slow city activists spoke about their relationship to their local environments in terms of sensory experience (Pink and Lewis, 2014) as a way to comprehend how their embodied and affective relationships to locality were part of their activism. Again I did not study the senses for the sake of defining the city or locality as a sensory context, but treated the sensoriality of the city and the local environment as a context for understanding people's actions in and concerning the areas they lived in. Likewise, my ethnographic work on organisations seeks not to study how the senses are used in those organisations, but the ways in which sensory experience and sensory ways of knowing are part of the ways in which people stay safe in organisations (Pink et al., 2015).

What the sensory ethnographer wants to find out is always inflected both by the disciplines through which she or he is working, or with which she or he collaborates, as well as with an assumption that the sensory ethnographer is seeking to understand the environments, activities and experiences that our lives come into contact with. These environments might have material, digital, invisible, intangible, social and other elements. Our respective interest in these will depend on a range of questions.

This is a departure both from the more traditional forms of ethnographic practice (e.g. Atkinson et al., 2007) that I outlined in Chapters 1 and 2. It also differs from the objectives of Howes and Classen (1991) whose idea of studying the sensory categories of any given culture resonates with conventional methods of investigating and documenting other cultures in twentieth-century anthropological practice. For example, for much of the twentieth century one of the first steps in doing anthropological research about another culture was to investigate and map out, diagrammatically, its kinship system (although towards the end of the twentieth century anthropologists became faced with questions about the validity of this approach – see for example Schweitzer, 2000). Howes and Classen suggested that another fundamental aspect of human culture should be given centrality – setting out an agenda for doing research that aims to elicit 'a given culture's "sensory profile" or way of "sensing the world"' (1991: 257). To do so they recommended attending to 'language', 'artefacts and aesthetics', 'body decoration', 'child-rearing practices', 'alternative sensory modes' (i.e. when people of different categories use different 'sensory orders'), 'media of communication', 'natural and built environment', 'rituals', 'mythology' and 'cosmology' (1991: 262–85). Their list is very inclusive and the areas they cover have been represented in several subsequent ethnographies that attend to the senses. For example, Geurts (2003) undertakes detailed analyses of both the linguistic aspects of Anlo Ewe sensory categories, practices surrounding birth and the care of children and ritual, and Grasseni has focused on how children learn to see (2007b); in my own work I have focused on the built environment (Pink, 2004, 2007b), rituals (2007b, 2008b) and what Howes and Classen call 'alternative sensory modes' (1991) (Pink, 2004, 2005b); and Desjarlais has examined how a man and woman interviewees used gender-specific sensory categories and metaphors to discuss their autobiographical experiences (2003). Yet, my argument here is that a sensory ethnography goes beyond this, and as it is presented here is aligned with a more processual and phenomenological approach.

Therefore, to return to the question of what the sensory ethnographer is trying to find out, we need to account for this context in which most ethnographic studies of the senses actually form part of research into other substantive questions. Thus, one response would be that the knowledge sought is always project-specific. However, more generally it is fair to say that the sensory ethnographer is trying to access areas of embodied, emplaced knowing and to use these as a basis from which to understand human environments, activities, perception, experience, action and meaning, and to situate this culturally and biographically.

REVIEWING THE EXISTING LITERATURE AND AUDIOVISUAL MATERIALS WITH PARTICULAR ATTENTION TO THE SENSES

Most good ethnographic research is concerned not only with the knowing produced through encounters with people and things and engagements with practices in fieldwork contexts. It is also dependent on existing related published ethnographic knowledge, local literatures (fictional and documentary), images and other texts (including online texts), and art forms that form part of the cultural knowledge that is inextricable from everyday practice and local ideologies. A review of such existing materials and materialities will help the researcher both reformulate their research question(s) and decide which methods are most appropriate for the task.

Howes and Classen suggest a systematic four-stage process for library-based research about the senses. This might involve working with an ethnographic text, a novel, a life history or a film. They suggest the researcher should: first, 'extract all the references to the sense of sensory phenomena from the source in question'; second, 'analyse the data pertaining to each modality individually'; third, 'analyse the relations between the modalities with regard to how each sense contributes to the meaning of experience in the culture'; and finally, 'conclude with a statement of the hierarchy or order of the sense for the culture'. As they point out, this method only allows the researcher to analyse the *representation* of the senses that is offered by the producer of the text, which will also represent the sensory subjectivity of that author (1991: 261).

Other forms of writing and representation can also become key sources in a sensory approach to ethnography. In my experience ethnographers always benefit from engaging analytically with fiction writing, film, other media representations, reportage and other literary statements connected with their topic. In fact existing discussions of the senses developed in architecture and design studies have often used both literary sources – fiction and poetry – and existing ethnographic description as sources to demonstrate the sensoriality of our experience of physical environments (e.g. Malnar and Vodvarka, 2004). Although literary writings on the senses will, like ethnographies, be based in the sensory subjectivity of their own authors, as well as possibly designed to portray particular experiences in ways that are morally inflected, they can offer insights into how sensory experiences are represented as part of specific cultural narratives, historical contexts and situated personal experiences. Fiction can also offer interesting sources that enable understanding of the ways that sensory experiences are expected to be or how they are framed in certain cultural and practical contexts. For example, 20 years after first starting my research about the bullfight in Southern Spain I was invited to write about the bullfight again. With no new ethnographic materials, but a growing interest in the sensory, embodied and effective elements of the performance, and its emplacement in the bullring, I returned to the historical bullfight literature in order to explore cultural narratives about the experience and sensoriality of the performance from the bullfighter's perspective. Using passages from the work of the well-known writer Blasco Ibáñez in his book *Sangre y Arena* (*Blood and Sand*) (1908), I reflected on representations of the sensory, affective embodied experience of the bullfighter. For example, in one particular passage, both Blasco Ibáñez's moral distaste for the bullfight and the sensation of being a bullfighter walking out into the ring are brought to the fore:

> They felt themselves different men as they advanced over the sand. They were risking their lives for something more than money. Their doubts and terrors of the unknown had been left outside the barricades. Now they trod the arena. They were face to face with their public. Reality had come. The longing for glory in their barbarous, ignorant minds, the desire to excel their comrades, the pride in their own strength and dexterity, all blinded them, making them forget all fears, and inspiring them with the daring of brute force.
>
> Gallardo was quite transfigured ...
>
> (Blasco Ibáñez and Gillespie, 2005: 41)

I argued that this scene might be understood through a theory of emplacement, as outlined in Chapter 2, and suggested that 'the wider implication is that a theory of emplacement might also be used to understand other performative contexts' (Pink, 2011a). Therefore, fictional texts, including historical fiction, can bring to the fore aspects of sensory experience in ways that are culturally, historically, politically and morally inflected. They therefore offer excellent ways in which to learn about the sensory ways of knowing that might be part of a specific context being researched, but as this example also shows they need to be situated so that we may comprehend how the experiences they are describing might be usefully meaningful in any one research project.

Another example of how a non-academic text has played an interesting role in enabling understanding of a research context emerges from my research about the Slow Food and Cittàslow movement. Here existing written materials about the aims and work of these movements have proved indispensable to my understanding of the role of the senses in the actual activities of their members. For instance, the Slow Food movement advocates and undertakes programmes of 'sensory education' (see Petrini, 2000), by which it hopes to convince people of the benefits of its ideology by teaching them about the meaning and importance of consuming and knowing about local produce, through the medium of food. Carlo Petrini, the leader of Slow Food, proposes that 'Reappropriating the senses is the first step towards imagining a different system capable of respecting man as a worker of the land, as a producer, as a consumer of food and resources, and as a political and moral entity' and 'To reappropriate one's senses is to reappropriate one's own life' (2007: 99). The analysis of such texts cannot provide researchers with first-hand knowledge of how people actually experience and give meanings to food. Rather, it allows us to gain an understanding of the sensory categories the movement's literature constructs, the moralities and values that it gives to particular types of sensory experience, and the wider activist agendas in which they are embedded. As such it provides a reference point from which to analyse the actual practices and meanings generated amongst research participants. For example, an appreciation of the Slow Food approach to the senses has helped me to analyse the ideological and activist strands of the sensory experiences that are structured into the composition of a Slow City carnival (Pink, 2007b) and in approaches to sustainable development in Slow Cities (Pink, 2008a). Not all texts that discuss the senses have similarly explicit political or activist agendas to that I have outlined above. For instance, other examples might be texts discussing clinical practice in bio-medicine or alternative therapies, or cookery books. Such texts will nevertheless be identifiable as attached to specific world views and ideologies and provide invaluable cultural resources for a sensory ethnographic study.

It is moreover not only written cultural *texts* that can offer researchers access to local discourses and representations of sensory experience. Sensory ethnographers should be open to other media and practices of representation. This includes viewing films and other audiovisual works in ways that are attentive to the senses but might also include performance as it is embedded in everyday life. For example, Marina Roseman discusses the significance of song amongst the Temiar people of Kelantan, Malaysia. The Temiar are an indigenous forest-dwelling people whose world, Roseman writes, is impacted on by 'rainforest deforestation, land alienation and Islamic evangelism' (2005: 213). Roseman shows how, as she puts it, 'In musical genres ... Temiars map out their experiential universe, locating that which is Other within reach of the self' (2005: 218). Thus to understand how discourses and sensory experiences are expressed and remembered in culturally meaningful ways, ethnographers can also benefit from looking beyond written and visual texts.

CHOOSING THE RIGHT METHODS

The discussions above have implied that the question of how close the ethnographer might get to 'sharing' the sensory embodied or emplaced experiences and the sensory subjectivity of their research participants might depend partly on the methods of investigation used. This does not mean that the method employed will determine the level of analytical *understanding* the researcher will arrive at, but rather that different methods take us into other people's worlds and ask them to reveal their experiences to us through different routes. In the following chapters I approach the question of what sorts of engagements are facilitated and what types of knowledge are produced through a series of different methods: interviewing, participating and digital methods. The choice of method should be matched to two key factors: the method should serve the research question – it should be the method that will best enable the researcher to explore the themes and issues and acquire the understandings that she or he is seeking; yet this first factor requires that the method must simultaneously be suitable for and amenable to the research participants in question. In some projects the methods used will be predetermined and the participants in the research to a certain extent self-select in that they will only ever be those people who are happy to collaborate in knowledge production using the predetermined methods. However, in projects with a more flexible design, it might be that different participants in the same project collaborate more or less enthusiastically with different methods. Or even that the methods used are often determined not by the researcher's own prior decisions about practical approaches but by the research events and scenarios created by research participants (see, for example, Pink, 2008b).

Above all, it is useful to recognise that in sensory ethnography practice, methods themselves are ongoingly changing – they are not static tools that we can take off a shelf after having been used by someone else. Rather, methods are malleable and flexible: they can change over time and between projects. In short, methods have biographies (Pink and Leder Mackley, 2013).

REFLEXIVITY IN SENSORY ETHNOGRAPHY

That reflexivity is fundamental to a sensory ethnography has already been recognised by some key contributors to the field. The anthropologist Geurts puts this particularly poignantly; in setting an agenda for a reflexive and sensory ethnography, she writes:

> We [ethnographers] often find ourselves drenched – not just in discourse and words, but in sensations, imaginations and emotions ... And yet, if we have become drenched, those we work with may also be soaked through and through. Such moments open up space, or sound a call, to body forth fine-tuned accounts replete with an ethical aesthetics of relationships in the field. (2003: 386)

A sensory ethnography calls for a form of reflexivity through which the ethnographer engages with how his or her own sensory experiences are produced through research encounters and how these might assist her or him in understanding those of others. The following chapters of this book reveal that there exists a growing body of academic and arts practice that suggests how this reflexivity has been engaged in practice. As Regina Bendix pointed out in 2006: 'how ethnographers are to acquire sensory reflexivity and, concomitantly sensory effectiveness in participant observation has thus far hardly been discussed, nor has there been much experimentation or explication as to how sensory ethnography might find its way back on the printed page' (2006: 8; see also Bendix, 2000). Contributors to Bendix and Donald Brenneis' (2006) co-edited volume and other scholars (e.g. Geurts, 2003; Lee and Ingold, 2006; O'Dell and Willim, 2013) have begun this task. In the following section I pursue this question through a discussion of the sensory subjectivity and intersubjectivity of the ethnographic encounter.

Such reflexivity is essential to ethnographic research, as conceptualised here. It is a collaborative process through which shared understandings (to the extent that they can be shared) are produced. It involves sets of encounters that when presented appropriately can serve to represent in powerful ways, the experiences of one group of people to another. The self-conscious and reflexive use of the senses in this process is an important and strategic act. By attempting to become similarly situated to one's research participants and by attending to the bodily sensations and culturally specific sensory categories (e.g. in some, but not all cultures, smell, touch, sound, vision, taste) through which these feelings are communicated about and given value, ethnographers can come to know about other people's lives in ways that are particularly intense. By making similarly reflexive and body-conscious uses of this sensory knowing in the representation of their work, ethnographers can hope to produce texts that will have powerful impact on their readers or audiences. This might involve using the written word, yet recent discussions suggest the potential of sensorial media to invoke empathetic and possibly (if properly contextualised) intercultural understandings. Such processes can be engaged in both academic and applied research. The implication is that empathetic understandings might be produced through the engagement of decision makers (whether policy makers or in industry) with evocative multimedia and multisensory representations that seek to represent the embodied nature of other people's experiences and concerns. This implies the possibility that they might become reflexive audiences, self-conscious about their own subjectivities. Such empathetic and reflexive texts might convince in ways that cannot be achieved through the 'dry' (even if passionately conceived) arguments made in the bullet points of written reports based on questionnaire data.

FROM SENSORY BIAS TO SENSORY SUBJECTIVITY

An important step towards understanding other people's sensory categories and the way they use these to describe their environments, activities, experiences and knowledge, lies in developing a reflexive appreciation of one's own sensorium. In much existing research methods literature produced originally in the English language, the 'we' who do research are assumed to be modern western subjects, who divide the senses into vision, hearing, touch, taste and smell (along with the oft added mysterious sixth sense). Howes and Classen stress that '*Other cultures do not necessarily divide the sensorium as we do*'. They note how, for example, the Hausa have two senses and the Javanese five, and that these senses do not necessarily coincide with modern western ones (1991: 257–8, original italics). As Howes has later commented (for the modern western ethnographer), 'it is not easy to cultivate ... cross-sensory awareness because one of the defining characteristics of modernity is the cultural separation of the senses into self-contained fields' (2003: 47). Nevertheless, it is important for ethnographers to be aware of sensoria that differ from their own. As Geurts argues, the 'Western model of five senses is a folk model' (2003: 227) and as such it is one amongst others. For the modern western ethnographer an awareness of the five-sense model provides a useful comparative apparatus that might be employed as a way of reflecting on cultural difference; it offers a ready-made reference point. However, it is also more deeply embedded in the practice of modern western scholarship since there the ethnographer, as a scholar or an applied researcher, is usually obliged to communicate her or his findings to audiences of modern western subjects who also understand the world through a five-sense sensorium. At the same time, not all ethnographers necessarily originate from cultures in which the five-sense model is used, which means there is no real justification for putting it at the centre of academic enterprise: it is a tool employed by ethnographers who use it as a way of life and a way of research, but it is not the only possible model.

To understand what they call the 'sensory biases' of another culture Howes and Classen recommend that a researcher must both develop an awareness of and 'overcome' her or his own 'sensory biases' (or as I discuss below 'sensory subjectivity') and then train 'oneself to be sensitive to a multiplicity of sensory expressions'. They suggest undertaking exercises in self-training that might involve 'taking some object from one's environment and disengaging one's attention from the object itself so as to focus on how each of its sensory properties would impinge on one's consciousness were they not filtered in any way'. From this they recommend that researchers develop what they call 'the capacity to be "of two sensoria" about things'. This entails 'being able to operate with complete awareness in two perceptual systems of sensory orders simultaneously (the sensory order of one's own culture and that of the culture studied), and constantly comparing notes' (1991: 260). The process of seeking to apprehend one's own sensory situatedness might be begun before starting ethnographic fieldwork. Exercises such as those suggested by Howes and Classen can encourage us to break down an experience into sensory categories; the result of doing so would allow one to be aware both of the categories one uses and of how one defines and gives meanings to different types of sensation.

The suggestion that the sensory ethnographer starts with a kind of auto-ethnography of her or his own sensory culture and of how she or he is situated in it proposes a stage of preparation for ethnographic fieldwork. This should equip the researcher with an awareness of how he or she uses (culturally and biographically specific) sensory categories to classify and represent multisensory embodied knowing. In addition, this involves accounting for her or his own sensory subjectivity, an ability to be reflexive about how this subjectivity might be implicated in the production of ethnographic knowledge, and an openness to learning how to participate in other sensory ways of knowing. It is also essential to recognise that there is significant variation within cultures – although people of the same culture might share certain sensory categories and classifications, they may use these in different ways or give different meanings to them. The sensory ethnographer needs to keep in mind that in any given culture any number of different ways of living out – for instance, gendered, ethnic, generational, professional or other – identities might be associated with different ways of practising, understanding, recalling and representing one's experiences sensorially. These insights need to be applied not only to the way we understand other people's culturally specific sensory worlds, but also to how we regard ourselves as being situated in and moving between different sensory cultures.

Researchers tend to begin their fieldwork from a wide range of different relationships to the subjects of their research. In some cases a researcher might already be a specialist practitioner of the activity they are studying. Good examples include John Hockey's auto-ethnography analysis of the sensory experiences of long distance running (2006) and Hahn's work on knowledge transmission in Japanese dance, having been a dancer before beginning the research (2007). Other ethnographers who seek to learn about other people's experiences and meanings through the senses may not have such an established basis of specialist embodied knowledge. However, there are different degrees to which existing bodily knowing will be involved. This can depend on whether the researcher is doing fieldwork in her or his own culture. Ethnographers might research practices that are already part of their lives, but that might be experienced and understood differently by others. For example, in 2000 I worked on a study of everyday domestic laundry practices in the UK (Pink, 2005b, 2007c, 2012) and in 2010–14 I led a UK sensory ethnography of the home which also covered laundry (Pink and Leder Mackley, 2013, 2014). I have been doing laundry myself for many years, yet I found that my own knowledge and embodied ways of knowing about laundry, and ways of interpreting the domestic environment in relation to laundry processes, differed – sometimes enormously – from those of the people who participated in my research. When I was working on the first study in 2000, their (varied) beliefs and values concerning how one should use one's senses to judge when and in what ways laundry was clean or dirty led me to different consciousness about how I made my own subjective decisions about laundry. However, this self-reflexivity also allowed me to understand that how one treats laundry is bound up with how one uses sensory categories and practices to create statements about one's self-identity. In this reflexive process however, I did not attempt to deconstruct my own sensory knowledge about laundry *before* starting the research. Rather, the self-awareness it entailed was generated *during* the research process as I began to use my own sensory values and practices as a means of comparison and a reference point through which to situate the different approaches of my various research participants. However, the reflexive process can, over a series of studies, go further than this. For example, by the time I began to work on the later studies, what I had learned from the first study and my own personal experiences of doing laundry through different spatial layouts in Spain and Malaysia, brought a new set of ways of knowing and experiences through which to understand participants' sensory engagements with laundry.

Likewise, in my study of the sensory home this process of self-awareness was not an exercise that took place prior to the fieldwork, but developed relationally as I explored other people's sensory homes with them. In this instance I was doing research in two cultures, English and Spanish, in which I had lived my everyday life through fairly conventional and culturally specific routines. Before doing the research I had often noted how, for example, washing up was done differently in England and Spain, but I never reflected on how in either cultural context and material environment I had used my own sensory experiences and knowledge to make decisions about how and when to clean something in my home, or to pass judgements about other people. I had not realised how I also used sensory strategies as ways of defining my own self-identity. Now, years since I undertook my first project in the home my own practices invoke a particular awareness of how I use embodied sensory knowing and categories – when determining if clothing can be worn or needs to be washed, when rooms need to be tidied, when the kitchen floor needs to be cleaned. These strategies are also identity practices through which I create a particular self and engage with culturally specific moralities through my decisions about the condition of my clothes and domestic surfaces.

To understand the complex ways in which we use sensory knowing and categories and develop sensory strategies in social interaction and self-representation I suggest two concepts are needed. The first is the idea of *sensory subjectivity*, mentioned above. The idea that ethnographic research is by nature subjective and requires the researcher to reflect on her or his own role in the production of ethnographic knowledge is by now a widely accepted paradigm. The ways individuals use sensory knowledge and practice can be understood as a form of subjectivity – a way of understanding the world that is at once culturally specific and might also be influenced by experiences and ideologies originating beyond the local, from how an individual is positioned in relation to social institutions and other individuals, and that should be understood in connection with any number of other identity markers (such as gender, sexuality, ethnicity, age and generation) and more. However, rather than essentialising the individual as having just one subjectivity we should recognise that people may shift between different subject positions, depending on the contexts in which they find themselves. Thus, building on the literatures and ideas discussed in Chapter 2, as our emplacement shifts and changes, we continuously move and learn (see Harris, 2007: 1) and our self-identities are continuously reconstituted. As our identities are continually completed in relation to place and our ways of embodied knowing and learning, this idea of sensory subjectivity is thus sensitive to the contingency of identity and it is also inextricable from our relationship with our total environment.

The second concept implied by the idea of sensory subjectivity is that of *sensory intersubjectivity*. Indeed, if identity is continually being negotiated through our intersubjective relations with others and our material/sensory environments, we need a way of conceptualising how this works in practice during our research encounters. Our social interactions are certainly not based simply on verbal communications and visual impressions. Rather, they are fully embodied and multisensory events – even if actual physical contact does not take place. The sensory ethnographer needs to account for how the senses are bound up with her or his relationships both with research participants and between the people participating in the research themselves, and indeed how these shift and change.

OTHER PEOPLE'S SENSORY CATEGORIES AND SENSORY INTERSUBJECTIVITY

The way we live, understand and communicate through our senses involves *social* relationships. This means that through our participation in social and material environments our sensory practices and indeed identities are lived out. The type of sensory intersubjectivity that these social and material encounters involves invites three strands of discussion: the role of sensory perception in how we interpret and interact with others; the implications of sensory intersubjectivity for understanding the research encounter; and the ethnographer's quest to share sensory experiences with research participants, attempting to apprehend their experiences and seeking to communicate about them with them through this sharing.

Sensory intersubjectivity

The self might be seen to be constituted through processes involving the transmission of sensory knowledge – as we enter into new ways of knowing in and about and engaging with our environments both our self-identities and understandings shift. Desjarlais proposes that 'Distinct types of sensory perception take effect at different times in people's lives'. Thus it is useful to look out for people's 'shifting orientations, and changes in time' (2003: 342). These shifts take place as a result of changes that occur throughout the life course, be they gradual, abrupt and occurring through a sudden realisation (e.g. Hahn, 2006) or developed through a training or apprenticeship process (e.g. Grasseni, 2004a, b; Downey, 2005; Hahn, 2007). In part such changes are related to our changing social environments and encounters – as such to the intersubjectivity between persons and to the way that our notions of self are continuously negotiated and reconstituted through our intersubjective encounters with others. As Desjarlais notes:

> Sensory engagements are as much intersubjective processes as they are personal ones. They regularly emerge in the course of interactions among people. Any considerations of a person's sensory engagements in the world must therefore be considered within the frame of a person in reflective action among other persons and other consciousnesses. (2003: 342)

Desjarlais' points of course are equally applicable to the intersubjectivity that occurs between research participants as to that between researcher and participants. He argues that 'The very substance of anthropological knowledge is founded on a sensory semiosis' (2003: 243). By this point, which can also be applied to ethnography as practised in other disciplines, Desjarlais is referring to a process of intersubjectivity. The researchers' actions are informed by their own sensory subjectivities while, simultaneously, their actions and the meanings of these are also 'shaped by local perspectives on sensory perception' (2003: 243).

Another perspective through which to consider how the senses figure in the relationships between people entails a sociological focus on social interaction as outlined in Chapter 1 (Low, 2005; Largey and Watson, 2006 [1972]; Vannini et al., 2012). This approach suggests we should attend to how cultural norms are invested in sensory categories and invites us to consider how the ways people judge others is informed by a sensuous morality. This is particularly relevant as one considers the importance of the senses to the research encounter in general and to the interpersonal relationships that researchers develop during ethnographic research in particular. However, the moralities and values associated with the sensoriality of human interaction should also be situated in relation to specific bodies and materialities. Christina Lammer's discussion of 'bodywork', through the case study of her research about 'how radiological personnel perceive and define "contact" as it relates to their interactions with patients' (2007: 91) brings these issues to the fore. Drawing from the phenomenological writings of Merleau-Ponty as developed by MacDougall (1998), Lammer suggests that (as MacDougall proposes for anthropological filmmaking) in 'the biomedical practice of (interventional) radiology ... Bodies are mutually interpenetrated, leaving deep though invisible somatic traces; filling perception with multisensual flesh' (2007: 103). In the particular case of interventional radiology touch is central (2007: 104), thus making the corporeality of human interaction all the more obvious. Nevertheless, although sensorial intersubjectivity need not involve actual physical touching it should always be understood in terms of its corporeality and as occurring in relation to a material environment.

The sensory intersubjectivity of the research encounter

Above I have outlined three strands of thinking about how interpersonal relationships are lived out in everyday social encounters that might range from the seriousness and intentionality of a surgical intervention to the serendipity of a fleeting encounter in a supermarket while shopping. The first stresses that our self-identities are constantly renegotiated through these encounters as our own subjectivities become engaged with those of others. As (to take a modern western model) we see, touch, smell and hear others, and perhaps seek to modify their sensory experiences of our own bodies, we are continually resituating ourselves and re-making ourselves in relation to others. I have suggested that to acknowledge that sensory experience and perception form a part of these encounters allows us to understand the sociality that our emplacement involves. The second strand of thinking, emerging from sociological approaches to social interaction, reminds us of the way normative and/or deviant behaviours and values are instigated and interpreted through culturally specific sensory expectations and memories. Finally, Lammer's (2007) work invites us to reflect further on the corporeality and multisensoriality of human interaction. These points are no less relevant to our understanding of the relationships and encounters that take place between ethnographers and research participants.

Martin F. Manalansan IV's (2006) discussion of the notion of the 'smelly immigrant', through the case study of his research with Asian Americans in New York City, is a good example. Manalansan describes how one of the concerns of the Asian Americans who participated in his research was with the (lingering) smells of Asian foods in their homes and on their clothing and bodies. He demonstrates how the culturally specific ways immigrants negotiate their identities through sensory strategies are set within political contexts and specific power configurations. Yet, Manalansan points out that his findings are not solely relevant for comprehending the sensoriality of immigrant lives. Rather, they are more generally applicable to the ethnographer. Reflecting on an excerpt from his field journal, which describes his visit to a Korean family home in the United States, he asks:

> In what ways were my own presuppositions about odors influencing my own actions, feelings and reactions in that domestic space? Was I – the anthropologist – authority figure, causing specific anxieties and emotions among members of the Park family? (2006: 51)

Manalansan's questions reinforce the importance of the ethnographer taking a reflexive approach to the relationships and encounters that she or he has with others, using this to situate and interpret both her or his own actions and reactions as well as those of research participants. Working with people from different cultures to one's own offers a useful way in which to encounter ways in which we feel the world differently to others, and on the basis of this to begin to consider how the world feels to them.

Such a reflexive analysis should be part of any good ethnography – it helps us to be aware of the ways in which we learn and know. Incorporated into a sensory ethnographic methodology it involves referring to: first, one's developing understanding of local sensory categories and meanings, how these are constituted, how they operate in everyday life, and the wider political and power configurations that they are entangled with; second, one's own sensory subjectivity to understand how this is informed by particular values and thus leads us to categorise others in particular ways; and finally, to how one's own sensory subjectivity shifts in the contexts of social and embodied encounters and negotiations with others, and how this in itself enables one to arrive at new levels of personal and ethnographic awareness and knowing.

MEDIA, METHODS AND SENSORY KNOWLEDGE

There has been surprisingly little discussion of the relationship between media and the senses in the existing literature. In this section I outline some of the most historical work in this field, before suggesting an alternative approach which will inform the way that media are treated in the methods discussed in later chapters and also provide the theoretical foundations for understanding the use of digital media methods for sensory ethnography, as developed in Chapter 6.

In this context whereby until very recently (Pink, 2014) the question of media and the senses seems to have been largely evaded by both sensory and media scholars, one of the texts that has retained influence in this field is the early work of Marshall McLuhan (2005 [1964]). McLuhan's suggestion was that 'our technical media, since writing and printing, are extensions of our senses' (2005 [1964]: 46). He argued that what he called the 'sense-ratio' shifts when different media are involved (2005 [1964: 47). 'Sense-ratio' referred to 'the proportional elaboration of the senses within a particular cultural logic' (Howes, 2005b: 23) and McLuhan proposed that 'any new medium alters the existing sense ratios and proportions, just as over-all colors are modified by any local shift of pigment or component' (2005 [1964]: 47). Thus the 'latest' media of the time of his writing – television – he proposed was 'an extension, not just of sight and sound but ... tangibility in its visual, contoured, sculptural mode' and thus a 'sudden extension of our sight-touch powers' that must have social effects (2005 [1964]: 46–7). Although as Howes notes, there are problems with 'the technological determinism and implicit evolutionism of McLuhan's theoretical position' (Howes, 2005b: 23), his work invites the important question of the relationship of different media to sensory evocation and communication.

There have been other older theoretical explorations of media, the senses and society, one of which is Rodaway's attempt to explain the sensory context of postmodernity by drawing from Jean Baudrillard's notions of 'the orders of simulacra and the concept of hyper-reality'. Rodaway sought to explain the 'socio-historical development of styles of sensuous experience and the consequent changes in concepts of reality through the introduction of new social practices and the employment of new technologies' (1994: 9). While Rodaway's discussion is dated through its association with late twentieth century conceptualisations of postmodernity, the questions he raises remain pertinent. Much social, sensory and material experience is mediated in multiple and diverse ways by (constantly changing and developing) media technologies. Thus, as Nick Couldry (2000) has suggested, we might understand much human practice as 'media orientated'. This invites a consideration of how our emplaced contact with media technologies and the mediation of experience might be conceptualised within a sensory ethnography.

Indeed, there are several ways that culturalist and non-representational approaches to the senses impact on how we might understand media as 'sensory' (Pink, 2014). As I have emphasised in the earlier chapters of this book there is a clear distinction between the culturalist approach to the senses developed by Howes (e.g. 2003) and the non-representational approach developed by Ingold (e.g. 2000, 2010). If we likewise apply these two approaches to understanding media, then similar trajectories develop. Yet as I have pointed out elsewhere, the shifts towards phenomenological and non-representational approaches across academic disciplines that I have discussed in Chapter 1,

> have led to only a very limited amount of discussion of the experiential and sensorial dimensions of how we perceive and engage with media in everyday life. In contrast, through the representational approach of Visual Culture Studies W.J.T. Mitchell (2005) engages the sensory to develop a semiotic approach to media. (Pink, 2015)

Above I have noted McLuhan's culturalist and representational argument, which is aligned both with the theoretical commitments of David Howes and those of the visual cultures scholar W.J.T Mitchell, mentioned above. These authors take approaches that are rooted in semiotic analysis, and that are undertaken at the level of culture, rather than at the level of seeking to understand human experience and perception. In contrast, the approaches of Ingold (see Ingold, 2010) and of Barbara Stafford (2006), who has brought together insights from research in the neurosciences and art history in her own work, offer us a very different way to understand representations and their experiential and sensory qualities (Pink, 2015). My point is that the analytical consequences of taking a representational or non-representational approach to media are rather different (Pink, 2015), as are the consequences of doing so in relation to the senses (Howes, 2011a, 2011b; Ingold, 2011a, 2011b). In this book where I engage with media and technologies, both as part of the world we research and as part of the toolkit we use to research in the world, I treat them in a way that goes beyond their status as technologies to disseminate representations or be used for communications, but as sensory technologies with other forms of presence, affordances and qualities (Pink and Leder Mackley, 2013).

In Chapters 4, 5 and 6 I identify how different media have been used in sensory ethnography research through examinations of how specific methods have been developed in different research projects and contexts.

ETHICS IN SENSORY ETHNOGRAPHY

Any research project needs to attend to the ethical codes of the academic discipline(s) it is located in (these are normally developed by the professional associations of the discipline) and of the institutions with whom they are involved. As I have discussed elsewhere (Pink, 2007a), researchers doing ethnography need to account for the ethical issues that are raised by specific cultural contexts and the culturally and personally specific moralities of their research participants. In this general sense ethical issues raised by a sensory ethnography need not vary from those of a visual ethnography (Pink, 2007a) or applied ethnography (Pink, 2005a, 2007b). Indeed, it is difficult to propose an ethics framework for an area of research practice that is already evidently cutting across academic disciplines and applied research agendas. Researchers working with different types of research question, participant and context will need to ensure that their ethical practices conform to those of their own professional associations and academic institutions. One of the keys to ensuring that research practice is ethical is to ensure that it is as far as possible collaborative. This means engaging the subjects of the research as participants in the project, rather than as the objects of an experiment. This is part of the collaborative and reflexive approach that is fundamental to sensory ethnography as it is conceived in this book. The idea behind this sensory ethnography is not so much to study other people's sensory values and behaviours, but to collaborate with them to explore and identify these. This is not to say that in some instances more experimental approaches are not interesting. However, generally before considering intruding on the sensory consciousness of research participants the ethical implications of doing this should be thoroughly considered. Indeed, Devon E. Hinton, Vuth Pich, Dava Chhean and Mark H. Pollard propose that 'Traumatic events are encoded into memory by auditory, olfactory and visual cues', all of which might be triggers or lead to flashbacks (2006: 68). Their report on psychiatric research into 'the phenomenology of olfactory panic attacks' amongst Cambodian refugees (2006: 69) is a powerful reminder that sensory memories do not always invoke the nostalgia of good times past.

Conventional approaches to research ethics, quite rightly, take a pragmatic approach to setting out how we might best prevent our research causing any harm or disrespect to others. However, the existing literature also implies a further role for a sensory ethnography, seeing a sensory approach itself as a moral perspective. Several writers have suggested that taking a sensory approach to understanding and intervening in the world might help to make it a better place. In Chapter 1 I argued that a sensory ethnography should be based in a collaborative and participatory approach to research that respects research participants and recognises that ethnography might have a role in the real world as well as in academia. The idea of a sensory approach as a moral perspective also links in interesting ways to the conceptualisation of a collaborative and participatory sensory ethnography.

The idea of a sensory approach as a moral perspective was first noted in humanist geography where the practical and ethical elements are interlinked. Porteous insists on there being practical implications of his notions of 'smell-scape' and 'sound-scape' for urban planning (e.g. 1990: 43–5, 62–5). He suggests that to 'live well', 'we need to improve the current imbalance of our sensory modalities, to moderate our current overemphasis on vision that distances us, and ultimately alienates us from our surroundings' (1990: 200). His moral message is that 'The non-visual senses encourage us to be involved, and being involved, we may come to care' (1990: 200). Tuan's notion of aesthetics also has a moral message. He compares what he calls the 'Shadows' of 'Human Frailty and Evil' (1993: 238–40) with the 'Light' of 'Moral beauty' (1993: 240–3). He sees the 'human story [as] one of progressive sensory and mental awareness', thus seeing culture as a 'moral-aesthetic venture to be judged ultimately by its moral beauty' (1993: 240). In a similar vein the anthropologist Paul Stoller has suggested that 'humility' should be at the foundation of a sensory ethnography. He closes his book *Sensuous Scholarship* by proposing that 'If we allow humility to work its wonders it can bring sensuousness to our practices and expression. It can enable us to live well in the world' (1997: 137).

These approaches suggest that a heightened sensory awareness and a sensitivity to sensoriality in the way we both design and appreciate our physical environment and other people's ways of knowing also resonate with recent literature in architecture and design studies and outside academia. For example, the Slow Food movement takes a similar view – suggesting that it is through the education of the senses that we might better appreciate our environments and create a better world (see Petrini, 2001); the Finish architect Juhani Pallasmaa suggests that 'the city of the gaze passivates the body and the other senses' (2005 [1999]: 142–3); and the design theorists Joy Malnar and Frank Vodvarka (2004) argue that a multisensory approach should inform design (see Pink, 2007b).

Thus a sensory ethnography has certain congruences with the ethics of those who hope to make the world a better place, seeing greater sensorial awareness as a route to achieving this. This does not mean that the sensory ethnographer is necessarily one who cares more. It does nevertheless imply that in applied research attention to the senses can lead to an appreciation of what is important in how people feel – the affective and sensory elements of – their social and material worlds.

This ethic of working towards a better world, and the existing connections between a sensory approach and design, open up the possibilities of us also thinking about the role of sensory ethnography as part of ethical and collaborative co-design processes. This ethic connects with the future-oriented focus of a sensory ethnography that engages with the imagination and the ways that the future is part of the present, outlined in Chapter 2. It also enables us to consider the ethics of the ethnographic place as discussed in Chapter 2 – suggesting that by bringing together the ethics of a sensory ethnography approach with the ethics of change making for a 'better' world, a sensory ethnography approach is well placed to further novel approaches to design research and practice, precisely by inviting us to address the future and its uncertainties in ways that go beyond verbal expression and the domain of representations that are the subject of the approaches to media critiqued in the previous section.

Summing up

In this chapter I have examined practical and ethical aspects of a sensory ethnography. I have stressed that doing sensory ethnography is an approach that leads researchers to understandings of a wide range of aspects of other people's lives and experiences – rather than simply involving a substantive focus on the senses. To develop this approach ethnographers might incorporate into their preparation for research, attention to the following: examining their own sensory subjectivity (from both cultural and personal perspectives); an awareness of how sensory experience might be associated with media use and communication; reviews of existing writings, films and other representations of sensory experience and practice relating to the people with whom they plan to research; and (in addition to existing discipline-specific ethical codes) the specific ethical and moral concerns that have been associated with sensorial understandings in existing literature. This, I have suggested, offers us a route to considering the role of the future orientation of sensory ethnography in designing for change.

Recommended further reading

- Desjarlais, R. (2003) *Sensory Biographies: lives and death among Nepal's Yolmo Buddhists.* London: University of California Press.
- Geurts, K.L. (2003) *Culture and the Senses: bodily ways of knowing in an African community.* Berkeley, Los Angeles, London: University of California Press.
- Hahn, T. (2006) '"It's the RUSH ... that's what drives you to do it": sites of the sensually extreme', *The Drama Review: the Journal of Performance Studies*, 50(2): 87–97.
- Howes, D. (ed.) (1991) *The Varieties of Sensory Experience: a sourcebook in the anthropology of the senses.* Toronto, Buffalo, London: University of Toronto Press.
- Pink, S. (2015) 'Approaching media through the senses: between experience and representation', *Media International Australia*, 254.

II

Sensory ethnography in practice

FOUR

The sensoriality of the interview

Rethinking personal encounters through the senses

The interview is arguably the most firmly embedded research method in contemporary qualitative research practice. In this chapter I re-conceptualise the interview through a sensory approach. I revise the way we understand and interpret the interview on two levels: first, I re-frame it as a multisensory event and as such a context of emplaced knowing; and second, I suggest how, through the interview, we might attend to participants' treatments of the senses in order to learn about how they communicate about and categorise their experiences, values, moralities, other people, things and more. For the interview to be used to its full potential, I suggest, such a revision in our understanding of it is needed.

INTRODUCTION: DEFINING THE INTERVIEW

The existing qualitative methods literature identifies several types of interview, each of which has its own epistemological foundations. As pointed out in Jonathan Skinner's review of interviewing in qualitative research, this includes disciplines such as journalism, health care, psychology, criminology, counselling, education and oral history (Skinner, 2012: 35). Taking two extremes as examples, to discuss the interview from a different perspective, Clive Seale contrasts what he refers to as the classical and idealist approaches to interviews. In the '*classical* tradition of social survey work' interviewees' accounts 'are assessed according to how accurately they reflect' a supposed 'real social world' (Seale, 1998: 202–3, original italics). In contrast to the '*realist* approach' of the classical tradition 'is an *idealist* one, ... in which interview data ... are seen as presenting but one of many possible worlds' (Seale, 1998: 203, original italics). In practice, qualitative researchers often combine these approaches, which need not necessarily be incompatible. Thus one might understand the interview as a *representation* of an experienced reality rather than a realist or authentic account of an objective reality. However, simultaneously it would usually be reasonable to treat certain knowledge represented in its narrative as a reliable account of, for instance, events that happened and persons who existed.

In the qualitative methods literature two aspects of interviewing have been emphasised. First, the interview itself is often seen and analysed as a 'social event' (Seale, 1998: 202), in which, as Tim Rapley puts it, 'two people, often relative strangers, sit down and talk about a specific topic' (2004: 15). Second, the interview is often described as a form of 'conversation'. Indeed, for some researchers this is why the interview as a method is so appealing. For instance, discussing a feminist approach to research Ann Oakley has characterised in-depth interviews as 'the face-to-face' method *par excellence* and 'as such the chosen method for feminist researchers'. Oakley suggests that 'Interviews imitate conversations; they hold out the promise of mutual listening' (2000: 47). Indeed, some researchers treat interviews as conversation in a more formal sense by applying the method of conversation analysis to them (Rapley, 2004).

Talking undeniably plays a central role in the interview. Yet a notion of the interview as simply an encounter that benefits from the intimacy of face-to-face conversation is insufficient. Rather, it is a social encounter – an event – that is inevitably both emplaced and productive of place. It has material and sensorial components. Interviewees refer to the sensoriality of their experiences not only verbally through metaphor, but through gesture, actual touching, sharing scents (e.g. perfumes, sprays and other products), sounds (playing music, demonstrating a creaking door), images (e.g. showing photographs) and even tastes (e.g. offering the researcher food or drink to try). An emphasis on 'talk' in discussions of what interviewing involves, and dependency on conversation analysis as a means of understanding the sorts of interactions that occur during interviews (e.g. Seale, 1998; Rapley, 2004), limits the ways interviews can be understood.

This focus on talk in conversation analysis has been extended, for example, by Charles Goodwin who demonstrates the role played by 'the gaze' in human interaction (Goodwin, 2001: 158), and by 'multi-modality' scholars (e.g. Kress and Van Leeuwen, 2001) who stress the different modes through which communication takes place, involving 'the abstract, non-material *resources* of meaning-making (obvious ones include writing, speech and images; less obvious ones include gesture, facial expression, texture, size and shape, even colour)' (Dicks et al., 2006: 82). A focus on interaction also offers a sociological interpretation of the multisensoriality of the interview, which reveals two interesting insights: first, it shows clearly the inadequacy of a dependence on talk in understanding human interactions; and second, it stresses how multiple modes and media come into play in these forms of 'meaning-making'. An interaction perspective has also helpfully been used to understand difficult moments and silence in interviewing (Montgomery, 2012).

However, that I suggest should be seen only as a starting point. The focus on the senses I am proposing here goes beyond the analysis of these observable aspects of human interaction. As I have stressed in the previous chapters, an understanding of research as *participation* rather than observation is fundamental to a sensory ethnography methodology. Thus I suggest interview encounters should be understood as instances in which interviewer and interviewee together create a shared place. Interviewer and interviewee communicate as embodied and emplaced persons, sometimes using media technologies in this process. Refiguring the interview in this way opens up possibilities for understanding how and what we might learn about other people's worlds through the interview. Thus ethnographic interviewing might be rethought in terms of a sensory paradigm. In line with the reflexive approach to sensory ethnography outlined in Chapter 3 and which is discussed in relation to more participatory ways of doing research in Chapter 5, in this chapter I suggest treating the interview as a route to understanding other people's emplacement through collaborative and reflexive exploration.

THE SENSORIALITY OF THE ETHNOGRAPHIC INTERVIEW

In the context of an ethnographic research project, interviews are not simply research events during which one person (the researcher) asks and audio records a set of questions of another (the interviewee). A consideration of some of the established literature about ethnographic interviewing offers a useful starting point from which to consider how a sensory ethnography approach to interviewing would be different. Barbara Sherman Heyl has defined 'ethnographic interviewing' as including projects

> in which researchers have established respectful, on-going relationships with their interviewees, including enough rapport for these to be a genuine exchange of views and enough time and openness in the interviews for the interviewees to explore purposefully with the researcher the meanings they place on events in their worlds. (2001: 367)

While Sherman Heyl's definition involves certain methodological conditions, it is also suitably open to reflect O'Reilly's fundamental point that 'there is no normal within ethnography'. Rather, as O'Reilly stresses, the ethnographer might draw from a 'range of interviewing styles', but 'the key is to be flexible, and to be aware at every stage about why you are using that approach' (2005: 116). A sensory approach to the ethnographic interview coincides largely with these points. As will be evident from the case studies discussed later in this chapter, interviewing styles, narratives and experiences tend to be context-dependent. They are negotiated in relation to the research aims and through the relationship and particular style of sociality that develops between the researcher and the research participant.

A sensory approach to interviewing also has sympathies with a feminist approach which, as Rubin and Rubin describe it, 'humanizes both the researcher and the interviewee' and empowers the interviewee by 'Allowing people to "talk back" (hooks 1989) [and thus] gives a voice through interviews to those who have been silenced' (2005: 26). This feminist approach also recognises the emotive nature of the interview, stressing the need for researchers to also be reflexive about *their* own emotions (2005: 26).

Building on these understandings, I see interviews as social, sensorial and affective encounters. In some instances they entail the sorts of sensory sociality between researcher and research participant that I outline in Chapter 5. Indeed, the similarities between participant observation and interviewing have been stressed in recent methodological discussions – as O'Reilly has pointed out, for ethnographers 'There might not be a clear distinction between doing participant observation and conducting an interview' (2005: 115). Atkinson and Coffey have made a similar point, arguing that observation and interviewing should not be seen as being in opposition to each other; they suggest that 'Actions are understandable because they can be talked about. Equally, accounts – including those derived from interviewing – are actions'. They thus propose that since 'Social life is performed and narrated we need to recognize the performative qualities of social life and talk' (2003: 110). These suggestions also support the point that interviews are not simply about talk. In emphasising the performative nature of talk, they imply the embodied nature of the interview. It is a short step from here to recognise that the talk of an interview is not simply performative and embodied, but that it is more fully situated in that it is an emplaced activity that engages not only the performative body but also the sensing body in relation to its total environment.

SITUATING THE INTERVIEW

It is not uncommon to find research projects that rely on interviewing as their main or sole source for ethnographic knowledge. However, even within more conventional discussions of qualitative interviewing researchers have expressed the inadequacy of studies that depend solely on interviews for their 'data' to 'understand people's *lived, situated, practices*' (Rapley, 2004: 29, original italics). Moreover, some, in the context of social anthropology, would recommend 'the interview as a part of participant observation and not apart from participant observation' (Skinner, 2012: 83). Indeed, the relationship between what *is* verbalised in interviews and knowledge that is not articulated in this way is itself an interesting question. For example, summing up his analysis of the sensoriality of gardening Chris Tilley points out that as an embodied activity gardening involves 'doing rather than saying' – it is in fact 'an escape from verbal discourse' (2006: 328). His article contains numerous quotations from interviews with 62 Swedish and 65 English gardeners (2006: 313) that demonstrate his point that 'touch, sound and taste especially, were not sensory dimensions of the garden that were either usually verbalized or explicit'. Nevertheless, this is not to say that gardening is a predominantly visual practice. Indeed, Tilley stresses that for most gardeners 'touch, sound and taste, unlike sight or smell remain part of the sensory unconscious of gardening ... rarely acknowledged, thought about or discussed' (2006: 314). Thus, the sensoriality of gardening cannot necessarily be directly accessed through verbal interviews. Gardening involves knowledge that is not verbal or articulated. Rather, as Tilley puts it, 'the intimacy of bodily contact through all the senses ... can be readily observed when you study the manner in which gardeners actually garden'. It is thus 'in their practice' (and not in their talk) that the senses are clearly significant (2006: 328).

In my own experience of doing anthropological research, interviewing has often, but not always, been developed in relation to other ways I have participated in the lives or cultural worlds of interviewees, either during the same research episode or in the past. This combination of prior experience and combining interviews with the video tour method (discussed in Chapter 5) and sharing other activities with research participants was essential to my research about the sensory home (see Pink, 2004, 2006, 2012). Using interviews in relation to video tours also forms part of the approach I take to researching uses of digital standby modes with digital media in Australian homes (discussed in Chapter 6). Likewise, other examples discussed in Chapter 5 involve the combination of interviewing and forms of participation, showing how they can effectively form part of the same research process, because they bring different elements of experience and ways to communicate and understand it to the fore. For instance, the anthropologist Judith Okely has stressed how her participation in similar practices that her elderly research participants had enjoyed before they lived in a residential home led her to better understand their interview conversations (Okely, 1994).

THE INTERVIEW, PARTICIPATION AND PLACE

In Chapter 2 I suggested that sensory ethnography itself entails a form of learning about other people's emplacement and experiences through participation in specific practices and environments. Interviewing can be understood according to a similar phenomenological approach, although there are some obvious specificities in the ways one would be able to participate. Indeed, recently anthropologists have reflected on the *experience* of interviewing in some depth (e.g. Hockey and Forsey, 2012; Rapport, 2012; Wulff, 2012). Moreover, the argument that 'sensory questions can enrich interview research' (Harris and Guillemin, 2011: 690) is demonstrated across a range of fields now, as shown in this chapter. In interviews researchers participate or collaborate with research participants in the process of defining and representing their (past, present or imagined) emplacement and their sensory embodied experiences. If we situate the interview within a process through which experiences are constituted, it might be understood as a point in this process where multisensorial experience is verbalised through culturally constructed sensory categories and in the context of the intersubjective interaction between ethnographer and research participant. However, this definition might be taken still further. As I have stressed above the interview is not simply a verbal conversation that can be audio recorded. The interviewer and interviewee do not need to be sitting down, immobilised and simply speaking. Although it is an ordinary everyday practice to sit and talk, other examples include Spinney's practice of talking with cyclists while riding alongside them (Spinney, 2006). Rather, throughout interviews, whether sitting, standing or moving, both ethnographers and research participants *continue to be* active participants in their environments, using their whole bodies, all their senses, available props and the ground under their feet, to narrate, perform, communicate and represent their experiences.

The sensoriality of these social encounters might be evident in the sharing of certain embodied experiences. For instance, in England, when I have arrived at people's houses to carry out an interview they have almost always offered and prepared a cup of tea or coffee for us both. Sometimes interviews take place with the television or radio on as a 'background' soundscape (or in the case of Vokes' (2007) work discussed below, as a purposeful medium of elicitation). An interview might happen in a public context over a shared drink or meal. An ethnographer and interview participant might walk together to the physical stopping point where the interview is to be done, to the railway station after it has happened, or an interview might be done in movement – during a walk. Equally important is to note that an interview is not an exclusively aural encounter or event but one that also involves the materiality of the environment and of artefacts. While this is not a new point it becomes particularly salient when re-thinking the interview through the senses. Tracing the history of the interview in anthropological research, Richard Vokes shows how the role of material objects in the ethnographic interview has long since been recognised. Vokes points out that, now nearly 100 years ago, Bronislaw Malinowski wrote: '"my experience is that direct questioning of the native [sic] about a custom or belief never discloses their attitude of mind as thoroughly as the discussion of facts connected with the direct observation of a custom or with a concrete occurrence" (1915: 652)' (cited by Vokes, 2007: 290). Significantly, he goes on to note that Malinowski argued that 'This effect was most easily achieved ... through the use of some object associated with that custom or occurrence' (Vokes, 2007: 290).

In my experience it is not only the introduction of objects into interview situations by researchers that can invoke important narratives. Rather, research participants themselves also use all resources available to communicate about their experiences, and spoken words only represent one of these strategies. They might pass researchers objects to touch and hold, to look at, smell and listen to or invite them to sense physical spaces (in my experience this has included photographs, cleaning products, cupboards, plants and more). They invite us to engage not only with what they are saying but with the material and sensorial qualities of the things they describe or actually interact with. Indeed, as Helen Wulff beautifully describes, in a discussion of her experiences of interviewing dancers, the moving/performing human body itself can become part of an interview:

> During interviews I did with dancers in my study of the transnational ballet world it often happened that the dancer would get up from the table and start illustrating a point he or she was making through a step or a combination of steps. It was also more common than not that the dancer I interviewed would move around while sitting down, flapping arms and lifting legs under the table. Once a male principal dancer I was interviewing over a breakfast table in a hotel on a tour got so excited over a role in a performance we were discussing that he over turned the table, sending coffee cups and croissants flying around the room, to the amusement of everyone present. (Wulff, 2012: 322)

Thus interviews can invite ethnographers to participate in multiple sensory ways of knowing by incorporating a whole range of different embodied experiences and emotions into the narratives that are audio recorded and taken away. For example, Wulff, who was a dancer herself, goes on to comment on the ways in which interviewing in this sense might engage the embodied experiences of movement shared by the interviewer and interviewee. Calling on both her own and Skinner's work she describes how:

> Writing about the interview Skinner did with the woman salsa dancer, he notes that it is 'a learning case study' and 'above all, one based around muscle and cerebral memories' for both of them (2010: 11). When I was interviewing ballet dancers, many of them, again, related to me as if we were dancing a duet together. (Wulff, 2012: 323)

When participants introduce objects or movements into an interview, this also creates routes to the forms of interviewee empowerment that the feminist approach to interviewing discussed above seeks to create. Engaging multisensorial communication and analysis can achieve this by allowing for the use of non-verbal types of communication and knowing. This might include socially marginalised forms of knowledge and communication. Finally, when research participants use words to describe their experiences, they are placing verbal definitions on sensory embodied experiences, and in doing so allocating these experiences to culturally specific sensory categories. Interviews can thus produce knowledge on different levels: through verbal definitions of sensory experiences; when the 'interviewee' introduces a range of other embodied ways of knowing into the interview process; and through the sensory sociality of the interview process and context itself. For the multisensory potential of the interview to be achieved researchers need to be open to these possibilities, to ensure that research participants know that they are not necessarily expected to simply sit still and talk. Rather, researchers invite participants to gather everything they need in order to communicate about the place they occupy in the world.

Whereas some existing approaches to the interview have tended to treat it as a realist account, a conversation or a narrative, here I suggest an alternative sensory methodology. If we treat the interview as a phenomenological event it is more appropriate to use the idea of place-making as a metaphor through which to understand the interview process. The place created by an interview involves a process of movement, through a narrative. As the examples discussed above have shown, as the researcher and interviewee move though their route they unavoidably verbalise, engage with and draw together a series of ideas, sensed embodied experiences, emotions, material objects and more. This is not so much the gathering of data that the researcher will take away to analyse, but rather it is a process of bringing together which involves the accumulation of emplaced ways of knowing generated not simply through verbal exchanges but through, for example, cups of tea and coffee, comfortable cushions, movement or performance, odours, textures, sounds and images.

For instance, by sitting with another person in their living room, in *their* chair, drinking *their* coffee from one of *their* mugs, or when drinking together in a café, one begins in some small way to occupy the world in a way that is similar to them. As the interview progresses, images, sounds, artefacts and emotions might be shared and other people may come and go. The interview and its environment create a place-event, where researcher and interviewee are mutually emplaced as they move along its narrative. They are in a situation where they interact in ways often more intense than in everyday life, producing heightened reflections and new ways of knowing. Interviews are not only places where researchers learn about other people's experiences, but where interviewees might arrive at new levels of awareness about their own lives and experiences. I have often left interviews feeling dislocated, as if suddenly emotionally and sensorially detached from an empathetic encounter, precisely because they generate more than a verbal interaction.

THE INTERVIEW AS A ROUTE TO UNDERSTANDING OTHER PEOPLE'S SENSORY CATEGORIES

In Chapter 3 I outlined how, in some sensory ethnography studies, one of the first steps taken by the researcher has been to identify the sensory categories and meanings of the people participating in the research. In this section I discuss how interviewing has frequently and successfully been used for this purpose – sometimes in combination with other methods.

It is commonly recognised that interviews cannot bring researchers into direct contact with life as it is lived and experienced or with the routine and other practices that people engage in on a day-to-day basis. However, one of the advantages of interviews is that they allow people to discuss their lives, beliefs, values, opinions, experiences, practices and more in a focused way in collaboration with a researcher within a circumscribed time. The interview creates a place in which to reflect, define and communicate about experiences; it is indeed a creative place where representations and understandings of experience rather than objective truths about what has been experienced are intentionally produced (and moreover often audio recorded for analysis). However creative the narratives and stories of interviews become they are nevertheless framed by cultural and personal experiences, values and moralities. These in turn are represented through interviewees' personal interpretations and appropriations of culturally specific sensory categories, metaphors and meanings. The ways these sensory categories, metaphors and meanings are used by people to represent their lives, experiences and opinions, can often offer a key to understanding their self-identities, what is important to them and why.

Nevertheless, it should not be assumed that in all research contexts simply asking people about or discussing with them the sensory categories they use and the meanings they attribute to certain experiences will provide the researcher with direct and comprehensible knowledge about local sensoria. In some cases, according to personal and cultural circumstances, research participants might find it easy and indeed interesting to reflect on how they, for instance, use smell or touch to make judgements about the status of particular artefacts they have in their homes, or about the personal hygiene of others. In other situations however they may find it impossible to articulate sensory categories and values. The following examples, from quite different cultural contexts, demonstrate this well.

The first example concerns my experience of doing research about the sensory meanings attached to domestic laundry. In 1999–2000 I collaborated with researchers from Unilever Research to undertake two projects focusing broadly on domestic practices of housework, home decoration and laundry (these are reported on in more detail in Pink, 2004, 2005b, 2006, 2007c, 2012). As part of the interviews about laundry in the home I asked participants to describe how they evaluated their 'clean' laundry. At this point in the research I was interested not so much in asking people to reflect on how they *experienced* the laundry process and the emotive and memory processes this involved, but in the ways they used different sensory modalities and categories to evaluate and to communicate about the cleanliness of their laundry:

> Jane: Um, well, when it's got no marks on it basically and it looks clean and pressed. I can't sort of say the smell would influence me on whether it be clean, whether it's just sort of nice, no marks on it and nicely ironed.
>
> Sarah: Yeah, yeah, and I mean in order for it to be clean what actually has to be done to it, what has to happen to it for you for it to be clean.
>
> Jane: For it to be fed through that washing machine, Sarah, with some ... [laundry detergent] ... in it, because as I say, I generally do rely on the ... [laundry detergent] ..., and um, and as I say, and then I check it when I'm ironing it. It's nice if it, nice if it's got a bit of ... [fabric conditioner] ... smell to it.

I was doing research in English homes, places in many ways very familiar to me. Nevertheless, as I learnt through the research process, the women who participated in the interviews had quite different experiences and knowledge about laundry to mine. They found it easy to articulate their knowledge and experience through the five-sense sensorium of modern western culture, commenting not only, like the participant quoted above, on the sight and smell of clean laundry, but also on, for instance, the feel of starchy shirts or soft towels. Later in this chapter I reflect further on these uses of sensory categories and their implications and in Chapter 6 I discuss the second stage of this research which involved video tours and performative representations.

Geurts' descriptions of doing research with Anlo Ewe people in Ghana, a culture quite different from the North American culture she had come from, provide an interesting contrast. The experiences of interviewing about local sensory meanings and categories that she describes in this context were quite different to those I experienced in my own culture, and required different solutions. Geurts discusses how she was initially unable to find a local cultural category that was the equivalent of the modern western notion of the senses. She writes how:

> there seemed to be little consensus about a precise cultural category that we could map into our domain of the five senses. In fact, at one point in the middle of my research, I seemed to have nearly as many configurations of sense-data as the number of people I had interviewed. (2003: 37)

In search of the answers to her questions she interviewed a local expert on Anlo 'history and cultural traditions'. However, neither did this interview provide her with a direct route into local cultural knowledge that she was seeking. Geurts describes the encounter, noting how on arrival she presented her interviewee with a bag of oranges, and 'he inhaled the fragrance from the bag'. Nevertheless, she continues: 'When I asked him a question about the senses, however, he emphatically replied "We don't have that in our culture"' (2003: 37), always insisting that 'Anlo-Ewe cultural traditions simply did not involve the cultivation of any kind of reified model of sensory systems that clearly spelled out a theory for *how we know what we know*' (2003: 38).

Another example of how the categories used to describe experiences might vary from those that the ethnographer might bring with her, is shown by Sandra Fahy, writing about her experiences of interviewing people about their memories of hunger in North Korea. Although she does not explicitly address the question of the 'sensory' experiences of the people who participated in her interviews, Fahy's work shows very well how the categories used to represent experience need themselves to be situated and understood in context. In this case the experience of hunger was considered to be 'unspeakable' in certain terms, both within the context that it was historically experienced and within the interview. In the first sense, as Fahy explains, this was because the political regime of the time would not allow hunger to be openly expressed, and therefore people developed alternative ways of expressing it, and alternative categories through which to speak about it. As Fahy expresses it:

> The language used by North Korean famine survivors in their oral accounts demonstrates consistent patterns in speech that I classify as ambiguous because they require context to achieve full meaning. These expressions can be understood as 'silencing' and making 'unspeakable' their experiences in the North because that original context is so impenetrable, both physically and somewhat ideologically, for many listeners. Indeed, it could be argued that these expressions continue to make experiences unspeakable after survival, in South Korea or Japan, because truly accurate communication could endanger family members and friends still living at home. (Fahy, 2012: 440)

Thus, interviewing people about sensory experience is not a straightforward exercise. Interviews that seek to identify sensory categories or to use them as a way of discussing different aspects of experience or practice cannot necessarily be approached in the same ways across cultures – or even for different groups with some degree of shared cultural knowledge. In some research contexts interviewing might turn out to be a less fruitful exercise in the search for knowledge that is better accessed through participatory and apprenticeship methods of the kind discussed in Chapter 5.

SITTING AND TALKING: SPOKEN NARRATIVES IN SENSORY ETHNOGRAPHY INTERVIEWS

Although much ethnography and certainly most ethnographic interviewing is done sitting down, little analytical attention has been paid to this (nearly) universal human practice. Yet sitting is no less a sensory embodied experience (for the interviewer and interviewee) than are walking and eating discussed in the next chapter. Further reflection raises a whole series of questions. These include more commonly raised issues concerning whether the interviewee is sitting comfortably, in familiar circumstances, near enough to the microphone, etc. Even these issues, when thought through a sensory paradigm, begin to provide a basis through which to understand how the sitter is emplaced. What might she or he see from where she or he is seated? Is there a pleasant breeze or cold draft from the window? Is the chair the same one she or he sits in to watch TV, read the paper, relax, work, eat, have an afternoon nap? In what might on the surface seem to be a relatively straightforward interview situation, a new layer of complexity is introduced if we pause to consider the meanings that might be invoked through the material and sensorial environment. There are moreover good reasons why many interviews take place sitting and talking. These are not simply qualitative interview conventions but cultural practices, sometimes part of everyday routines or story telling and other oral narrative traditions. Thus when undertaking 'sitting and talking' type interviews it is useful to first gain some ideas about local cultural conventions regarding these practices – for instance, what does one *also* do (and not do) while sitting and talking/listening. This might indeed include eating, drinking, listening, tapping one's foot and more.

The reflexive analysis of the sensoriality of the interview context aside, the key motive that researchers have to undertake interviews is to learn about, for instance, other people's experiences, understandings and values. Although there are limits to the extent to which we can access other people's embodied experiences through the interview, there are strong arguments for using this method. In this section I first discuss Robert Desjarlais' (2003) argument that biographical audio recorded interviewing can serve as a phenomenological research method that provides insights into other people's sensory experiences through their own spoken narratives. I then demonstrate through a discussion of my own research materials how talk that uses sensory metaphor while also discussing sensory experience can provide insights into other people's worlds, everyday practices, values and moralities.

Desjarlais' (2003) *Sensory Biographies: lives and deaths among Nepal's Yolmo Buddhists* 'explores the life histories of two Yolmo elders, focusing on how particular sensory orientations and modalities have contributed to the making and telling of their lives' (back cover). While biographical interviewing is a common method for life history research (e.g. Plummer, 2001), Desjarlais' approach demonstrates the significance of such interviews as multisensory processes. Although recorded conversations are central to his methods Desjarlais points out that these were not undertaken in isolation from his wider involvement in the everyday lives of his research participants (2003: 18). While talk is the focus of his analysis, it is clearly set within a wider set of everyday and extraordinary individual and cultural practices that in turn inform the analysis. His descriptions bring to the fore not only words uttered, and linguistic meanings, but how the interview involves experiences and communication across different sensory modes. Thus, when discussing the interview context, Desjarlais comments on how, during an interview with Mheme, an 85-year-old man: 'his [Mheme's] daughter served us cup after cup of salt-butter tea' and how Mheme was 'usually relaxing cross-legged in the center of his bed with a cup of tea by his side'. Of particular interest is that Desjarlais remarks on how 'There were also occasions, especially when I visited Mheme on my own, that he looked at me in ways compared with that earlier gaze of his' (Desjarlais, 2003: 23). The 'gaze' that Desjarlais refers to is, as he explains in a later chapter, an important form of communication amongst Yolmo people for whom, he writes, 'sustained, mutual visual rapport can involve moments of intimacy, affection, and concern'. Such 'shared consciousness or an agreement of minds' might be developed or sustained through 'eye contact in tandem with a host of linguistic practices' (2003: 60). Therefore, while Desjarlais has a declared interest in 'talk' (2003: 18), his approach goes clearly beyond those of Rapley (2004) and Seale (1998) who use conversation analysis as a basis from which to understand human interaction in interview contexts.

Desjarlais' work is also interesting because his analysis of the interviews reveals the importance of sensory metaphors as forms of expression both within and in structuring the narratives through which people tell stories about their lives. His study was centred around the life histories recorded with Mheme Lama, mentioned above and Kisang Omu, an 88-year-old woman (2003: 1–3). He comments that as the interviews progressed:

> I realised that while Mheme's recounting of his life was dominated by motifs of vision and bodiliness, of knowing the world though visual means, and of acting and suffering through the medium of his visible body, Kisang Omu's accounts of her life largely entailed a theatre of voices: when narrating significant events in her life, she often invoked, in vivid, morally connative terms, the voicings of key actors in those events. (Desjarlais, 2003: 3)

Desjarlais notes that this striking difference invites a further and more general question: 'How ... do a person's ways of sensing the world contribute to how that person lives and recollects her life?' (2003: 3). This question is applicable not only to Desjarlais' own research (readers interested in his analysis are recommended to read his text) but alerts us to the point that individual, gendered, generational, ethnic, class-based and of course culturally specific ways of sensing the world will inevitably impinge on how research participants recount their lives in any interview context. An analysis of their 'talk' contextualised as recommended above (to incorporate also looking into other forms of sensing), offers routes into understanding how people situate themselves and their experiences through specific sets of moralities, relationships and more. Attention to the way they use sensory metaphors to express these experiences, comment on their own and other people's moralities, and the qualities of their social relationships can offer important insights. In the next section I demonstrate this further through a discussion of an example of how sensory categories were used in interview talk about domestic practices.

TALKING ABOUT DIRT, CLEANLINESS AND 'FRESHNESS'

In this section I discuss one aspect of my research about domestic laundry, introduced above: the question of how the people who participated in my research talked about dirt. The research was structured into two parts – an initial in-depth interview, which explored questions that included themes about self-identity, lifestyle, home, the senses and notions of clean and dirty and the moral connotations of these; this was followed by a video tour of the home (see Chapter 5). Here I reflect further on how in one interview the idea of dirt as something that was experienced and evaluated sensorially was discussed. The transcript below is an extract from an interview with a middle-aged woman who was responsible for most of the domestic work at home. In this extract we were discussing the question of how she knew when laundry items were clean and could be worn/used or needed to be washed:

Sarah: And what about clothes and things, if you had a little stain that just wouldn't come off?

Jane: It all depends where it would be. Em, I wouldn't discard it Sarah, I'd probably, I'd wear it sort of for every day, I would, but I wouldn't discard a thing if it had just a tiny stain on, no.

Sarah: Would you wear if sort of ...

Jane: Not for best,

Sarah: but if you could see it though, if you were going shopping would you wear it or would you ...

Jane: No, no, not if people could see it Sarah but I mean, if it sort of meant like a little bit under the arm or, (pause) oh I don't know.

Sarah: Or if you could wear a jacket over it and it didn't show ...

Jane: That's right, yes, and probably get, and prob ..., if I liked it enough Sarah, I probably would still utilise it, yeah.

Sarah: [is that] because you think it would be clean?

Jane: Well I do, yes, as long as I say it's gone through there [through the washing machine], even if it's got a teeny little stain, and I couldn't get it out with the ... [laundry detergent], I mean but generally I've not got, no I don't think I've got anything like that ...

Sarah: ... and do things feel different when they're clean?

Jane: Ooh yes I think so definitely, yes, they do.

Sarah: How do they feel?

Jane: Um, they just feel, well as I say, nicely pressed they do, fresh and certainly fresher, yeah.

Sarah: What do you mean by fresher?

Jane: Um, just, well as I say when they are dirty and all that they've got that sweaty smell about them and grimy on the collar and everything, so as I say, just, they're just, they're nicer to put on.

Sarah: Yeah, and um how do you know if something is dirty? ... You said it might smell of something.

Jane: It's smelly! It's smelly! Because as I say I know when it's dirty ... but if it's white you cannot help but get a grimy colour. Ever so strange, so [with shirts] as I say, usually by the collar Sarah.

This part of the interview was guided by a part of my checklist that reminded me that I wanted to explore how participants in the research thought about different sensory modalities as ways of understanding cleanliness and dirt. In doing so I was specifically relating their experiences to the modern western five-sense sensorium. Therefore, I consciously probed them to tell me about how vision, smell and touch figured in their understandings of their laundry. However, they also related sensory categories to me unprompted – for example, to stress how even if something might visually have a permanent stain on it, one might not know if it was actually dirty until it had been smelt. By prompting interviewees to introduce other sensory categories into their evaluations I was gradually able to build a picture of when different people thought that the smell, feel and visual appearance of their laundry became an important signifier of its cleanliness. In the transcript above the research participant also introduces the concept of 'freshness', which she relates to the textures, smell and visual appearance of an item of clothing. The idea of 'freshness' being an ideal characteristic of laundry recurred throughout the interviews and tended to refer to the total experience of a laundry item, although smell was often used as an identifying feature. However, different people approach their laundry differently. They therefore use different sensory categories and experiences through which to discuss cleanliness, dirt and freshness. Therefore, through the *variety* of their responses to these questions I was able to assess how different people constructed their self-identities through their approaches to the sensorial quality of their laundry. They also used these categories when making moral judgements about the visual and olfactory states of laundry done (and clothes worn) by others. The interviews thus provided me with a set of discourses about laundry, cleanliness, dirt and morality and the ways these are experienced. As the research went on I began to self-evaluate my own clothing through the perspectives of different interviewees as I got ready to go to an appointment: Would it be acceptable for me to wear a top that had a small 'permanent' olive oil stain on it, if this was under my jacket? What if I took my jacket off? How would the people I was interviewing judge me through my own laundry?

This full interview was an hour long and then followed by another hour of video tour interview. Thus the extract discussed here is only a fragment of the whole interview encounter. It is a fragment on one level because it represents only a short period of time within a longer meeting. It is also just a fragment of an encounter that included a cup of coffee, the ringing of the telephone, the visual context and the textures of the carpet and sofa in the living room where we sat to talk, and more. Taken as a whole, the interview can be seen as part of a place-making process. The interview and the video tour became a place-event, creating a self-identity and home, through a series of verbal and sensorial engagements.

SENSORY ELICITATION: THE INTERVIEW AS A RESPONSE TO SENSORY STIMULI

Elicitation as a method

The use of material objects to elicit responses or evoke memories and areas of knowledge was and has long since (see Vokes, 2007) been employed in anthropological research (see also, for example, Hoskins, 1998). In my own research both research participants and sometimes my own physical, olfactory, visual and tactile engagements with material objects were central to our explorations of the meanings of home (see Pink, 2004). In Chapter 6, through a discussion of the video tour method I examine such multisensorial engagements further. Here, I discuss how researchers have focused single modern western sensory categories as routes to knowledge in what we might call elicitation interviews. In contrast to situations where objects that are already present serendipitously become part of a research encounter, elicitation interviews involve the researcher intentionally presenting research participants with a series of objects or experiences. An early template for this method was developed in the practice of photo-elicitation as presented by John Collier Jr (1967) (Vokes, 2007: 292), now commonly used across academic disciplines (see Harper, 2002; Lapenta, 2011). Photo-elicitation relies on the idea of the photograph becoming a visual text through which the subjectivities of researcher and research participant intersect. It can evoke memories, knowledge and more in the research participant, which might otherwise have been inaccessible, while simultaneously allowing the researcher to compare her or his subjective interpretation of the image with that of the research participant. The photographs shown are moreover not simply *visual* images, but also material objects with sensory qualities, or when shown on a computer screen, invested with a different type of materiality.

Sensory image elicitation

A conventional photo-elicitation practice would involve showing research participants images of other people or objects and asking them to discuss aspects of these images in interviews. In the context of a sensory ethnography this might involve inviting people to interpret other people's embodied experiences, or to suggest what it might feel like to be involved in a particular activity or to use a particular object. Such methods might indicate how research participants interpret and categorise other people's sensory experiences as well as inviting biographical and memory work regarding their own experiences. Another method involves showing research participants images of themselves engaged in particular activities and then exploring how they experienced these activities verbally in interviews. This method is particularly useful if one is trying to understand physical practices and activities which it is difficult to interrupt when they are in progress, yet which are so embodied that it is also problematic to disengage the discussion of them from the practice of them.

For example, Spinney discusses how he used video as part of a 'mobile ethnography' (2008: 79) in which he sought to understand 'what people's experiences of cycling were, how it becomes meaningful to them, why they move in particular ways, and how these practices define and reproduce particular identities' (2008: 76). To achieve this he combined cycling with and video recording research participants, with interviews during which he showed them sections of video footage. Spinney highlights the 'kinaesthetic and embodied approach' to understanding riders' practices and talk that his method allowed (2008: 92). Using video in addition to riding with other cyclists he was able to 'elicit embodied understandings from participants' through the playback of 'fleeting and ephemeral moments' (2008: 98). Through such research practices Spinney suggests that 'we begin to construct a vocabulary for the unspeakable and thus language can begin to play more of a role in how we understand and represent the embodied, the fleeting and the sensual' (2008: 101–2).

A further use of image elicitation involves inviting research participants themselves to produce images. Recent projects have applied similar principles to exploring sensory experience. Samantha Warren has developed this practice further in the context of what she refers to as a 'sensual methodology' in organisational aesthetics research. One of the concerns of this subdiscipline is with the feelings employees have about 'their organisational lives based especially on their sensory encounters with the world around them' (Warren, 2008: 560). Warren's own research was based in an organisation that had been refurbished to create a more 'playful' and 'fun' environment (2008: 567). To explore research participants' feelings about their environment Warren combined three methods: 'semi-structured biographical interviews'; 'respondent-led photography'; and 'aesthetic ethnography' which involves using the researcher's own aesthetic experience to inform her or his understandings (2008: 568). Participants were invited to photograph their experiences of the department as they chose and the photographs were then discussed in interview. Warren notes how her own 'aesthetic experiences and judgements were useful "empathetic framing" of the experiences of others' and provided a comparative perspective when they differed (2008: 569). The photographs in turn, she reports, worked in three ways: 'as a window on participants' aesthetic worlds'; 'evoking and "recreating" aesthetic experience during the interviews'; and as 'sites through which to explore the socially constructed nature of the participants' aesthetic judgements' (2008: 570–1). As such, using photographs in this way, Warren was able to combine her own empathetic knowing with interviewees' representations of their own experiences and an analytical acknowledgement of the constructedness of the categories they would use to express this.

Although image elicitation often involves the use of photography, some interesting uses of participant-produced drawings and paintings have also been developed.

In visual anthropology these include the work of Ian Edgar (e.g. 2004) and Gemma Orobitg (2004). The cultural geographer Divya P. Tolia-Kelly has also developed particularly interesting uses of participant image making to explore sensory and affective experiences in collaboration with the artist Grahame Lowe. Tolia-Kelly discusses the 'Nurturing Ecologies' project which investigated how the landscape of the Lake District National Park in England was experienced beyond the frame of a singular 'English sensibility' by working with migrants from Eastern Europe, India, Ireland and Scotland (Tolia-Kelly, 2007: 329–31). Using drawing and painting, she suggests, offered a route to 'a set of affective registers that are normally not encountered in representations of this cultural landscape', thus aiming to 'make tangible a divergent set of sensory responses to this landscape and show how affect and emotion are experienced' (2007: 331). Tolia-Kelly's collaborative methodology is particularly interesting in terms of sensory ethnography practice because it links to several of the research practices already discussed in this book, including talking, the representation of embodied knowing, and walking. First, it involved biographical workshops, thus acknowledging the role of biography and memory; second, in visual workshops participants were invited to produce collages to represent their own 'valued landscapes'; and finally, the groups took a walk through the Lake District after which the researchers asked them to 'record (using paint and paper) their responses to their experiences of the Lake District' (2007: 339). Tolia-Kelly demonstrates how this use of painting, connected to other collaborative methods, allowed new routes of expression creating 'alternative grammars that are not always encountered or expressible in oral interviews' (2007: 340). Her example invites us to consider how the sensory ethnographer might engage visual practices, combined with verbal discussion, to explore research participants' biographically situated encounters with material and social environments.

These examples demonstrate how sensory ethnographic image-elicitation methods can have some key uses including: offering research participants alternative media and frames through which to express their emplaced, sensory and emotional experiences and ways of knowing; inviting engagements with sensory memories; providing gateways through which research participants and researchers might imagine themselves once again engaged in an embodied practice or actual environment represented audiovisually; potentially evoking previous embodied experiences of such practices; enabling researchers to create empathetic connections to the experiences of research participants; and inviting verbal reflection along these themes. While image elicitation could be accused of privileging the visual it would be erroneous to associate this method with merely the production of visual knowledge. Indeed, by recognising the role of visual images as a standard medium for communicating about and invoking other sensory experiences, ethnographers can engage its potential for representation and forms of communication across modern western sensory categories.

Sound in sensory elicitation

Vokes has suggested extending the idea of elicitation to include not only the visual/material but sound, through a 'radio elicitation' method, which he has used in both an 'unstructured' and a more controlled form (2007: 295). In contrast to the interview methods discussed in earlier sections of this chapter, Vokes' 'radio elicitation' method is not designed to research local culturally specific sensoria. Rather, it is situated within his wider understanding of the role of radio in the local 'soundscape'. Before undertaking radio elicitation exercises he engaged in a series of 'radio walks' (similar to some soundwalk methods as reviewed by Adams and Bruce, 2008), in which he 'moved around the village along a predetermined route of about three miles long' in order to 'build up a record of the village "soundscape", by noting down all the sounds that could be heard along the way', with particular attention to radio sound (2007: 293). Thus the method uses elements of existing local soundscapes to elicit or inspire commentaries from people participating in his research. Vokes describes how when carrying out 'unstructured radio elicitation', he gradually moved from a stance where he did 'little more than sitting with people as they listened to the radio as part of their normal daily routines' to one where he 'began to "take control" of the listening situation' by asking more and more questions and eventually began to use a notebook (2007: 293). He then introduced a more structured method of '"radio elicitation" based on the classic focus-group model', by which he would invite a selected group of people to his house to listen to and then discuss a series of pre-recorded clips from radio shows. This method was particularly appropriate in the context of Vokes' research in rural Uganda where they are 'a common part of the normal, everyday flow of social relations' (2007: 264). Although Vokes' focus is primarily on one sensory modality – sound – his work provides a useful counterbalance to the existing writing on photo-elicitation, reminding us that interviews (either pre-structured or those that bounce off the flow of everyday life) indeed occur in multisensory contexts.

Another example of the use of sound in group discussions is outlined by Stephen Feld. Feld describes how during his research with Kaluli people in Papua New Guinea he made audio recordings of 'everyday sounds' and 'night time forest sounds' and then invited people to listen to these to 'identify and discuss all of them'. His intention was 'to create a pool of sensate material' on the basis of which he and Kaluli people could develop discussions, and thus lead him to better understand 'everyday Kaluli meanings and interpretations' of sound (2001b: 428). Whereas Vokes' audio-elicitation method aimed to understand how people spoke about the issues he was researching, Feld's method involved using sound as a way of investigating the meanings of the sounds themselves. In common these two case studies refer to the use of sound recordings in elicitation methods. This phono-elicitation is perhaps the most obvious way to use sensory stimuli in research since, like visual images, sound is recordable. However, as demonstrated by the soundwalks Adams and Bruce (2008) produced as part of their urban soundscape research (discussed in Chapter 5), audio recording does not necessarily form part of all sound elicitation methods. Adams and Bruce accompanied their research participants on predetermined urban routes before interviewing them about the soundscapes they experienced during these walks.

Olfaction in sensory elicitation

In contrast to sound and images, of which one can make permanent recordings, smell is much more elusive in that its temporality has different limits and cannot be controlled to the same extent. Although, as I discuss in Chapter 8, exhibitions and books of scents are possible, the incorporation of smell into ethnographic representation is more challenging. Yet smell has already been used as a form of elicitation in the sociologist Low's research into 'the role of smell in everyday life' (2005: 407). As I have noted above, interviewing is frequently used in combination with other methods – particularly in sensory ethnographies – and Low's work is no exception. He used narrative interviews in combination with what he calls 'breaching experiments' and 'participative observation' (2005: 407). Although experimental methods are relatively uncommon in ethnographic research, Low's use of them is interestingly close to the impromptu or serendipitous type of interview that might occur during participant observation, although in this case it is of course planned. He describes how the breaching experiments were designed to elicit responses as follows:

> In the case of 'gender-ed' smells, I wore fragrances that were commercially marketed for females, and sought to test how such scents may/may not provoke responses from those around me. In addition, I deliberately asked what others thought of the fragrance, in a bid to elicit any reflective evaluation or interpretation. (2005: 407)

Once he had established these initial responses both through and to the olfactory sense he then began to probe further verbally to explore 'what social actors mean when and if they ascribe "race" or "gender" to certain scents that they pick up or have pointed out to them', and to ask people to define the meanings they intended when using terms such as 'pungent' and 'smelly'. Through this method Low claims he was able to uncover 'the sense-making/rationalizing processes as to how social actors orientate themselves in the construction of their social realities, with smell as an intermediary' (2005: 407). Low's work shows how, by approaching everyday life through one sense modality, researchers can begin to learn both about what is important to people and how that particular culturally constructed sensory category functions as a way of creating and understanding a social order.

Sensory elicitation and the interconnected senses

Sensory elicitation interviews can offer researchers new and valuable routes to other people's experiences, knowledge and values. Each of the examples discussed above focuses on a specific modern western sensory modality as a route towards understanding. When working in this way it is important to remain aware of the conceptual issues raised in Chapter 2 and at the beginning of this chapter. This means keeping two points in mind: first, the interconnectedness of senses, and the capacity of audio recording, for example to communicate not only about sound; and second, the multisensoriality of the interview event itself, for example an interview centred on olfactory elicitation will inevitably also involve textures, vision and more.

Summing up

In this chapter I have suggested re-thinking the interview through a sensory paradigm. This means departing from the notion of interview as a type of special conversation, questioning an emphasis on talk, and going beyond the idea of the interview as part of a wider complex of communication and practices. Instead, I have suggested that the interview be understood through a theory of place. This involves understanding the narrative of the interview as a process through which verbal, experiential, emotional, sensory, material, social and other encounters are brought together. This process creates a place from which the researcher can better understand how the interviewee experiences her or his world. Abstracting the idea of an interview in this way offers a means of understanding the interview encounter as a place-event.

Within this place-event ethnographers have opportunities to learn about both others' embodied ways of knowing and their verbal narratives and ways of defining sensations, emotions, beliefs, moralities and more. In this chapter I have elaborated on a series of techniques that might be used to create these routes into other people's ways of knowing through both talk-based and sensory elicitation interviews.

Recommended further reading

- Desjarlais, R. (2003) *Sensory Biographies: lives and death among Nepal's Yolmo Buddhists*. London: University of California Press.
- Low, K. (2005) 'Ruminations on smell as a socio-cultural phenomenon', *Current Sociology*, 53(3): 397–417.
- Skinner, J. (2012) *The Interview: an ethnographic approach*. Oxford: Bloomsbury.
- Vokes, R. (2007) '(Re)constructing the field through sound: actor-networks, ethnographic representation and "radio elicitation" in south-western Uganda', in E. Hallam and T. Ingold (eds) *Creativity and Cultural Improvisation*. Oxford: Berg.

FIVE

Sensory research through participation

From observation to intervention

In this chapter I discuss how ethnographers might become sensorially engaged through their participation in the environments and practices they share with others. I draw from examples from my own and other ethnographers' research experiences to propose a re-thinking of participant observation with particular attention to the multisensory and emplaced aspects of other people's (and the researcher's own) experience. I therefore reframe ethnography as a participatory practice in which learning is embodied, emplaced, sensorial and empathetic, rather than observational. I argue for the concept of the 'research encounter', which refers to the shared moments through which ethnographers learn and know about other people's experiences. Such participation produces multisensorial and emplaced learning and knowing.

INTRODUCTION: BEYOND 'PARTICIPANT OBSERVATION'

'Classic' participant observation

The use of participant observation in its 'classic' rendering for sensory research has been discussed by Howes and Classen, for whom 'If one's field research involves participant observation, then the question to be addressed is this: *Which senses are emphasized or repressed, and by what means and to which ends?*' (1991: 259, original italics). They suggest investigating this on the levels of both the particular and the general. The former would involve questions such as: 'Is there a lot of touching or very little? Is there much concern over body odours? What is the range of tastes in foods and where do the preferences tend to centre?' (1991: 259). The latter would include asking: 'Does the repression of a particular sense of sensory expression correspond to the repression of a particular group within society?'

and 'How does the sensory order relate to the social and symbolic order?' (1991: 259). This earlier methodology, which is part of Howes and Classen's agenda to uncover the 'sensory profile' of the culture being studied, is also represented in some contemporary work such as Atkinson et al.'s (2007) classic approach to ethnography. Arguing for attention to the senses in participant observation, their focus is on how sensory phenomena are 'culturally significant', thus 'how they are meaningful to a given group or category of social actor' (2007: 180). They thus identify the task of the ethnographer as to 'make sense of ... sensory codes and to recognize them within broader analyses of social organization' (2007: 204). These classic approaches to participant observation are focused on understanding cultural and social systems, of values, organisation and more. While they are concerned with relevant elements of culture and society, they are limited by their lack of attention to the experiential aspects of doing ethnography. In the work of Atkinson et al. for whom 'there is no doubt, however, that the visual is the most important mode of understanding' (2007: 180), this neglect of experience leads to a stress on visual observation.

A phenomenological approach to participation

An alternative way to investigate other people's experiences through participation is by taking a phenomenological approach. This enables us to conceptualise experience as multisensorial and as such *neither* dominated by *nor* reducible to a visual mode of understanding (see Ingold, 2000; Grasseni, 2007a). While the visual does not cease to be relevant, it needs to be situated in relation to the other senses, and to be opened up to new interpretations. For instance, whereas methods of observation tend to assume the importance of light, Tim Edensor has argued for attention to 'attributes of darkness that have been sidelined in the quest for bright space'. As he points out, this opens up 'the potential for conviviality and intimacy to be fostered in the dark, the aesthetics and atmospherics of darkness and shadow, the affective power of the star-saturated sky, the possibilities for looking at the world otherwise and apprehending it through other senses' (Edensor, 2013: 447–8).

Learning through emplaced sensory participation

The questions posed in classic approaches to participant observation often cover central areas of human practice, sociality, social organisation and more. They certainly should not necessarily be dismissed as irrelevant. Nevertheless, taking the questions they pose seriously should not preclude actively engaging with the methodological strand which understands participation in sensory ethnography as a process of learning through the ethnographer's own multisensory, emplaced experiences. This approach means going further than interviewing and observing to entail what Okely describes as drawing 'on knowledge beyond language' where knowledge is 'embodied through sight, taste, sound, touch and smell' and 'Bodily movement, its vigour, stillness or unsteadiness ... [is] ... absorbed' (1994: 45). For Stoller this begs that 'ethnographers open themselves up to others and absorb their worlds', indeed he stresses how ethnographers can 'be consumed by the sensual world' (1997: 23); this approach involves not only ethnographers seeking out ways to share others' experiences but also their situating their experiences within other people's places – or, put another way, learning how to recognise their own emplacement in other people's worlds. For example, Tripta Chandola describes how her sensory 'listening' ethnography developed in India. Chandola writes of how 'the importance of sound and practices of listening in the everyday life of the slums' developed, partly through the intimacy that she shared with the women who participated in her research (Chandola, 2013: 58). Yet, as she reflexively describes, emphasising the importance of having the 'humility' that for Stoller is fundamental to a sensory scholarship, she learned how to listen:

> my initial listening(s) were limited as my ears were closed (Murray Schaffer, 2003) to a sonic regime, and its nuances, outside of my middle-class construction. Once conscious of my own middle-class informed listening(s) into the Govindpuri slums, I was able to raise questions outside of this sensibility – 'Who's listening? What are they listening to? And, what are they ignoring or refusing to listen to?' (Murray Schaffer, 2003: 25). I became aware of my own sonic prejudices and a different way of listening to the space. I listened in to what people listened to and did not listen to, whether consciously, subconsciously, covertly or overtly. I heard them listening in to others. I listened in to what they heard as others. (Chandola, 2013: 58)

Understood through a theory of place, the idea of ethnographer-participation implies that the ethnographer is co-participating in practices through which place is constituted with those who simultaneously participate in her or his research, and as such might become similarly emplaced. Indeed, she or he becomes at the same time a constituent of place (one of those things brought together through or entangled in a place-event) and an agent in its production.

Auto-ethnography as sensory participation

Sensory participation is in some ways akin to auto-ethnography, a method that allows ethnographers to use their own experiences as a route through which to produce academic knowledge. For instance, John Hockey has used auto-ethnography to examine the sensoriality of the 'routine activity' of training in long distance running. Hockey argues that in the case of his research: 'For the author and his co-researcher who wished to portray the relationship between the distance running "mind" (emotions, sensations, knowledge) and its embodied activity, it [auto-ethnography] constituted the best means of accessing and depicting that relationship' (2006: 184). While such closeness to the experiences one is seeking to understand might not always be possible, methods that require the ethnographer to draw on the similarities and continuities between her or his own experiences and those of others can lead to understandings of how it feels to be emplaced in particular ways. Thus the sensory ethnographer would not only observe and document other people's sensory categories and behaviours but seek routes through which to develop experience-based empathetic understandings of what others might be experiencing and knowing.

Okely, who reflects on her research about 'the changing conditions and experience of the aged in rural France' (1994: 44), has shown how through active participation one can also find routes to knowledge and memories perhaps otherwise inaccessible. Okely used her contemporary sensory experiences as a way of understanding other people's biographical experiences. Through her experiences in environments similar to those in which her elderly research participants would have lived, worked and celebrated in the past, she found ways to 'create correspondences' with *their* past experiences and her own embodied experience. She writes: 'my residence in the villages, and work on a small farm similar to those the aged had once known, gave embodied knowledge of something of their past' (1994: 44). This was a two-way process. Okely not only learned something of the sensoriality of her participants' past experiences. Rather, her having learnt in this way provided a way for her ageing research participants to remember their own pasts and empathise with her experiences (1994: 45–6).

The scholars whose work I discuss in this chapter have variously been guided by either classic observational approaches or experiential methodologies. While a classic participant observer approach to other people's sensory experiences alone is limiting, as the discussions demonstrate it can provide useful insights. The methods and approaches of conventional participant observation benefit from being combined with the reflexive and emplaced methodology proposed in this book, and disassociated from the idea that vision is necessarily the dominant sense. In the following sections I discuss a set of themes and issues that form the basis of the 'participant sensing' of the sensory ethnographer. These have been identified through a review of recent sensory ethnography literature and represent currently salient topics.

THE SERENDIPITOUS SENSORY LEARNING OF 'BEING THERE'

In Chapter 3 I pointed out that often moments of sensory learning are not necessarily planned processes through which a particular research question is pursued in a structured way as it might be in the context of a survey or even a semi-structured interview. Rather, these are often unplanned instances whereby the researcher arrives at an understanding of other people's memories and meanings through their own embodied experiences and/or attending to other people's practices, subjectivities and explanations.

Long-term ethnographic research of the 'classic' kind that has dominated social anthropology (particularly in the past) provides researchers with some significant luxuries. It means they are able to follow through both the sensory routines and rhythms of life as lived on a daily, monthly and even annual basis. It allows them to follow through a sensory hint, hunch or moment of realisation by waiting to see how, over time, this occurrence or experience fits in and thus might be comprehended in relation to other elements of knowing, yet to be experienced or understood. Donald Tuzin's discussion of his research with the Ilahita Arapesh people of East Sepik Province in Papua New Guinea shows how ethnographers might, by attending to an initial cue, piece together sensory meanings. Tuzin writes of how the 'first inkling that the people with whom I lived had (what by western standards must be) an exaggerated olfactory aesthetic, occurred early during my fieldwork' (2006: 62). During his fieldwork, Tuzin's cat had had kittens and when removing the family of cats from its original birthplace in his book box, he had accidentally left one kitten behind, only to discover its decomposing body a few days later. His local assistant was horrified by Tuzin's request that he dispose of the body. Evidently using his own sense of smell as a comparative measure, he noted that 'the stench seemed hardly sufficient to incapacitate' the assistant (2006: 62). It was at this point that he realised that smell held a particular significance for the Arapesh. This meaning unfolded during his ethnography and Tuzin provides a detailed discussion of how smell is implicated in a number of domains of Arapesh life. Significantly, he concludes that 'olfaction in Ilahita is the vehicle and vocabulary of moral reckoning'. There 'One's moral character is formed by smells taken into the body, while the unavoidable constancy of inspiration means that one is always vulnerable to unwelcome changes in that character and in the existential contours of life itself' (2006: 66); thus explaining why his assistant had been so horrified by the idea of the smell of the dead kitten.

Long-term fieldwork also enables ethnographers to live in the same environment as their research participants, experiencing the sensory rhythms and material practices of that environment. The benefits of this are demonstrated clearly in Erik Cohen's (2006 [1988]) analysis of the olfactory context of 'the slum areas of a *soi* (lane) in Bangkok [Thailand]' where he 'lived for extensive periods of time between 1981 and 1984' (2006 [1988]: 120). Cohen's analysis unravels why these *soi* residents paid great attention to avoiding and morally judging body odours while they appeared oblivious to what Cohen describes as the 'stench of disintegrating refuse' in the *soi* (2006 [1988]: 120), like Tuzin (2006, discussed above) using his own sensory reactions and categories as a point of comparison. Based on his experience of living in one area Cohen is able to report on the routines and cycles of garbage accumulation and removal, its smell (as he experienced it) and the activities that people engaged in, adding cooking and food smells. Because local people did not complain about these odours he concludes that they did not find such smells that 'are not of human origin' offensive. Contrasting this with the meticulous attention that the same people paid to their own and other people's body odour, Cohen raises the question of why they were so unconcerned with what he refers to as the 'stench' in the *soi*. His explanation however relies on his knowledge of another Thai environment. Cohen explains that most *soi* residents were migrants from rural Thailand where garbage is usually left to rot, burned or used as fertiliser in the household compound (2006 [1988]: 122). Thus it decomposes as part of a normal cycle. In contrast, in the urban *soi* this ecological cycle is 'broken' (2006 [1988]: 125). He suggests that thus there is a 'cultural lag' through which 'the stench of disintegrating garbage has not yet acquired a negative cultural connotation for the slum dwellers' (2006 [1988]: 125). Such insights about sensory meanings clearly depend on long-term engagements in specific cultural and environmental contexts. Those ethnographers who are able to relocate for sufficient time to benefit from the possibility of undertaking comparative research will thus learn much from attending to how sensory understanding might be embedded in long-term routines and processes. It is clear from Tuzin's (2006) and Cohen's (2006) discussions that they both used their own sensory experiences and reactions as a point of comparison with those of the people participating in their research. In doing so they take as analytical foci other people's sensory experiences and categories, and how these might be understood in relation to culturally specific moralities.

These classic approaches can be contrasted with more recent ethnographic practice which concentrates on the sensory and embodied nature of the ethnographer's own experience and demonstrates the essential contribution this can make to ethnographic understanding. Indeed, such practices reveal a further dimension to how the ethnographer's being there can produce knowledge. A good example is provided by the work of Edvardsson and Street (2007), developed in a healthcare setting. In their discussion of the nurse-ethnographer as a 'sensate' researcher Edvardsson and Street outline what they refer to as a series of 'epiphanies' that occurred while Edvardsson was doing research about how different environments affect ways of provision and understanding of care. They define these epiphanies as 'sudden intuitive realizations that the use of his [the researcher's] senses in these environments was gradually changing the way he asked questions and conducted observations' (2007: 26). Edvardsson and Street describe six of these moments of realisation, each connected to different types of sensory experience: movement; sound; smell; taste; touch; and sight. As an example here I briefly relate their discussion of walking – a theme that will be taken up again below. They write:

> While being at the ward as a participating observer, DE found that he instinctively joined in the brisk pace habitually used by the nurses as they moved around at the unit ... he found that the brisk movement and sound of the hurried steps of staff prompted the sensation of wanting to move with the pace of the unit ... [this] led him to understand the way that corridors were used in these units as spaces for passage and not for lingering or chance encounters ... This epiphany stimulated his curiosity to explore further how people moved around the unit and what this movement might mean. (2007: 26)

Such forms of ethnographic learning are characteristic of 'participant sensing' where the ethnographer often simultaneously undergoes a series of unplanned everyday life experiences and is concerned with purposefully joining in with whatever is going on in order to become further involved in the practices of the research participants. When we participate in other people's worlds we often try to do things similar to those that they do (although we might not fully achieve this) or play roles in the events, activities or daily routines that they invite us to participate in. Such forms of participation do nevertheless usually involve us also participating in some 'ordinary' everyday activities, including eating, drinking, walking or other forms of movement or mobility that our research participants are also engaged in. This relates to participation in both actual activities and more generally through 'being there' in a shared physical environment.

VISITING OTHER PEOPLE'S SENSORY ENVIRONMENTS

In other circumstances where long-term relocation of the researcher is not possible ethnographers might learn by participating sporadically in events. For example, my own research about the Cittàslow movement is multi-sited – spread across several British towns – and involves a series of return visits to encounter specific individuals, activities or special events. In 2007 I attended a Community Partnership event organised in Diss, a Cittàslow town in Norfolk, UK. Here I helped to lay out the food to be offered to visitors, including cutting the Cittàslow cake and arranging the snail symbol biscuits, as well as helping to eat and hand out the food to visitors and passers-by later in the day. That food was central to this event was not surprising for two reasons: first, because food is often part of celebratory activities; and second, because food, with a focus on local produce and commensality, is a key theme of the work of Cittàslow, also manifested in its close relationship to the Slow Food movement. Below I explain how as an ethnographer I was able to make my food- and drink-related sensory experiences at the event meaningful both in terms of the Slow principles that were part of the event itself, and in academic terms.

My experiences of handling, cutting, laying out and eating the food at this event were part of a wider complex of activities and experiences I was involved in. I also undertook some short interviews, photography and generally helped out where I could during the day. However, for the sensory ethnographer it is important to attend to the meanings of tastes, smells and textures and the significance of their presence. For instance, the cake was accompanied by freshly brewed coffee supplied by one of the local small shops that the Cittàslow movement strives to nurture. The striking aroma of the coffee itself signified its 'quality' and participating in its appreciation could be seen as a way of also participating in the articulation of the values of the Slow Food movement as outlined by its leader Petrini who stresses that to be regarded as 'quality' food should be 'good, clean and fair' (Petrini, 2007: 93). I was reminded of this still later as I did some shopping in the town and smelled the odour of fresh coffee coming from the doorway of the shop. At this Community Partnership event I thus found myself participating in the practices of the Cittàslow movement, while also producing ethnographic materials for my research. I was able to theorise how the visual, olfactory and gustatory effects of the foods and drinks in the hall formed part of the processes through which a place-event was constituted. The hall was transformed multisensorially through these practical engagements with Cittàslow principles. Analysed through modern western sensory categories this could be said to happen visually (through stands and displays as well as the visualisations of the Cittàslow snail on the cake and biscuits), through olfaction (for example through the smell of the coffee) and through tastes and textures (of the local produce and locally made foods on offer), thus offering visitors an embodied experience framed by Cittàslow principles. Situated as such, visitors to the event became emplaced, albeit temporarily, and participated in an environment both purposefully framed by Cittàslow's discourses and in which the movement's aims were explicitly verbalised in printed materials. Nevertheless, this sensory research experience alone was not enough. Making it meaningful as ethnographic knowledge involved my connecting my own experiences with the principles of Slow living outlined in the texts produced by the movement's leaders, and theoretical understandings.

Other examples in the existing literature also show how researchers' participation in other people's activities, in slightly more structured ways, can enable them to learn by connecting through the senses. Susan Buckingham and Monica Degen have discussed their experiences of doing sensuous ethnography focused on how women experienced their bodies in activities that were not related to sex work. Part of their work involved exploring 'how abused and vulnerable women feel about, and relate to, their bodies, and how they therefore respond to the intersubjectivity and/or intercorporeality of the research/practice relationship we have developed through the teaching/practice of yoga' (2012: 331). They note that they had not initially intended to focus on sensory experience *per se* but 'As our time in the field evolved we became aware that we could not use a traditional ethnographic framework to get closer to the women we wanted to work with' (2012: 331). The teaching of yoga to this group of women enabled them to achieve what they call 'carnal sorority' (2012: 337); for instance, they describe how 'By physically assisting women into positions, we became aware of their physical stiffness or flexibility, which gave us some access to unspoken aspects of their lives' (2012: 337). Indicating the potential power of this approach, they also write how:

> Practicing sensuous ethnography has shocked us into an awareness of the physical, material, psychological, and emotional trauma that many of these women experience. Their limitations in the yoga positions reveal the exigencies of street work, drug abuse, rough living in damp hostels: from asthma to arthritis. (Buckingham and Degen, 2012: 337–8)

Visiting can take many forms and needs usually to be carried out in such a way that is coherent with the types of activities or environments that are being studied. A different pattern was developed by the sociologists Dawn Lyon and Les Back in their visual ethnography of the 'sensory and embodied experience of working with fish' in a London fish market (2012: 1.2). Focusing on the work of two fishmongers over two years they made about 20 visits to the market (2012: 2.2), using observations, photography and sound recordings as part of their methods (2012: 1.3). Here they developed a relationship between audio recording and photographing because they were keen to bring certain aspects of sensory experience to the fore, writing that:

> We could of course have filmed the fishmongers at work but felt that this would have led us to 'relive' the confusion of market activity and exchanges in our viewing of the films rather than help us to notice what we were not able to see when things were in motion. Instead, we preferred to limit the sensory data we collected, paradoxically in order to grasp more of it. (Lyon and Back, 2012: 2.3)

They also, using photography, attended to the detail of the work of the fishmonger – as his gloved hand worked with the fish, focusing on the timing, rhythms, temporality, sound and tactility of this work (2012: 5.12–15). One of the important sociological arguments that they conclude with is that through these techniques they were able to learn about the skill and experience of working with fish, but also about the social 'landscape' of the market that is an inevitable part of the environment that they were researching in (2012: 8.2). Thus pointing to the ways in which environments 'feel' can be important in underpinning our understandings of the social worlds that they connect with.

Collectively, the examples discussed in this section demonstrate how attention to our own, and other people's, unanticipated sensory embodied, or emplaced, experiences can lead researchers to new routes to understanding. This might mean the ability to make connections with others and their experiences, and it may raise questions about the meaning of actions of others and how these are embedded in visible or otherwise not immediately obvious realms of meaning. Attending to sensory experience can invite researchers to analyse from new perspectives those activities that might on the surface seem to be standard and often familiar everyday practices.

THE ETHNOGRAPHER AS SENSORY APPRENTICE

The idea of the ethnographer playing a role of apprentice who learns about another culture by engaging and learning first-hand the practices and routines of local people has long since been part of the idea of participant observation. Greg Downey notes how amongst others 'Esther Goody (1989: 254–255) and

Michael Coy (1989: 2) both suggest that apprenticeship is not only an excellent way to learn a skill: it is also an ideal way to *learn about* it, and to *learn how one learns*' (Downey, 2005: 53). With more specific relevance to a sensory ethnography Grasseni has argued that 'The call for "sensuality" in anthropological scholarship should ... contain recommendations to maintain close attention and discernment of the actual techniques and apprenticeships thanks to which embodied knowledge emerges' (2004b: 53). Harris has likewise drawn on a notion of apprenticeship to suggest that 'a "way of knowing" is the movement of a person from one context to another' and 'a path to knowledge in terms of an apprenticeship' which involves 'work, experience and time' (2007: 1). As these and other ethnographers have come to focus more closely on the senses, the idea of the ethnographer-apprentice learning to know as others know through embodied practice has become firmly embedded in existing literature. This focus has developed in tandem with theoretical investigation of questions concerning learning and knowledge transmission (see Chapter 2).

Connections between the idea of a 'sensory scholarship' and the ethnographer as apprentice were introduced in the 1990s through Paul Stoller's excellent discussion of his own apprenticeship in Songhay sorcery (in Niger), which is 'learnt through the body' (Stoller, 1997: 14). In an essay entitled 'The Sorcerer's Body' Stoller describes how, having previously begun to learn about sorcery, when he returned to Niger for a research trip he became ill and was advised by several local people to return home. They told him he had been the victim of sorcery, since, as Stoller explains once someone has, as he had, even 'taken only a few steps along sorcery's path' they are likely to be attacked by other sorcerers. The form of attack in this case was that sickness had been sent to him and he had been insufficiently protected to resist it. Stoller describes how once he had become an apprentice sorcerer he had joined a world where 'the sentient body is the arena of power' (Stoller, 1997: 12–13). Stoller describes part of the sensorial experience of illness as follows: 'My head throbbed. In the morning I took a few more chloroquine tablets, but my condition didn't change. By the next day my eyes blazed with fever, I took two more chloroquine tablets. By noon my body was incandescent with fever' (1997: 10–11). He was diagnosed with malaria. However, seen through the prism of Songhay sorcery rather than western bio-medicine, as Stoller's discussion reveals, his illness can be understood as being embedded in a complex of local relationships and rivalries, in which he was also implicated.

More recently the idea of a sensory apprenticeship has been developed further both theoretically and practically. Ingold has argued that technical skills are transmitted not through 'genetic replication' but through '*systems of apprenticeship*, constituted by the relationships between more and less experienced practitioners in hands-on contexts of activity'. Ingold gives the example of the 'novice hunter' who 'learns by accompanying more experienced hands in the woods'. Such a learning process would be as follows:

> As he goes about he is instructed in what to look out for, and his attention is drawn to subtle clues that he might otherwise fail to notice ... For example, he learns to register those qualities of surface texture that enable one to tell, merely from touch, how long ago an animal left its imprint in the snow, and how fast it was travelling. (2000: 37)

This form of apprenticeship involves learning how to sense one's environment in a culturally meaningful way. However, Ingold insists the form of learning that occurs when the novice hunter becomes an apprentice should be understood as an 'education of attention'. Thus, drawing from Lave's (1990) work he argues that culture cannot simply be transmitted to the apprentice, but rather 'the instructions the novice hunter receives – to watch out for this, attend to that, and so on – only take on meaning in the context of his engagement with the environment' (2000: 37). Ingold's ideas have implications for the idea of the ethnographer as sensory apprentice: it is through actually engaging in the activities and environments we wish to learn about that we come to know them. On the basis of such participation the ethnographer then has to unravel the academic implications of such learning and of the ways of knowing she or he has experienced.

Grasseni, following a similar analytical path to that set by Ingold, has discussed how she learnt about cattle through a 'master–apprentice' relationship with a high-ranking Italian cattle expert during her fieldwork with dairy breeders in the Italian Alps (2004b: 43). Grasseni describes the 'skilled vision' of the breeder as 'never detached from a certain amount of multisensoriality – especially from tactility' (2004b: 41). She followed the inspector as he toured cattle sheds collecting data on the cattle, describing how 'He positively directed my attention, with the aim of getting me to learn to see like he did, so that we could agree in our judgement of a cow' (2004b: 43–4). Learning to see was a long process. Grasseni relates that it was after touring around 50 stables, accompanying a breed inspector, that she could identify, for instance, 'the "superior" look of my host's herd, of which they were particularly proud' (2004b: 45). She argues that on having learnt to see in this way one has 'access to a different quality of attention' and 'perceptive hue'. This way of seeing becomes a 'permanent sediment, an embodied way of accessing the world and of managing it – in other words an identity' (2004b: 45). To conceptualise how the ethnographer learns in this way through apprenticeship Grasseni draws on her experiences to propose that 'Through participation in a practice, one eventually achieves flexibility, resonance with other practitioners and an attunement of the senses' (2004b: 53).

As other recent studies demonstrate, vision is not the only sensory practice that might be understood as a skill to be learnt through apprenticeship. Doing research about sound in a hospital setting Tom Rice describes his methodology as '"stethoscopic" in itself' (personal communication). Learning to use the stethoscope became a part of his research. It facilitated his relationships with others – as he suggests, 'Perhaps I could let the stethoscope provide a means of bringing me into contact with people? It would be a novel way of making connections' (Rice, personal communication). Rice describes one of the aspects of this methodology as learning 'to hear as a doctor would myself'. As he puts it: 'I wanted to be able to hear with the doctor's ears, and realised that training in auscultation would bring me closer to inhabiting the perceptual world of the doctor' (personal communication). In taking this approach Rice moves beyond existing approaches to listening in ethnography. These, he notes, are exemplified in Clifford's (1986) focus on the multi-vocality of texts and Anthony Cohen and Nigel Rapport's (1995) treatment of the 'ethnographic ear' whereby speech is considered 'the expression of the speaker's consciousness' (Rice, 2006). Instead, in common with the ethnographers whose work is discussed above, Rice writes: 'I anchor my fieldwork in the "apprenticeship" of student', in this case through 'his practical acquisition of listening skills'. The benefit of this 'Participant observation in "learning the ear"' was to enable Rice 'to understand how auditory knowledge was applied, reproduced and disseminated in the medical setting through gaining a grasp on the embodied nature of medical skill' (Rice, 2006).

Greg Downey similarly acknowledges the role of 'the apprenticeship of hearing' in training for the art of Capoeira (2005: 100), in this case suggesting that 'music can be a medium for educating the senses' (2005: 101). Brazilian Capoeira is 'an Afro-Brazilian art that combines dance, sport, and martial art' (2005: 7) and Downey's research was based partly in his own training in Capoeira between 1992 and 2000 (2005: xi). His work demonstrates particularly well the embodied nature of physical fieldwork engagements, describing how his physical self was changed through this training, in that: 'My muscles strengthened and stretched, I lost weight, and distinctive calluses formed on my palms, just below my middle finger' (2005: 25). Thus Downey emphasises the relationship between the body and the senses in such apprenticeship since 'learning a physical skill requires that one develop both the necessary body techniques, robust and modifiable, and the sensory skills they depend on' (2005: 28). Learning to sense and make meanings as others do thus involves us not simply observing what they do, but learning how to use all our senses and to participate in *their* worlds, on the terms of their embodied understandings.

In some ethnographic projects researchers might find the step between becoming a participant in other people's ways of sensing the world and then analysing their practices and values to be relatively unhindered. However, Hahn, whose research also involved a form of apprenticeship draws from her experiences to stress some of the difficulties of studying 'transmission' or 'the physical internalization of aesthetic practices' for the participant observer (2007: 59). Hahn's research involved her learning Japanese dance in the context of the relationship between herself the student and her dance teacher (2007: 67). She notes how 'as the practice unfolds a myriad of cultural patterns, these patterns become physically internalized and often seem less accessible on a conscious level' (2007: 59). However, as Hahn's analysis shows, she was able to interpret the sensory embodied experience of Japanese dance, and the learning process she was studying, first in relation to the Japanese philosophy and aesthetics that inform it, and second in terms of academic analysis *as* a transmission process.

Although of course there are variations in detail and across projects, this pattern of analysis should by now start to sound familiar to the reader: in my own research I interpreted my olfactory experiences in relation to the principles of the Slow Food movement; Stoller (1997) interpreted his sensory embodied experiences of illness through the prism of Songhay sorcery while showing that an alternative explanation was also offered by modern western bio-medicine; Grasseni (2004b) understood the 'skilled vision' she learnt from the cattle breed inspector through the 'standards' of that particular 'community of practice'; and Hahn's (2007) experience of dance could be rendered meaningful through Japanese philosophy. Emplaced knowing is inevitably involved with and thus open (in Massey's, 2005, sense of the term) to discourses that extend beyond the direct immediacy of actual practice.

Learning through apprenticeship requires an emplaced engagement with the practices and identities that one seeks to understand. This involves a reflexivity and self-consciousness about this learning process, establishing connections between sensory experience, specific sensory categories and philosophical, moral and other value-laden discourses (and the power relations and political processes they might be connected to), and creating relationships between these and theoretical scholarship.

INTENTIONALLY JOINING OTHERS IN (NEAR) UNIVERSAL EMBODIED ACTIVITIES

The previous section focused on the idea of the ethnographer as apprentice. An apprentice usually works in close relation to a teacher in order to learn specialised skills. The apprentice thus takes on the ways of knowing and identities associated with this skill. In this section I continue the discussion of how ethnographers learn through participation with a different focus, by focusing on their engagements in the more commonplace activities of eating and walking. Other everyday practices could be discussed in a similar way – such as talking, sitting or dressing oneself. I focus on eating and walking here because there are rich, albeit emergent literatures on both these topics that have already started to illustrate the benefits of sharing such practices and experiences with research participants. The insights from these works might be transferred to imply the benefits of applying a similar approach to other practices of everyday life.

Eating together or commensality

Along with a general increasing academic interest in food questions concerning the meanings of the tastes, textures, sights and smells of foods and the experience of sharing, meals are becoming increasingly prevalent in the work of social scientists (e.g. Stoller, 1989; Okely, 1994; Seremetakis, 1994; Sutton, 2001; Law, 2005; Walmsley, 2006; Hayes-Conroy, 2010). Stoller's well-known example of how he was given a 'tasteless' or bad tasting sauce to eat during a research trip to Niger provides an insightful starting point. By situating the taste in relation to his understanding of the culture and the specific social relations in which the cook was living, Stoller interprets the sauce's taste as an expression of the cook's frustrations with her situation (Stoller, 1989: 15–34). The practice of eating food prepared by people with whom one is doing research (or preparing food with and for them) is an obvious way to participate in their everyday lives. But in order to understand the tastes and meanings of different dishes and foodstuffs one needs to do more than simply eat and drink. Seremetakis has defined commensality *'as the exchange of sensory memories and emotions, and of substances and objects incarnating remembrance and feeling'* (1994: 37, original italics). This approach means going beyond the idea of commensality as simply 'the social organization of food and drink consumption and the rules that enforce social institutions at the level of consumption' (1994: 37). Indeed, it begs the ethnographer's own participation in eating with others and her or his engagement with eating as a way of knowing and remembering. It moreover requires a form of reflexivity that will allow her or him to acknowledge and communicate gustatory knowledge academically.

To demonstrate how food substances might be both shared and invested with memory Seremetakis evocatively outlines examples of Greek food practices. For instance, she describes how the Greek grandmother would 'cook' a baby's food in her mouth using her own saliva:

> She takes a piece of crustless bread ... crumbles it with her fingers and puts a few crumbs in her toothless mouth. The tongue, rotating, moistens the bread with saliva till it becomes a paste, 'clay.' She molds the bread till its texture signals that it is ready for the child

and then places it in the child's mouth (1994: 26). Seremetakis suggests 'the food is not only cooked by saliva, but also by emotions and memory'. In her interpretation, 'Cooking food in grandma's mouth with saliva imprints memory on the substance internalized by the child', leading her to assert that 'Memory is stored in substances that are shared, just as substances are stored in social memory which is sensory' (1994: 28). This relationship between food, its tastes and textures, and memory is significant to the sensory ethnographer in two ways. First, if we are seeking to understand other people's memories, sharing the tastes in which these memories are embedded might serve as a starting point for this task. Second, taste memories form part of all of our biographies. Therefore, attending to gustatory memory is relevant for understanding not only how other people make memories and meanings through food-related practices, but also for the reflexivity that is integral to a sensory ethnography. As ethnographers we are bound to interpret new taste experiences through comparison with our existing gustatory repertoires *in relation with* any instructions and verbal or other knowledge about these foods and tastes suggested to us by people with whom we are eating, drinking and doing research.

The significance of my own biographical experiences emerged clearly to me one December morning as I sat drinking a cup of half-milk coffee in a temporary café set up in a Town Hall function room in Mold, the first Welsh town to become a Cittàslow member (see also Pink, 2008b). As a child I had drunk half-milk coffee, made from instant coffee granules dissolved in a cup of hot milk combined with hot water. This is different from the other practice of boiling a kettle of hot water which is poured onto the instant coffee before milk is later added. I remembered us taking half-milk coffee on family picnics, kept warm in a flask – as the coffee I was served that day in the temporary café had been. Now living a life where instant coffee is much less mainstream and many cafés offer 'real' Italian-style coffees, re-tasting this coffee led me to two sets of insight. It evoked memories of picnics, the rug, the flask and my own past. But as a comparative example it gave me a sense of something rather British that had been superseded by Italian-style coffees in many public spaces. By attending to this taste, linking it to my own biography and considering it comparatively I was able to grasp what it was about the temporary café that led me to understand it through its cultural specificity. It was not simply the sociality of the context where local people could meet and have a drink, biscuit and chat. Rather, it was the practices by which the coffee was prepared, the way it was described as 'half-milk', its being served from the flask and its very taste that together facilitated that understanding. Rather, I was drawing from my own taste experiences in Britain to create a comparison. Our biographical taste experiences inevitably inform how as ethnographers we might interpret current ones.

Eating with others during their special or celebratory events might also bring to the fore the importance of food practices and specific tastes. For example, the geographer Lisa Law (2005) discusses her experiences of participating in Sunday meals in Hong Kong held by Filipino women domestic workers. Sunday was the women's weekly day off and they tended to spend it in a part of the city referred to as Little Manila due to its occupation and transformation through the presence of Filipino migrant workers on this one day of the week. As part of her discussion Law describes a birthday meal she attended, held outdoors, at which they consumed Filipino dishes rather than the Chinese food the women tended to eat with the families they worked for during the week. She writes:

> We were all provided with a paper plate and chopsticks and helped ourselves to the food. About halfway through the meal however I noticed that the chopsticks were quickly being replaced by thin plastic gloves that Deenah [the host] had also brought along. Deenah looked at me and queried 'You like?' Asserting my own cultural capital, I abandoned my clumsy attempts at chopstick etiquette and opted for these more pliable eating utensils. (2005: 234)

Law explains that Filipinos enjoy eating with their hands, but use the gloves because there are few places for washing their hands or utensils in Hong Kong's parks. In a context where few of the women ate Filipino food during the week, as they lived with Chinese families in Hong Kong, Law interprets their exchanging the chopsticks for the gloves as 'a moment of casting off Chinese customs to enjoy the *taste, aroma and texture* of home' (2005: 234, original italics).

In Chapter 2 I introduced Allison and Jessica Hayes-Conroy's notion of the visceral in human geography research. Allison Hayes-Conroy has written about this further in relation to the methods she developed for understanding Slow Food experiences in the USA. Hayes-Conroy used a range of different methods in her research with the Slow Food movement, including interviews, a survey and designed events. However, of particular interest here is how she describes what she refers to as starting with 'a series of informal chats', which happened with a participant who did not want to participate in a designed experience. As so often happens in ethnographic research this was a spontaneously generated research event. Hayes-Conroy discusses how, while the method of conversing with Steve (the participant) was not productive, they began to communicate through food:

> For over an hour Steve, Jessica, and I chatted as we moved between various back rooms, walk-in refrigerators and kitchens of his restaurant, sampling this odd array of foods. During this time, it was especially intriguing that Steve suggested to me that our research interests were being resolved through our expressions after sampling the foods, because it indicates his sense that visceral intensities of food can be shared. Although the ways in which Jessica and I reacted and responded to the various foods were undeniably different from the ways in which Steve's body was affected by them (particularly the raw sea urchin, which at 9:30 in the morning induced in me a mix of nausea, intrigue and anxiety), he nevertheless suggested a sense of shared energy. (Hayes Conroy, 2010: 738)

She suggests that by involving them in his experiences of food 'he was able to convey how SF [Slow Food] felt and worked in him', arguing that thus 'For Steve, the acts of seeing, smelling, and sampling fresh, local, unique, artisanal, ecological, and/or fairly produced foods were what SF was all about, and these experiences generated vigor for continued association with the movement' (Hayes Conroy, 2010: 738).

As these examples show, in different contexts we learn different things by eating with others. However, since the tastes people enjoy or dislike and the memories that are related to them, are so inseparable from processes through which self-identities are constituted in the present, it is always likely that an ethnographer will learn *something* by sharing a meal or more spontaneously presented and shared foods with others. Thus sensory ethnographers can benefit from being attentive to the possibility of learning through the sensory sociality of eating with others, and recognising how the sharing of tastes, textures, eating practices and routines can bring otherwise unspoken meanings to the fore.

Walking with others

The idea that walking with others – sharing their step, style and rhythm – creates an affinity, empathy or sense of belonging with them, has long since been acknowledged by ethnographers. I have already emphasised the importance of the encounter in sensory ethnography practice. Walking with research participants is another instance of this, as it offers ways in which to do research *with* people. Indeed, examples of how ethnographers have walked or run in harmony with research participants were already developed in some classic ethnographies of the twentieth century. For example, in his monograph *The Forest People* Colin Turnbull describes how his ability to walk through the forest in a way that corresponded with that practised by the Mbuti Pygmies could be understood in relation to their approval and acceptance of him (Turnbull, 1961: 75–6). Likewise, Lee and Ingold highlight how in his *Interpretation of Cultures* Clifford Geertz (1973) describes how his having run away from a police raid on a cockfight *with* the local people changed his relationship with the villagers by enabling him to participate in their everyday lives (2006: 67). More recently both a more systematic interrogation of the role of walking in ethnography and a focus on the ethnography of walking have been developed (e.g. Ingold and Lee-Vergunst, 2008). This work moreover recognises the multisensoriality of walking.

In this section I explore how walking has been used in sensory ethnographic practice. In Chapter 6 I discuss how walking has been combined with the use of digital technologies in both human activity and in ways to research experience, and in Chapter 8 I reflect on the possibilities of walking in ethnographic representation. However, I situate this theme in two ways. First, walking is not the only form of mobility that ethnographers can share with research participants. In fact when working with people with disabilities and impairments walking may not be an appropriate form of mobility to share (Pink, 2008e). In other cases, forms of (technologically mediated) mobility may present alternative forms of participation through, for example, climbing (e.g. Lund, 2006) or cycling (e.g. Spinney, 2008). Second, a *walking with others* method should also entail a commitment to self-reflexivity. Just as our experiences of eating the same foods as others will always be subject to comparisons from our own biographies, the routes we walk and walking rhythms we share with others will always be shaded by the steps we have taken in the past.

A focus on walking is instructive for two reasons: first, because a literature is developing around the possibilities of walking with others as a research methodology; second, because walking is moreover a near-universal multisensorial activity that most ethnographers will engage in with their research participants, albeit only for a few metres or a couple of steps, at some point in their research. Lee and Ingold's essay 'Fieldwork on foot: perceiving, routing, socializing' (2006, and see also Ingold and Lee-Vergunst, 2008) is a key starting point for any ethnographer interested in walking as a sensory ethnography methodology. Lee and

Ingold both outline a 'series of resonances between walking and anthropological fieldwork' and discuss their experiences of fieldwork which 'involved participant observation in the form of sharing walks with a variety of people' (2006: 68). Of particular interest for the discussion here is their emphasis on 'the sociability that is engendered by walking *with* others' (2006: 69, original italics), and their understanding of walking routes as a form of place-making. Seeing walking as place-making brings to the fore the idea that places are made through people's embodied and multisensorial participation in their environments. In Lee and Ingold's understanding of the sociality of walking, the body and the senses are equally important. Referring back to Geertz's (1973) experiences (and as is also shown in Turnbull's (1961) commentary), they assert that 'Sharing or creating a walking rhythm with other people can lead to a very particular closeness and bond between the people involved' (2006: 69), and show through examples from their ethnography how when walking together people might share a rhythm which produces 'closeness', demonstrating how 'social interaction during walking is a full bodily experience'. This, they point out, has implications for ethnographic practice in which 'This physical co-presence, emphasised by common movements, is also important ... as we attempt to live and move as others do' (2006: 69). Therefore, amongst other things Lee and Ingold's approach opens up the possibility of seeing walking with others as a sensory ethnography method. It can bring ethnographers 'close' to the research participants with whom they share rhythms and routes, and can allow ethnographers to participate in the place-making practices of the people whose worlds they are learning about. Good examples of this are developed in the work of Katrín Lund who has participated in both hill-walking in Scotland and festive processions in Spain as part of her ethnographic research. Describing her experiences of hill-walking and climbing with a group of mountaineers in Scotland, Lund sees walking as

> a bodily movement that not only connects the body to the ground but also includes different postures, speeds and rhythms ... [that] ... shape the tactile interactions between the moving body and the ground, and play a fundamental part in how the surroundings are sensually experienced. (Lund, 2006: 28)

At the beginning of her (2006) article Lund's descriptions of her own embodied experiences of hill-walking provide an entrance point into her discussion of the relationship between touch and vision in the way the moving body perceives its environment. This experience provides an important context through which the reader of Lund's article can understand the quotations from her research participants' discussions of their experiences later in the article. By walking with someone it is thus possible to learn to inhabit a similar place to them, although, as I have pointed out, for any 'shared' experience, here again similarity does not mean sameness. This impossibility is often recognised in existing writing (e.g. Okely, 1994; Downey, 2005). Thus while Lund (2006) does not describe the actual embodied experiences of the research participants, her descriptions of her own experiences offer us a route through which to imagine what such experiences would be like. In another publication, drawing on her research in Southern Spain, Lund demonstrates how walking with others might produce understandings of festive events through her discussion of an Andalusian religious procession. Here Lund's varying forms of participation and involvement in the event allowed her to understand its local significance. She suggests that 'in order to understand what is produced through and meant by the activity of walking with the patron saint, one needs to locate oneself within the ritual by taking part in the walking'. She continues, stressing the sensorial and corporeal aspects of this, to point out that: 'For participants in the performance, authenticity cannot be seen, but is imprinted in the sonic rhythm of synchronised movements' (Lund, 2008: 97). By emphasising the experiential dimensions of both ethnographic practice and local ways of knowing, Lund's work shows how walking with others can bring ethnographers closer to the sensory and affective dimensions of other people's everyday, leisure or festive practices.

I have also developed ways of participating by walking with others and walking routes created by others. However, in contrast to those studies cited above, this has involved walking routes that have already been self-consciously created by others with the purpose of 'showing' an urban environment to an audience. As part of my fieldwork in the Cittàslow town of Diss in Norfolk, UK, I have participated in locally designed walks around the town. One route involved my participating in a guided 'history walk' in the town with a group of others during the town's History Festival. With a group of walkers including Bas, the local historian, I was led along a route that introduced me to buildings, historic carvings and pathways. Like the experiences described by Lee and Ingold (2006) and Lund (2006, 2008) this was a multisensorial event. We toured the town on foot, navigating its different surfaces at the same time as attending to the verbal commentary of our guide, the changing weather (we thought it might rain) and the visual and material environment that we were instructed (how) to see. In particular we were invited to look at buildings, carvings, and more and to *see* their significance. For example, when we visited the church I initially looked at the windows, admiring their patterns and colour. But it was when I was told what to look for that I learnt about their special characteristics, including words inscribed on them, possibly by the craftsmen who were involved in building the church. By participating in the history walk I had set myself the task of engaging with local 'ways of seeing' (Berger, 1972) features of buildings that I would otherwise have looked at differently. However, I was not only seeing, but I was seeing in step with others, and as part of a route that had been pre-designed. As we walked we listened and looked; the narrative of the walk depended on the idea of learning about the town in movement. Walking with others therefore enables us to access elements of their sensory experiences of the world that might otherwise not be available to us.

A number of other good examples of using walking as a sensory research method are now available. For instance, Monica Degen and Gillian Rose have used walking with participants in UK urban contexts along with photo-elicitation methods to research their experiences of 'designed urban environments' (Degen and Rose, 2012). Another good example is presented by Andrew Stevenson, who describes his experiences of walking with a visually impaired person and her dog – and how this led him to a 'reprioritization of the senses and first-hand experience of inter-subjectivity'. Indeed, in this case, as he emphasises, the implication of what he learned from walking with this participant and her dog was that in 'disability studies a more relational acknowledgement of inter-corporeality, of the construction of vital spaces between people, animals and technologies, leaves us less likely to regard people without sight as isolated, tragic individuals' (Stevenson, 2013: 1166).

In ethnographic practice where walking is intentionally used as a research method other ethnographers have used walking methods that emphasise sound (although not to the exclusion of vision), inviting their participants to engage with aural environments while walking. Mags Adams and Neil Bruce have identified two research uses of the soundwalk. They describe how 'some have used it as a means through which the researcher immerses themselves into the urban soundscape while others have used it as a way of engaging others in to the practice of listening to and describing the city' (Adams and Bruce, 2008: 553). Their own method entailed the researcher accompanying participants during urban soundwalks which followed a set route around Manchester. Adams and Bruce describe how, following a brief interview, 'The soundwalk was conducted in silence and participants were asked to concentrate on what they could hear as they walked and to look at the urban environments they passed through ... in order to make connections between what they could see and what they could hear' (Adams and Bruce, 2008: 556). However, during this process the interview and soundwalk methods were combined, since at five locations during the walk participants were interviewed about aspects of that location and its soundscape, and the walk was concluded with a final interview. Adams and Bruce's soundwalk method differs from the idea of 'walking with' people along *their own* routes. Here the researchers intended to 'open up participants' ears to ... different soundscapes' along a pre-designed route, so that the participants would then discuss these new experiences. However, simultaneously this method of mixing walking with research participants and location-specific interviews allows researchers to benefit from some of the sensory sociality and sharing that the writers discussed above emphasise. Adams and Bruce note that 'it was possible for the researchers and the participants to have a shared sensory experience of the urban environments' (2008: 557). As part of a mixed method this was also important because, as they continue, it enabled 'a deeper and more meaningful semi-structured interview to take place' (2008: 557).

Movement is also emerging as part of a theme in auto-ethnography practice – particularly notable in the work of John Hockey (e.g. Hockey, 2006; Hockey and Allen-Collinson, 2006) discussed earlier in this chapter. Other examples focus on urban walking, including Heide Imai's (2008) accounts of the sensory experience of urban walking in Japan. More recently Edensor's very evocative auto-ethnographies of his experiences of walking in the dark at night in two different locations (2013) have shown us how the kind of attention to sensory experience that this practice brings to the fore can help us understand how elements of the environment are constituted culturally and experientially – in the case of Edensor's research, an investigation into 'the dark'. On the basis of his experience of night walks Edensor argues that 'the affects generated by the coalescence of dark, temperature, silence and closeness to others penetrate the body, enfolding it into the field (Brennan, 2004). This potency is perhaps intensified in a world in which deep darkness is unfamiliar' (2013: 463). In considering how to express the experiences of walking through one outdoor area in the dark conceptually, Edensor suggests using 'the metaphor of flow', which he connects to feelings whereby he writes:

> We became detached and attached to points in the landscape, sometimes lost our bearings, focused on finding the way, became absorbed in the atmosphere, tuned into sounds, sights and smells, tried to make things out and were occasionally subsumed by a powerful impression such as the owl's shrieking and the uncanny lights. (2013: 459)

This again exemplifies the utility of sensory approaches for inviting us to consider alternative ways to understand how we experience our environments.

While walking with research participants is, and has perhaps 'always' been, integral to ethnographic practice, in contemporary writing the theoretical and methodological implications of ethnographic walking are coming to the fore. As the examples outlined above have shown, different walks – such as soundwalks and night walks or dog walks – might be interpreted to emphasise different elements of experience. It is moreover significant that this is occurring as part of the move towards elaborating sensory methodologies in ethnography.

Summing up: emplaced and active participation

Both classic and experiential approaches to ethnography have been applied to research concerned with the senses. The being there of participating, observing, asking questions and interviewing involved in classic ethnographic practice can lead to analyses of culturally specific meanings of sensory categories and understandings of how people might operate these in everyday and ritual practices. However, this approach should be rethought through a paradigm that rejects the assumption that the visual would be the dominant or most important sense in either everyday life or research practice. An experiential approach does not preclude visual observation (although it would refigure this as a form of participation and a visual practice). Rather, it suggests a way of ethnographic learning and knowing by which the ethnographer seeks to participate in the emplaced activities of others through her or his own embodied engagements, thus, offering an alternative route to ethnographic knowledge.

(Continued)

(Continued)

Therefore, the methodological developments discussed in this chapter indicate how a notion of *emplaced and active participation* can accommodate some of the characteristics of the classic approach while acknowledging that through our own emplaced experiences we can gain insights into those of others. This means that all the senses need to be accounted for. By this I mean not only 'all the senses' in terms of modern western sensory categories. Rather, in line with the argument that these are culturally constructed categories, I refer to all the sensory categories that are in play in the culturally specific context in which one is researching. Indeed, one of the tasks of the emplaced active participant ethnographer is to learn how to interpret her or his embodied sensory experiences through other people's cultural categories and discourses, and as such to participate not only in their emplaced practices but in their wider ways of knowing.

Recommended further reading

- Downey, G. (2005) *Learning Capoeira: lessons in cunning from an Afro-Brazilian art*. Oxford: Oxford University Press.
- Grasseni, C. (2004) 'Skilled visions: an apprenticeship in breeding aesthetics', *Social Anthropology*, 12: 41–55.
- Lee, J. and T. Ingold (2006) 'Fieldwork on foot: perceiving, routing, socializing', in S. Coleman and P. Collins (eds) *Locating the Field: space, place and context in anthropology*. Oxford: Berg, pp. 67-86.
- Okely, J. (1994) 'Vicarious and sensory knowledge of chronology and change: ageing in rural France', in K. Hastrup and P. Hervik (eds) *Social Experience and Anthropological Knowledge*. London: Routledge.
- Sutton, D. (2001) *Remembrance of Repasts*. Oxford: Berg.

SIX

Mediated sensory ethnography

Doing and recording sensory ethnography in a digital world

Digital technologies have become integral to much sensory ethnography practice. They are already used in some way in most of the processes of research discussed in earlier chapters - for instance, for audio recording ethnographic interviews, writing up transcriptions and fieldnotes, taking photographs and video, and geo-locating. In this chapter, however, I focus beyond such routine uses of digital media to explore further the novel ways in which we might think theoretically and methodologically about the use of these technologies in sensory ethnography practice.

INTRODUCTION: DIGITAL MEDIA AND SENSORY EXPERIENCE

The use of digital media in ethnography has been discussed in a range of recent publications (Hine, 2000; Ardévol, 2012; Boellstorf et al., 2012; Pink, 2013). When we consider that contemporary digital technologies involve forms of corporeal and sensory engagement – which bring together touch, vision and sound – in ways that were not afforded by analogue media, then it is clear that their use in sensory ethnography calls for further theoretical development and practical experimentation. As Ingrid Richardson has argued, 'in an environment of multiplying handsets and frequently upgraded portable game consoles it is salient to examine the perceptual specificity of our interactions with and experiences of such devices' (Richardson, 2011: 421). Moreover, this context has implications for the ways in which we understand the ways of learning and knowing that are integral to sensory ethnography practice. As Vaike Fors has put it, 'The interrelationship between perception, embodied learning, and digital technology has pedagogical implications' in both more obvious learning contexts and in 'the "pre-reflective" knowing that emerges in our daily use of keyboards (Crossley 2001) and computer mouses (Nunes 2006)'. Therefore, drawing on existing literature she points out how 'what emerges in these human technology situations is embodied knowing and funds of pedagogies, what Tomlinson calls a set of "acquired habits and sensory-bodily rhythms" (2007: 109)' (Fors, 2013: 278).

In this chapter I explore the use of digital video, touch screens and haptic technologies, digital sound recording and phonic or audio ethnography methods, and also comment on the potential of the relationship between body data and sensory experience in ethnographic practice. I do not discuss specific technologies simply because technological change and the ways technologies are appropriated by their users is a continuous process, and the discussion would most likely be out of date before this book is even published. Instead, I refer to the categories above. Much of the discussion is dedicated to uses of digital video and audio recording as ways of producing sensory ethnography knowledge. The simple reason for this is that these remain the most established uses of digital media in this field, and indeed there continue to be interesting innovations in their development, some of which I discuss below. In a more tentative way I introduce the possibilities offered by other technologies, such as body-monitoring devices for investigating sensory experience.

First, in the next section I account for the ways in which digital technologies have become part of the sensory environments in which many people now live. I then discuss the relationship between the idea of multisensorial research and the tendency to think of different media as engaging primarily (with), or privileging, particular sensory modalities. The chapter is then organised to represent a set of themes in sensory ethnography research practice, and to examine how digital technologies have been and might be used in response to the questions posed in these areas. Readers should keep in mind that part of this discussion is necessarily speculative given that this area of sensory ethnography research practice is still emergent and holds many opportunities for future development and advancement. These three themes connect with the broader theoretical frames that I use to situate sensory ethnography in this book: movement, environments and bodies.

DIGITAL MEDIA AND SENSORY ENVIRONMENTS

Sensory ethnography, as I have outlined in Chapters 1 and 2 of this book, is a way of approaching the world that accounts for the ways in which we are emplaced – that is, how we are part of the everyday environments in which we live, how we perceive these environments and how we contribute to their constitution. This includes, as I have indicated, accounting for what Ingold (2010) would call the 'weather world' as well as the built environment, what I have called the 'sensory home' (Pink, 2004, 2012), the ways in which our relationships with other people entail forms of sensory intersubjectivity (Chapter 3) and a reflexive engagement with our own sensory embodied experiences (Chapter 3). However, these elements of our environments and everyday activities and the ways in which we experience them are increasingly digitally mediated – for example, when people use smartphone apps to find out about the daily weather forecast before planning activities or what clothes to wear.

Indeed, the ways in which we experience the human-made and the 'natural' elements of our environment are often inextricable from the ways they are digitally mediated. One example is the increasing presence of urban digital screens, discussed in the work of Scott McQuire (e.g. McQuire et al., 2009, 2012), which have become part of contemporary public space in cities. Another is the use of digital maps and photography to find or gain a sense of what physical localities we wish to visit are like, when we track our movements to find particular localities using platforms such as Google Maps or Street View (see Pink, 2011b). Indeed, the physical routes and traces we make through the world are often accompanied by digital traces, because we have chosen to upload photographs and comments relating to these routes to platforms such as Facebook or Instagram (see Pink and Hjorth, 2012; Hjorth and Pink, 2014). In other contexts, as I have found working with Jennifer Morgan and Andrew Dainty, the very experience of having a mobile phone with them made participants in our research about occupational safety and health feel more secure when travelling or walking through and working in uncertain environments (Pink et al., 2014).

Likewise, workplaces are usually in some ways digitally mediated environments; perhaps one of the less obvious of these is the construction site – itself a fascinating example of a place that is ongoingly changing in its human and material composition. Again working with Morgan and Dainty, when we focused in on the question of the multisensoriality of the construction site, we expected to learn about the sensory and embodied ways of knowing that workers used in their everyday working practices, and indeed these were part of our findings. However, we also learned about the ways the experience of the environment was digitally mediated, and how this formed part of our research topic, which was worker safety and health. As we describe it:

> Construction sites are generally experienced as mediated environments in relation to industry signage (sometimes digital), and uses of broadcast media in construction work. In addition to mobile phones, on construction sites the ongoing presence of the 'crackle' of radio and constant talking on it became part of the sensory experience of the site for Jennie. Thus, while media are not explicitly part of OSH [occupational safety and health], they are part of how the workplace setting is made to feel sensorially and affectively 'right' for workers as they settle into working in what is otherwise a continually changing and often uncertain environment. For example, one 'gang' of bricklayers that Jennie spent time with always took their 'jobsite' radio with them, and this was the first thing that they set up in their work place, with different radio stations audibly crossing over with each other in some areas of the vast and complex building site. Each station became part of the specific sensory-affective working environments of different groups of workers or trades. (Pink et al., 2014: 345–6)

Indeed, the ways in which many (but not all) people, to differing extents and in different ways, experience the world and move through it does not happen without having some kind of relationality to digital media (see also Pink, 2013).

The home also offers an interesting example of how localities and elements of our everyday worlds are constituted in part through digital media, thus meaning that the sensory environments in which we live are themselves partly made up of digital technologies and characterised by the qualities and affordances of these technologies. This has become evident across projects in which I have been doing research about how digital media and other forms of energy use, including lighting, are part of everyday life in the home in the UK and Australia. As part of a research project based in Melbourne, Australia, called *On/Off/Standby*, Yolande Strengers and I have been looking at households who use multiple digital devices in their homes in order to understand what the ambiguous states of media on/offness mean to people and for their energy consumption. This builds on the LEEDR research project I worked on from 2010 to 2014 where we looked at digital media and energy demand in UK homes. There are many ways to interpret the meaning of 'standby' mode, for example in engineering-oriented energy use measurement studies it might be thought of as a way of wasting energy, whereas when we look ethnographically at how it is used as part of everyday life, it can be understood as a way of using energy as part of creating particular experiences and within processes of activity (see Pink and Leder Mackley, 2013). Digital media and lighting also create other elements of the sensory aesthetic of home, for example the giving of warmth or a humming sound. As my research with Leder Mackley with UK households demonstrated, this becomes very much part of the habitual way the home is experienced:

> This contingent live-ness of devices also formed part of the unintended but 'felt' experiential sensory environment of the home during the day, for example by generating warmth (e.g. Laura and Paul's flatscreen TV), light or sound (such as the electronic humming of games consoles). Where TVs, radios and video or computer games prominently featured in the audio-visual environment, the home tended to become less directly infused with media content at night. Yet in at least seven of our participating households people drift off to sleep to mediated sounds including radio, TV, iPods, mobile phones or stereo systems. (Pink and Leder Mackley, 2013: 688)

Likewise, in Australia as Strengers and I toured our participants' homes and garden sheds and workshops with them, we experienced a similar degree of presence from media and lighting. For example, as we explored her husband's shed with her, one participant noted how

> There's the TV, a radio, a CD player and a set top box of … it's an old TV from one his work clients … we used to have a … one of those massive ones that's sat on its own unit … flat screen thing … ah there's a humming if you can hear it, I don't know which light that is … I think that's an emergency fluoro I think that's if the power goes off … it's a proper emergency back-up light.

We also heard the hum of the light and observed with her the good number of digital media that surrounded us, even though none of these were actively being used at the time. As we toured the home indoors the same participant took us into the study. Here she showed us around; in one place on the table there were some chargers and a docking station which she explained were to use with one of the laptops, as well as a camera that they don't usually use, and pointed out that she knew that there were 'other gadgets under there'. There were also some speakers connected to the docking station, some storage devices, and another device, which had blue lights moving on it. This, she told us, was also a storage device, but pointed out, speaking of her husband, 'I just use it, he sets it all up', telling us also that 'There are multiple printers up there that we don't use', and we looked up at the shelves which were piled up with IT equipment boxes. Here in the study there was for our participant a certain taken-for-granted assumption that these technologies were there and were active in some way, which, although she did not have an understanding of their technical elements, she knew were 'working' somehow. The little lights indicated this presence.

Therefore, we could understand the home, working through our video recordings and interview transcripts as a sensory domain that was felt partly through the presence of lighting and humming. As these examples show however, if we want to understand light we need to go beyond thinking of it as something that is only involved with visual contemplation (see Chapter 5) and rather as something that creates sounds such as humming and as little lights that communicate about the states and activities of technologies. Technological presence is part of the sensory environment of home, but this happens, as these examples show, in ways that go beyond the idea of us using technologies to create desired atmospheres through music or candle-light, to the other affordances of technologies which create a background of sound, lighting and warmth in our environments that tends to not normally be spoken about. Our tours of the home, with digital video, enabled us to bring these to the fore, by engaging specifically with this materiality and sensoriality of the intangible affordances of technologies, as we found them, and in discussion and in sharing those very environments with participants.

In this section my aim has been to demonstrate how in both public and private domains of everyday life, many people (but not all) live in worlds that are somehow digitally mediated and impacted on by the sensory qualities and affordances of the technologies and their content. The above examples do not stand for any definitive universal account of how people experience everyday environments as digitally mediated. However, more generally a sensory ethnography needs to account for the different, culturally, socially, technologically and materially diverse ways in which everyday environments *are* increasingly mediated, and, as I also discuss further below, as ethnographers we need to consider how and when this very environment, the technologies that are part of it and the human activities that are performed within it, might themselves be harnessed as routes to understanding other people's sensory and affective experiences of the world.

Therefore, the understanding of place developed in Chapter 2 also assumes that place is constituted in part through the digital technologies and platforms that are part of everyday life, and the kinds of relationships, activities and experiences that are able to emerge as their qualities and affordances are realised in relation to other materialities and intangible flows as well as human life itself.

SENSORY DIGITAL MEDIA AND THE INTERCONNECTED SENSES

In this section I examine how we might think of digital media as being multi-sensory. By way of example, I examine this in relation to digital video. While for some scholars the use of digital video in research might be to generate 'visual data', in the context of sensory ethnography the approach is quite different. I use the example of digital video to explore the relationship between vision, touch and sound in sensory ethnography and to enhance the discussion in this chapter by bringing to the fore how we might think of digital media as multisensory, rather than viewing it through the limited prism of a five-sense sensorium.

Audiovisual media as sensory media

Over the last two decades researchers and scholars already working with visual and digital technologies and methods have incorporated an appreciation of the embodied and sensory nature of their practice. This shift is evident in visual anthropology (e.g. MacDougall, 1998, 2005; Pink, 2004, 2006, 2013; Irving, 2013), visual sociology (e.g. Lammer, 2007), learning studies (e.g. Fors, 2013), video studies of interactions (e.g. Hindmarsh and Heath, 2003; Hindmarsh and Pilnick, 2007), in the use of theories of multi-modality in digital sociology (e.g. Dicks et al., 2006; Hurdley and Dicks, 2011) and in the ethnographic filmmaking of the Sensory Ethnography Lab at Harvard University in the USA, which 'is an experimental laboratory ... that promotes innovative combinations of aesthetics and ethnography. It uses analog and digital media to explore the aesthetics and ontology of the natural and unnatural world' (http://sel.fas.harvard.edu/). Here I attend specifically to the relationship between digital visual media and sensory ethnography practice, and refer readers interested more broadly in the use of visual digital media to other publications (e.g. Pink, 2013). However, there has in parallel been a history of research that has involved using audio recording (including soundscape studies, discussed in Chapter 8). This field of research is particularly interesting for sensory ethnography practice, especially in a context where Michelle Duffy and Gordon Waitt tell us that geographers are 'rethinking sound in relation to space as a process rather than representation' (Duffy and Waitt, 2013: 469). Within this area of sonic research, more recently the geographers Michael Gallagher and

Jonathan Prior have developed a framework for what they term 'phonic methods', which they suggest involve 'three ways in which audio recordings can be understood in relation to inquiry: as capture and reproduction; as representation; and as performance' (Gallagher and Prior, 2014: 8). I discuss this further in the following sections and connect the discussion to audio methods where relevant.

Multisensory media: the example of digital video

It has been argued that visual methods and media can provide us with routes to privileged insights into human relationships to their material environments. The emphasis on the role of the visual in leading us to other elements of sensory experience has not been because digital (audio)visual media are thought to directly record other sensory experiences. Rather, it is normally accounted for through the understandings of the senses as *interconnected* that I discussed in Chapter 2. This understanding refutes concerns that refer to the use of any visual media in sensory ethnography and not only the digital. Yet, there are also qualities and affordances that are specific to digital video that need to be accounted for, precisely because they are part of the ecologies of digital media that participate in constituting the everyday mediated environments I have discussed at the beginning of this chapter.

In debates about the use of video in sensory research, for instance, an understandable doubt is expressed through the supposition that digital video or photography would not adequately record non-visual modalities of sensory experience. The question becomes, as the film theorist Laura Marks posed it more generally:

> How can the audiovisual media of film and video represent non audiovisual experience? There are no technologies that reproduce the experiences of touch, smell, taste, and movement. There are technologies that attempt to simulate the effects of these experiences, such as virtual reality's audiovisual synthesis of movement or IMAX movies, whose disorienting audiovisual cues induce vertigo in viewers. But there is no way to mechanically reproduce the smell of a peach, the texture of concrete, or the feeling of falling off a cliff. (2000: 211)

Marks is of course not arguing that film and video are inadequate for representing 'non audiovisual experience'. In fact she offers an approach to understanding film as a multisensorial medium that is also applicable to understanding the use of digital video in ethnographic research. Indeed, these concerns that an audiovisual medium cannot represent other sensory modalities of experience are largely misguided. They can, as Marks (2000) and others have suggested, be resolved by taking an approach that acknowledges the interconnectedness of the senses and the embodied, emplaced nature of viewing video or photographs.

The anthropological filmmaker and theorist David MacDougall has advanced the debate in his discussions of the sensoriality of the context of filmmaking through the concept of 'social aesthetic', which he uses to refer to 'the creation of an aesthetic space or sensory structure' (2005: 105). It is significant that MacDougall developed these ideas specifically in the context of his having begun to use digital video to record in his filmmaking practice, which enables longer takes and different ways of immersing oneself in other people's worlds. This is not to say that digital video is more 'sensory' than analogue film, but to suggest that digital video has certain qualities that make it useful in sensory ethnography research. Reflecting on his video practice MacDougall suggests that such 'social aesthetics, as both the backdrop and product of everyday life, could only be approached obliquely, through the events and material objects in which it played a variety of roles'. This might include anything from 'simple hand gestures' to celebratory events (2005: 108). MacDougall's work shows the benefits of using visual media to research social aesthetics very well, and also emphasises the potential multisensory element of this. He suggests that to describe 'the phenomenological reality' of social aesthetics 'we may need a "language" closer to the multidimensionality of the subject itself – that is, a language operating in visual, aural, verbal, temporal, and even (through synesthetic association) tactile domains' (2005: 116). In my own work (e.g. Pink, 2006) I have extended this discussion to connect it more explicitly with more conventional ethnographic research methods. There, using examples from my research about the 'sensory home', I demonstrate the evocative nature of digital video materials that both represent the research encounter and at the same time investigate sensory domestic practices. I also suggest that when the lone ethnographer is working with her or his own materials these materials become meaningful in terms of the ethnographer's whole biographical experience of the research process. In this situation the materials help to evoke the sensoriality of the research encounter itself (and concomitant memories and imaginaries), rather than just suggesting, for instance, textures and smells. In contrast, when watching a film, the viewer must grasp at her or his own experiences and memories, and engage her or his imagination in trying to reach the sensory experiences of others (see Pink, 2006; and also Pink and Leder Mackley, 2012; Pink, 2013). The same issues, I suggest, form part of the ways in which ethnographers working with audio recordings also work with these materials.

Video ethnography and the ethnographic place

MacDougall takes the interconnectedness of the senses as his starting point. Drawing from the work of the neurologist Oliver Sacks and the philosopher Merleau-Ponty, he follows a similar analytical route to that discussed in Chapter 2, to suggest that 'Filmmaking requires interactions of the body with the world in registering qualities of texture and shape, which do not exist independently of such encounters'. Thus he argues that 'The world is not apart from, but around and *within* the filmmaker and viewer' (1998: 50, original italics). The same can be said for the digital video ethnographer (and also for sensory ethnographers who use audio recording and other techniques in their research) and this idea invites us to consider how such work connects with the idea of ethnography as a place-making practice. We can see the camera, audio recorder or other recording devices that might be used, as another aspect of the ethnographer's emplacement, and as such as part of the entanglement (see Ingold, 2008) of place. On the one hand these technologies are elements of the material environment the ethnographer is participating in. Yet on the other hand significantly the camera or audio recorder is also essential to the ethnographer's forms of engagement in that environment, ways of experiencing and *mode* of participation. It moreover moves with, rather than independently of, the ethnographer as she or he moves.

Moreover, because it is a recording device, the digital video camera lends a further layer of complication to the analysis. In his later work MacDougall stresses how we 'see with our whole bodies, and any image we make carries the imprint of our bodies; that is to say of our being as well as the meanings we intend to convey'. Thus, what MacDougall calls 'corporeal images' can be seen as 'not just the images of other bodies; they are also images of the body behind the camera and its relations with the world'. These are 'inherently reflexive' – whether photographic images that 'refer back to the photographer at the moment of their creation' or filmic images where 'each successive scene further locates the author in relation to the subjects' (2005: 3). Therefore, a research event, activity or encounter that is video recorded can be interpreted as place-making on a second level. In the first instance, place is made through the coming together of social, material and sensorial encounters that constitute the research event. However, additionally place is simultaneously remade as it is recorded in the camera. Similar assumptions could also be made for the ways in which sound recordings are used to make senses of place and in ethnographic place-making. As such, places are re-made as a representation of the experienced environments from which they have emerged. Place can indeed be said to be re-made on a third level when viewers of those visual or audio recordings – including of course the ethnographer – use their imaginations to create personal/cultural understandings of the representation. Thus ethnographic uses of audiovisual and audio media can be understood as both a research technique and as practices that become co-constituent of an ethnographic place.

Thus we can consider digital recording devices to be part of the ethnographer's embodied mode of engagement and participation in her or his social, material and sensory environment. Using digital recording devices might therefore be seen as invoking not only the visual or verbal knowledge that might be produced through interviews or observations, but also implies that such research materials can provide a route into the more complex multisensoriality of the experiences, activities and events we might be investigating. They do not *record* touch, taste, smell or emotion in the same way that they record images and sounds. Indeed, in this sense they provide an incomplete record. However, an understanding of the senses as essentially interconnected suggests how digital video recordings can evoke or invite memories of the multisensoriality of the research encounter (see Pink and Leder

Mackley, 2012). This potential might also, as I discuss in Chapters 7 and 8 respectively, be engaged in the processes of analysis and representation of ethnography.

Multisensory screens: thinking beyond video

However, while sensory ethnographers might be likely to use video, photography and audio recording in their work, and indeed my review of the research discussed in this book implies that these are predominant practices and technologies used in sensory ethnography, we also need to think outside these more conventional methods and towards the ways in which contemporary and new technologies might be engaged in our practice. As I have outlined elsewhere (Pink, 2015) there has been varied interest in the sensoriality of digital media, some of which has followed the 'culturalist' approach of McLuhan, which understood technologies in terms of what he called their 'sensory ratios' (McLuhan, 2005 [1964]). Ingrid Richardson, who takes a more phenomenological approach, emphasises the corporeality of our engagements with media through her relational concept of '*technosomatic involvement*' (2010) which she describes as going beyond 'the confines of "sensory ratios" applied to specific media, to include the way in which the body–media relation is also moored by sedimented cultural habits, body-metaphors and tropes surrounding our engagement with screens, and the impact of the situated or built environment upon that engagement' (Richardson, 2010: n.p.). For Richardson 'both body and screen are imbricated in a number of complex ontological and embodiment metaphors' (2010). She argues that mobile devices present 'a significant shift in the relational ontology of body and technology. This relation is perhaps more intimate, ever-present and affective than any we have thus far experienced', thus proposing that 'What we need, then, are ways of thinking through new body-screen metaphors that more effectively capture the distracted, discontinuous, motile, peripatetic and tangible nature of mobile media engagement' (2010). This therefore alerts us to the idea that through a reflexive and theoretically informed approach to the ways in which mobile media are becoming part of everyday life, and research practice, we might harness their qualities and affordances as part of sensory ethnography practice.

DIGITAL TECHNOLOGIES AND RESEARCHING THROUGH ENVIRONMENTS

Because digital video and audio recorders tend to be portable they lend themselves to researching environments as people move around in them. In the next section I focus in on their use for researching movement in everyday life. However, because these technologies are mobile they are likely to move around with the researcher or participant when researching everyday environments. I first examine two examples of the use of digital video to research the environments of homes and gardens before going on to consider audio recording and phonic methods.

Digital video for researching the sensory home

The first example draws on my experience of researching laundry as part of the everyday environments and activities of people in the UK. This research was developed with Unilever as an applied study. With each research participant I first shared an interview (see Chapter 4) and then collaborated to develop a 'laundry tour' (lasting about one hour), involving my following the research participant around their home from room to room, video recording with my camera and prompting from my checklist when necessary. We examined and discussed the laundry items in each room. However, since the home is actually made up of a great number of items that might potentially become laundry (curtains, rugs, cushion covers, towels, tea cloths, clothing, bed linen and more) this actually meant that we were exploring the sensory meanings of the domestic environment. We were also using these items as prompts through which to discuss the sensory *processes* that this environment went through, since doing laundry itself is a process through which the sensory qualities of domestic objects and environments are transformed. I was interested in finding out how my research participants evaluated these items, in terms of their sensory qualities, and what these sensory qualities meant to them. Therefore, for instance, when we examined towels I was interested in how people interpreted their textures, odours and visual appearance as indicating that they were clean, ready to be used, or needed to be washed, immediately or in the near future. Using video in the research process was essential as a facilitating tool in that it allowed us to examine the material and sensory qualities of these items performatively. Thus some participants would *actually* stroke, feel, smell, visually show and as such engage sensorially with items in their homes as ways of expressing their sensory qualities while also verbally articulating their meanings and decision-making processes. Video encouraged research participants to use their whole bodies and material environments and communicate as such about the multisensoriality of their experiences through these performances (for discussions of the findings of this study see Pink, 2005b, 2007c). The everyday practices through which the sensory environment of the home is created through laundry practices can be interpreted as part of the process through which places are made. Indeed, it is integral to how the material and identity-constituting features of both home (Pink, 2012) and self are created, including in UK homes the use of the home for indoor drying (Pink et al., 2013). Exploring this using digital video enabled me (Pink, 2012), and colleagues in a later study (Pink et al., 2013), to understand how people made and experienced the environment of home sensorially, and simultaneously to conceptualise this through the idea of place as event or process, as constantly changing.

Walking with video and the experience of place

My later use of the video tour as part of a study of a community garden project took a different approach. In this case, although I was concerned with analysing how the sensoriality of the garden project was essential to the practices, socialities and activities the participants engaged in, I was not directly investigating the sensory categories they used. Nevertheless, in common with the studies of the sensory home, the community garden study can be seen as an analysis of how sensory embodied practices are engaged in the constitution of place.

To understand the video tours of the community garden I have linked the idea of the video tour with the idea of 'walking with' as a sensory research practice to discuss the idea of 'walking with video' (Pink, 2007d). This idea of filming while walking with others is not at all new to social sciences; it has long since been an important technique in anthropological filmmaking demonstrated well in David and Judith MacDougall's film *Lorang's Way* (1977) as well as other more recent films and in applied visual ethnography practice (Jhala, 2007). The community garden was developed as part of the Cittàslow (Slow City) process in Aylsham, a town in Norfolk, UK. Between 2005 and 2007 I undertook several tours of the garden with David, the chairman of the project, some of which I recorded on video. I have discussed two of these tours, which examined the early and middle stages of the garden's development elsewhere (Pink, 2007d, 2008c). Here I reflect on the (to date) final video tour undertaken in 2007, at which point the garden was much more fully developed, although since such projects are always in a state of progress, it would not be proper to ever say it was absolutely complete. The video tours aimed to catch the garden project at certain moments in its development. This development can be seen as part of the process of the multisensorial transformation of the site, which developed from a piece of disused land to a beautiful garden with plants, trees, seats, a path and more. The material transformation involved the production of textures, smells and sights, which in turn also involved new sounds, for instance of steps underfoot, and socialities.

Because the final tour was undertaken at a point that both signalled a stage of advanced development of the garden itself and a final stage in the funded period of my own research, this tour had something of a reflective and conclusive feel to it. As such this tour was also in itself a memory practice – since it was used as a way of thinking through not only how the garden had most recently developed, but also differences between our previous tours and this tour. In the following example I demonstrate how MacDougall's ideas about the relationship between touching and seeing can be understood as part of the use of video as a sensory research method. Indeed, MacDougall's notion of seeing as a form of touching (1998, 2005) extends beyond the idea of the physical sensation of touch, to the idea of touching the consciousness of others (1998: 51–2). These interpretations can enable the researcher to create routes into understanding of how others inhabit and create their worlds, and as such the possibility of using video materials to communicate about aspects of these experiences to others.

As we walked into the garden David told me, 'as you can see there's a little bit of change now. That's the new garden, all the way down at the back there ... take a walk over shall we'. My camera followed David's gaze as he invited me to 'see' the new garden, and then followed him as we went off the brickweave path. We walked over the softer grass, towards the area that he had indicated, now 'in' the new garden to experience it close-up and as such engage more intensely with its sensory qualities. This closeness meant attending to the colours and textures of the plants and materiality of the garden. We approached the wooden surrounds that had been constructed around the big flower beds. David said they had become overcrowded with flowers and pointed out the types of plants and their colour to me. However, this was not just a visual survey, since actually *in* the garden David was much more physically involved with the flowers, many of which he had planted and/or tended himself. He took me to where the unusual red sunflowers had fallen in the quite violent rains of that summer, now touching each flower as he showed them to me. He then raised one of the fallen sunflowers to its former height before it had been lost in the gales. In the now calm, quiet garden the restoration of the plant in this way emphasised for me the physical power of the destructive gales. It also involved David's own embodied and tactile engagement with the plants, a theme that continued throughout our tour of the garden as he touched each of the plants he led me to, seemingly bringing them forward to the camera and at the same time drawing the camera towards them. At times we used the plants as memory objects, to reminisce about when they had been planted, by whom they had been donated and more. Before video recording the tour of the garden I did not plan to follow David's hands as he touched different flowers. Rather, what was striking about the experience of doing the tour was that the relationship between touching and seeing that is stressed by MacDougall (1998: 4–52) was drawn out in significant ways – first, because we began by 'seeing' but soon proceeded to come close enough to the flowers for them to be touched; second, because touching the flowers became a way of showing them to me and showing them for the video; third, by touching the flowers David showed his relationship to them; it was he (with others) who planted and tended them and his very relationship with them was tactile and physical rather than simply as someone who would visually appreciate them from a distance as they walked through; David walked in the garden and inhabited it with the flowers; and finally, touching is not simply physical but we can also be touched emotionally. The restoration of the red sunflowers to their former height was indeed a moment in which I felt sad for the effort that had been put into their planting and more generally for the garden having lost them. The garden itself can be understood through interweaving material and emotional narratives, and this represents one of these.

Elsewhere (Pink, 2007b, 2008c) I have discussed the importance of the pathway that goes through this garden. Because the pathway was designed and commissioned by the committee of residents that is responsible for the garden's development it has played an essential role in the production of the garden as a renewed sensory environment. It has changed the way that it is experienced under foot and as such the possibilities that people have for engagement with it and mobility through it. Now David began to show me how two new paths would be incorporated. To do this he walked the route of one of the planned paths across the grass, as it would divert from the main pathway. He stopped at its proposed end, where a bench would be placed. The positioning of the benches was important because, as David put it, 'lots of people sit on that bench there but ... it's under trees – look – and it's in permanent shade'. The new benches would mean that people could have an alternative sensory experience of sitting in the garden, in the sunlight. Plans for the garden, based on the sensory embodied experience of already being *in* and engaged with it over time, thus are intended to make possible imagined new sensory embodied experiences of it. The video tour of the garden presented this in terms of movement and of being there in the garden. Its future orientation also represented not simply how the garden would look different, but also how it would *feel* different.

By the time this collaborative video tour of the garden was undertaken the garden project had been up and running for over two years. As we stood at the entrance at the end of our tour David compared the 'field' to how it used to be – 'bare' and 'muddy', a place that one could not walk through to the town on a wet day. He noted how it now had a path through it and was filled with flowers. These reflections are highly significant because they not only describe the sensory transformation of the 'field' into a garden, but they also refer back to our previous digital video tours. We had visited the garden when it was 'muddy' and 'bare' and we had video toured it in the rain, on the wet grass avoiding the mud on the ground (see Pink, 2007d, 2008c). This time in contrast we had walked on the firm dry path. Before, there had been no flower beds, but now the garden is a place of flowers; as David's tactile tour of the flower beds brought to the fore, they are part of the way that he has both created and experiences being in the garden. Being there, in the garden, with the video camera, offers a way of accessing these sensorial aspects of the process of the development and experiences of it as well as some understanding of the memories and imaginaries associated with it. It does not offer the researcher a way of knowing how the participant(s) in the research experience the garden, but it does provide a route into using one's own experiences to imagine those of others. It allows research participants to use their whole bodies and senses to touch, show, smell and verbalise what is important to them about the environments they make and inhabit. As such it enables researchers to co-produce materials that offer rich opportunities for reflexive analysis. Ultimately, these video sequences might also be used to communicate something of these experiences to research audiences.

Audio recording to research the experience of place

Turning now to uses of digital audio recording, Gallagher and Prior make a case for what they call phonographic research methods. This is part of the move towards sonic geography, but as they point out, while sonic research might attend to sound in a number of ways, phonography involves using sound recording. They argue that 'phonographic methods can help researchers get to grips with the sounding of what Lorimer (2005: 83) describes as "our self-evidently more-than-human, more-than-textual, multisensual worlds", in ways that add considerably to what can be achieved using well-established research methods' (Gallagher and Prior, 2014: 2). They describe how, in an example from their own research in a Scottish coastal town, using audio recording brought to the fore local experiences and meanings of place:

> A focus on sound was chosen as a way to access some of the more-than-representational aspects of their [local residents'] everyday experiences of place: the immaterial, invisible, taken-for-granted atmospheres and emotional resonances of their local area. The researchers produced audio recordings of sounds identified by participants as being important to them. For example, audio recordings of the local harbor were used to document the chug and clank of boats, the cries of nesting kittiwakes, waves crashing against the sea wall, and a band playing an outdoor concert – sonic features which contributed to the distinctive ambience of that particular place. (Gallagher and Prior, 2014: 3)

Duffy and Waitt (2013) have also developed sonic audio recording research methods in geography in their work about sounds in homes in Australia. Their research was undertaken in an area where 'alongside an understanding of Bermagui as a rural idyll, homemaking practices in Bermagui are embedded in questions and concerns around forestry, fishery, drought, climate change and Indigenous sovereignty' (Duffy and Waitt, 2013: 471). Their method – the 'sound diary' (Duffy and Waitt, 2013: 471) – as they put it, 'asks participants to explore the more intuitive and affective aspects of our social lives through audio recording'. It actually involves participants recording during their everyday lives and then being interviewed about the recordings, in 'follow-up conversations' (Duffy and Waitt, 2013: 472). Duffy and Waitt used this process of listening to the recordings to 'explore the affective intensities and emotional responses of sounds'. They argue that

> Sounds happen across a range of performativities and are embedded within a diversity of representations. In any one fleeting moment, sounds that resonate with our own sense of self have the capacity to re-assemble the serendipity of things called home. Shifting the participants' focus to sound enables us to explore the various assemblages out of which such individual subjectivities and home places are forged. (2013: 472)

This again focuses on sound recording as a route through which to understand the experience and making of place. Here also Duffy and Waitt connect their findings to a sustainability agenda, as by using this method they were able to understand how everyday sounds are part of the way sustainability issues are experienced by people. They conclude that:

> the sounds of rain, bird calls, boat engines and the hum of fridges trigger affective responses that have important implications for how individuals engage with sustainable politics. We suggest that understanding more about how sustainability politics are fashioned at a visceral level is a productive line of future enquiry. (2013: 479)

As the examples presented in this section have shown, digital recording technologies – here video and audio – are starting to play an important role in the ways in which researchers gain understandings of how people make and experience place as part of everyday environments. Significantly, the projects discussed above have not been undertaken for the sake of studying the senses *per se*, but rather they have used digital technologies in studies of people's relationships with their environments that have allowed researchers to produce new knowledge and insights about sustainability relating to a range of environmental questions linked to energy, water and environment.

DIGITAL SENSORY ETHNOGRAPHY FOR RESEARCHING MOVEMENT

Small and lightweight digital technologies, in addition to the tracking potential of such technologies, are ideal for combining with the ways of moving with participants in research that are often characteristic of the emphasis in sensory ethnography practice on doing research *with* people as they move through the environments we share with them. In existing research the use of digital video, photography, audio recording, and digital tracking and checking in, as ways of following and sometimes also experiencing elements of the routes that people take through the world, are emerging as interesting research methods. Such methods, because they engage digital media as part of their practice, offer ways of engaging with the senses that are mediated and that need to be understood in relation to a theory of the interconnected senses. In this section I discuss examples of how mobile research using digital media has been developed, through a continuation of the focus on movement as a sensory ethnography methodology, which was developed in Chapter 5. This is not to say that walking is the only form of movement in which such sensory ethnography methodologies might be developed, however because it has been a key focus in existing literature it offers a useful example, which can be followed up through further reading.

Digital audio and video might be used with participants to re-trace with them habitual routes of everyday movement in their lives. I next discuss how in my own work participants have re-enacted everyday routines to retrace their habitual routes to bed at night and when getting up in the morning, through their homes in the UK (Pink and Leder Mackley, 2014), and how the anthropologist Andrew Irving invited people to participate in his research by verbalising and audio recording their thoughts, while being video recorded, as they continued the walks they were already intending to make across bridges in New York.

In the 2010–14 Lower Effort Energy Demand Reduction project (LEEDR) my colleagues and I developed the video tour method further to understand how the sensory aesthetic of everyday home environments is constituted. As part of that project we developed the video re-enactment method, which involved using digital video to record participants as they performed for us their everyday bedtime and morning routines. In developing this method we were specifically interested in learning about the tacit, unspoken, usually invisible, mundane everyday ways of knowing that were part of these routines. This type of sensory way of knowing the environment concerns the kinds of things that people do not need to speak about, and might never tell anyone about, precisely because they are so mundane and habitually repeated. However, for us as researchers these were very interesting everyday moments. For example, Kerstin Leder Mackley and I (Pink and Leder Mackley, 2012, 2013, 2014) write about how we asked participants in our research about everyday life, energy consumption and digital media to re-enact everyday routines. Participants showed us how everyday activities, such as going from switching off the TV in the living room, to getting into bed at night, were 'normally' done. These were of course not observations of what is referred to in some literatures as 'naturally occurring' activity, but our participants' ways of engaging with the camera to show us these experiences. We were particularly interested in how these re-enactments showed us how people sensed their everyday environments. In Chapter 5 I discussed Tim Edensor's work on light and darkness. In our re-enactment encounters we were similarly interested in how people experience environments in darkness. We recorded activities in daylight that would normally be performed in the dark, to ask participants to explore with us, in slightly different from normal situations, their tacit ways of doing and knowing as they moved through their night time homes (Pink and Leder Mackley, 2014).

Andrew Irving has used video and audio recording together as part of a project based in New York, USA, that 'explores the relationship between the thinking, feeling, moving body and a city's industrial architecture, infrastructure, and buildings' (Irving, 2013: 292), taking as his fieldwork sites four bridges – the Brooklyn Bridge, Manhattan Bridge, Williamsburg Bridge and the 59th Street Bridge (2013: 293). Videos from Irving's project are available online at http://blog.wennergren.org/2013/06/interview-dr-andrew-irving-new-york-stories/. Irving takes as a starting point the argument that

> The types of emotion, mood, and memory that are brought to life through everyday movements shape the empirical content and character of people's sensorial experience and generate different possibilities for being and expression, while simultaneously

> reinforcing the idea that experience and consciousness are ongoing fluid properties generated through action. (Irving, 2013: 292)

He was interested in exploring 'how the human body relates to, and is affected by, these massive industrial structures, including the different moods, emotions, and sensations people experience when they find themselves on, underneath, or close to them' (Irving, 2013: 293). To do this he developed a practice-based research project – *New York Stories* – which involved him audio recording the interior thoughts of participants as they walked across the bridges. Noting that he was surprised at how willing people were to participate, he describes his method as follows:

> The method was very simple: I stood at different points in the city and asked people what they were thinking about in the moment immediately before I approached them. I then invited them to wear a small microphone and narrate the stream of their thoughts as they continued their journey while I walked about 10 yards behind filming the street and surroundings. (2013: 297)

In his article, Irving presents the transcribed accounts of his participants along with his images (this is discussed further in Chapter 8 in relation to publishing sensory ethnography). Telling the stories of each of his four participants he brings to the fore how their sensory and affective states are expressed as they cross the bridges. Irving argues that

> bridges need to be understood as specific sites of cognition, sensation, and experience, which are not only good 'to think with' and 'about' but open up practical ways for researching and understanding how thought and sensory perception relate to the specificity of place, movement, and action. (2013: 307)

We might say the same for other architectural and natural environments. In his article Irving provides a short cultural history of bridges, which shows that there is some specificity in the ways they are conceptualised, experienced and in what they are used for. The use of any such environment would likewise need to be informed by such understandings of the specific affordances and qualities of, and cultural narratives already associated with, the specific environments that we might seek to research through sensory walking methods. The use of video and images and audio and transcriptions in his work helps to bring to the fore something of the sense of 'being there', although as he acknowledges such methods can only ever bring us the ways in which the sensory and perceptual experiences of participants are represented, rather than those experiences themselves.

Walking, which has been the main form of movement discussed here, demonstrates how audiovisual research methods might serve a sensory ethnography that recognises the significance of movement. Other forms of mobility might also be engaged in and for audiovisual research, for instance the geographer Justin

Spinney (e.g. 2008) developed ethnographic research, cycling with and video recording London cyclists. More generally a sensory video-ethnography-in-movement approach thus offers exciting possibilities for ethnographers seeking to combine their empathetic co-presence with participants in movement *and* verbal reflection about participants' everyday practices.

MOVING BODIES AND DIGITAL TECHNOLOGIES

In Chapter 2 I outlined how the shift towards the idea of sensory and emplaced ethnography emerged to a certain extent from existing discussions around the concept of embodiment, and the ways in which the body became, at the end of the twentieth century, a central focus, particularly in the ethnographic disciplines of anthropology and sociology. I have also suggested above that we live in a digitally mediated world where our experience of technologies is embodied and sensory. I now explore how the body is implicated in relation to the use of digital technologies in sensory ethnography research through a focus on mobile media, touch screens, body-monitoring technologies, computer keyboards and digital video. Readers should keep in mind that these technologies have rarely been discussed in existing examples of sensory ethnography research and that therefore this section is necessarily more speculative than those above. However, these technologies are in some cases already and in others fast becoming part of ordinary everyday life for many people, therefore a first nod towards their relevance is a timely move, and extends an invitation for further exploration through actual research practice.

Mobile phones and locative media are increasingly ubiquitous in everyday life, and media theorists have understood their uses in relation to their potential for communication and content, as well as for what has been called the 'co-presence' (Beaulieu, 2010) of being able to be 'with' others online through locative media when they are not physically present. James Miller has called for a focus on 'the phenomenological experience of personal smartphone use in the global West and North' (2014: 211). Calling on the work of mobile media scholars he notes how

> In a mobile life, the smartphone is used for affective and aesthetic purposes. A smartphone user achieves 'ambient intimacy,' a state of mind which Larissa Hjorth, Rowan Wilken, and Kay Gu (2012, p. 56) describe as 'an intimately audio, visual, sometimes haptic, "hand" and visceral awareness, a mode of embodiment which demands the ontological coincidence of distance and closeness, presence and telepresence, actual and virtual'. (2014: 215)

This characterisation of the smartphone starts to give us a sense of how it might be part of people's sensory experience of the world (see Pink and Hjorth, 2012;

Hjorth and Pink, 2014), and at the same time, how it might be harnessed for ethnographic research. The smartphone of course records audio, video and photography and, like many ethnographers, I have used it as a video and stills camera and as an audio recorder (see Pink, 2013). Yet if the smartphone has the qualities and affordances that enable such forms of intimacy, sensoriality and affective experiences, this implies that it could play further roles in the ways in which sensory ways of knowing are generated in ethnographic research (and in ethnographic representation, as discussed in Chapter 8).

MONITORING AND MEASUREMENT IN SENSORY ETHNOGRAPHY RESEARCH

Sensory experiences when researched ethnographically cannot be measured. Indeed, ethnography is specifically not a measurement technique. Yet the availability of increasingly sophisticated technologies that can be used to measure elements of both our environments and our bodies offer us new ways of thinking about both the body and the environment that we are part of and as such invite new questions for the sensory ethnographer.

For instance, body monitoring technologies are also becoming increasingly ubiquitous in everyday life. These include technologies such as sleep monitors, platforms where calorific intakes can be calculated, digital pedometers and more, and they create digital data which can be reflected on, shared and more. Often these are accessible through smartphone apps, thus linking the qualities and affordances of the smartphone discussed above to the use of body data. While not a mainstream pursuit such activities are promoted through the Quantified Self movement, through which people who engage in body monitoring are able to share and compare data and meet online and face-to-face. As Minna Ruckenstein has shown, those who use these technologies are able to reflect on their bodies, health and activities in new ways (Ruckenstein, 2014) and Mika Pantzar and Ruckenstein recommend 'following emotional reactions that the data produce' (Pantzar and Ruckenstein, 2014: 14). Although these works do not focus on the sensoriality of the experiences that body monitoring is applied to, body monitoring technologies are clearly interesting in the context of sensory ethnography practice because they lead us potentially to the ways people experience their bodies. Such technologies are precisely for measuring the body, and in doing so they are quantifying what is otherwise, or also, a sensory embodied experience – for instance of walking, running or eating, which are the areas covered in Chapter 5, as examples of sensory embodied activities through which we might research. Such technologies do not express the sensoriality of such experiences, but as they become part of people's everyday lives, they become an integral element of those experiences. Indeed, they become a way in which elements of the experiences and body functions associated with them are materialised and visualised – that is, they make the body visible in new ways and make the experience of the body something that is representational when, as suggested in Chapter 5, these might often be seen by researchers as non-representational elements of everyday experience. Therefore, as suggested above, video makes visible the ways in which the body is experienced by interrogating the ways in which people perform by considering their practical physical activity in the world, and listening to their verbalisations enables us to understand their categories. In contrast, working with participants via their uses of monitoring technologies, and data-visualisations of their embodied sensory experiences offers us another route towards understanding how they experience the body–environment relationship, that is, how they feel they are emplaced in the world. These and other studies (e.g. Fors, 2013) therefore all imply the potential for the camera phone, as an intimate and sensory artefact, which has certain affordances that generate everyday and potential research environments for sensory ethnography practice.

Indeed, it is not only the measurement and monitoring of the body that might offer us new routes towards understanding sensory experience in ethnography, but also the use of other monitoring technologies – such as those used to measure energy consumption in homes, and sensor technologies to detect and measure movement. These combined with experiential and ethnographic research can invite new research questions and agendas that surpass those usually asked by the ethnographic disciplines.

Summing up

In this chapter I have brought to the fore the ways in which digital media are implicated in sensory ethnography research practice. Questions around their use in the dissemination of sensory ethnography are discussed in Chapter 8. As I have shown, it is difficult to do contemporary ethnography without engaging in some way with the digital environments and technologies that are part of everyday human activity for many people. At the same time the very technologies that form part of everyday life and that are becoming increasingly ubiquitous are also emerging as research technologies. Some of these technologies still remain to be engaged for ethnography, and indeed new technologies are always emerging, therefore it would be difficult to end this chapter in any definitive way. Rather, I conclude by suggesting that as sensory ethnographers we need to keep aware of and alert to the roles of digital technologies in people's lives, and to how, at the same time, these technologies themselves might become part of the ways in which we do research, part of how we create entry points through which to learn about other people's sensory experiences and environments.

Recommended further reading

- Hjorth, L. and S. Pink (2014) 'New visualities and the digital wayfarer: reconceptualizing camera phone photography and locative media', *Mobile Media and Communication*, 2: 40-57.
- Irving, A. (2013) 'Bridges: a new sense of scale', *The Senses and Society*, 8(3): 290-313.
- MacDougall, D. (2005) *The Corporeal Image: film, ethnography, and the senses*. Princeton: Princeton University Press.
- Pink, S. (2007) 'Walking with video', *Visual Studies*, 22(3): 240-52.

III

Interpreting and representing sensory knowing

SEVEN

Interpreting multisensory research

Organising, analysing and meaning making

In this chapter I explore how we might conceptualise analysis and interpretation in sensory ethnography. In ethnographic practice analysis tends to be undertaken across the research process and is sometimes not so easy to disentangle from other parts of the research process. It may happen during the fieldwork as part of an ongoing ethnographic-theoretical dialogue, as well as through the materials produced by it, after those ethnographic encounters with people and places in situ have ended. Subsequently, the analysis of experiential, imaginative, sensorial and emotional dimensions of ethnography is itself often an intuitive, messy and serendipitous task. Here I introduce a reflexive approach to working analytically with sensory experiences, categories and materials.

INTRODUCTION: ANALYSIS IN SENSORY ETHNOGRAPHY RESEARCH

As often stressed in ethnographic methods texts, the idea that there are real rigid distinctions between fieldwork and analysis, making them separate stages of an ethnographic research process, would be misleading. Some ethnographic projects are structured into data collection and analysis stages, which are distinguished spatially (i.e. the ethnographic fieldwork takes place in one location and the analysis in another) and temporally (i.e. the ethnographic fieldwork is completed first and the analysis is carried out later). Yet even in projects of this kind analytical processes, theoretical thought and critique, and interpretative understandings cannot be separated from the ethnographic encounters from which they emerge.

Therefore, an initial and fundamental way to situate analysis is to place it within the knowledge production process. In this formulation analysis can be understood as a way of knowing. However, the practice of analysis can also be conceptualised as emerging at moments in the research where there are particularly intense and systematic treatments of research materials – interview transcripts, video, photographs, notes, and memories and imaginaries. This process often involves some degree of human intentionality in that the researcher might aim to impose an order on and deduce patterns within qualitative research materials. Such activities are often performed away (although not totally in isolation) from the location and relationships through which these materials were created.

Below I review some examples discussed in the existing literature, as well as my own experiences, to ask how an analytical process might attend to sensory categories and experiences. However, it is not my aim to create a method or template for sensory analysis, or for the analysis of materials specifically produced through a sensory methodology. It would be impossible to provide an answer to the question of 'how to' carry out a sensory ethnography analysis. And really no 'standard' procedure does or should exist. Rather, what follows is an approach to analysis that accounts for and attends to the senses and a set of suggestions regarding how an analytical process might acknowledge sensory experience and knowing. As for any ethnographic process the ways these approaches are incorporated in particular projects and used in relation to existing methods of analysis will depend on the creativity of individual researchers.

First, however, a key question needs to be addressed: What is analysis? Here I treat analysis as a process of abstraction, which serves to connect the phenomenology of experienced reality into academic debate or policy recommendations. The variation lies in the methods, theory and subject matter. In qualitative research these methods range from very systematic approaches to more intuitive forms of thinking through the meanings of ethnographic materials and experiences. However, creating an analysis is not an activity that is itself isolated from 'experience' or from the researcher's embodied knowing. To some extent this is a process of re-insertion, through memory and imagination work. However, in Chapter 2 I discussed ethnographic learning and Downey's point (2007) that embodied learning should be understood as involving physiological as well as cognitive and affective changes. Likewise, analysis does not just happen in our heads, but involves all our corporeality. Thus using the concept of place to understand analytical practice in ethnography involves understanding analysis as the process of bringing together or entangling a series of things in ways that make them mutually meaningful. We can understand ethnographic places as events that bring together combinations and interweaving of memory, imagination, embodied experience, socialities, theory, power relations and more. Massey's (2005) understanding of places as 'open' is important here since it allows us to conceptualise the places of *doing ethnography* and of *ethnographic analysis* as mutually open.

SITUATING ANALYSIS: A PRACTICAL PERSPECTIVE

The idea that fieldwork and analysis form different stages of the ethnographic process can create the misconception that after the fieldwork the remaining task of the ethnographer is simply to analyse the *content* of the research materials. While the analysis of the content of ethnographic materials can form part of the research process, it is more beneficial to take a broader and more flexible approach to how, where and when analysis occurs and what it involves. Thus analysis can be situated in two ways.

First, analysis is situated within the fieldwork process. It would be unlikely that an ethnographer would become so totally immersed in the sensorial and emotional ways of being and knowing lived by the people participating in the research that she or he would have no reflexive or analytical thought about these experiences. Indeed, analysis is an implicit element of ethnographic fieldwork, and as we have already seen, particularly in the discussion of participant sensing in Chapter 5, happens as part of both the reflexivity of ethnographic practice and within the ongoing dialogue between ethnographic research and theoretical and critical thought. Analysis can in this sense be thought of not as a structured or structural phase in the research process, but rather as a way of knowing engaged in by the researcher during the research. It is also part of the reflexivity of the sensory ethnographer who both seeks to understand other people's ways of being in the world and is simultaneously aware that her or his involvement is part of a process that will eventually abstract these experiences to produce academic knowledge. It is also a process of continual re-shaping that involves ways of relating forms of ethnographic learning and knowing and theoretical ideas – the ethnographic–theoretical dialogue – as new understandings emerge and their meaning becomes shaped by, or re-shapes, theoretical thought. This continuous analysis that forms and informs the research process also influences the systems ethnographers use for organising their materials during research, and can influence the themes identified when systematic desk-based analyses are conducted with the materials.

Second, analysis may be situated spatially or temporally away from the site(s) and moments of ethnographic fieldwork. Here a sensory ethnography approach explicitly seeks to maintain (or construct) connections between the materials and the ways of knowing associated with their production. Therefore, the analysis itself should be situated *in relation to* the phenomenological context of the production of the materials. This means treating the materials themselves as texts that can be evocative of the processes through which they were produced. Research materials can be used as prompts that help to evoke the memories and imaginations of the research, thus enabling us to re-encounter the sensorial and emotional reality of research situations. Such bringing together of research materials creates the ethnographic place as a new event.

These uses do not preclude the rather more systematic analysis of the themes and content of research materials that allows ethnographers to detect patterns and idiosyncrasies in people's practices and in the details of how they discuss and represent themselves and the worlds they live in. Such systematic analysis might also focus on the ways in which research participants use particular sensory categories and corporeal actions as ways of organising and communicating about sensory experience and knowledge.

In projects where one lone researcher is working with her/his own materials and experiences this process is relatively simple. However, projects with larger research teams may require greater practical effort so that research materials can be shared. To situate the analysis in relation to the research context in these circumstances it is important to annotate research materials. This might involve providing written notes to go with (audio)visual texts, additional notes to describe the contexts of interviews, fieldnotes, etc., which might provide a 'way in' for other researchers attempting to comprehend something of the phenomenological reality of the way knowledge was produced through the research encounter, and of the non-verbal ways of knowing that the researcher experienced. I discuss how this has been achieved through examples from two team-based projects I have worked on below.

RESEARCH MATERIALS AS SENSORY TEXTS

In Chapter 4 I stressed the multisensoriality of the material and visual culture that might be part of an interview encounter. Ethnographers might treat the material culture of their own disciplines as being equally multisensorial – the notebooks, photos, printed transcripts, computer screens, videos and more. They are sensorial in that they are themselves material objects, embedded in their own biographies and memory objects that are connected to the research process. However, as in the analysis of photographs, the researcher is not only interested in the materiality and biographies of these objects, but also in their content in terms of what they *represent*. In the case of a sensory approach to ethnography one of the objectives must be to treat the content of the research materials – by which I mean the written words, visual images, material objects, utterances and more – as evocative of the research encounter through which they were produced, and of the embodied knowing this involved. There is also a case for treating these materials as representations of knowledge that can be analysed systematically and thematically. In this section I attend to the idea of research materials as evocative of the sensoriality, and thus of the embodied, emplaced ways of knowing, that formed part of the research encounter. It is in discussions of visual ethnography that these ideas have been most fully developed to date. Therefore, I first outline this area and then suggest how similar ideas might be applied to understanding other research materials.

In Chapter 6 I introduced David MacDougall's understandings of the role of the body and senses in ethnographic filmmaking. MacDougall's insights are also relevant to understanding how an ethnographer might view visual material produced as part of the research process. Although his comments are directed towards analysing how audiences view documentary film, they can also be applied to the idea of the ethnographer as audience/analyst of her or his own video footage or photographs. MacDougall suggests that 'Our film experience relies upon our assuming the existence of a parallel sensory experience in others' (1998: 53) and, drawing from the work of Merleau-Ponty, he proposes that the 'resonance of bodies ... suggests a synchrony between viewer and viewed that recovers the prelinguistic, somatic relation to others of infancy, a capacity that still remains accessible to us in adulthood' (1998: 53). In MacDougall's analysis this process of resonance between bodies involves 'the viewer ... usually responding to not only the content of the images ... but also to the postural schema of the film itself, embodying the filmmaker' (1998: 53). However, if the viewer is the ethnographer her- or himself who is viewing video footage or photographs that she or he has produced in collaboration with research participants, then the 'resonance of bodies' may be understood differently. Indeed, this implies a much more direct resonance, a re-gaining of one's past experience and a re-touching of relationships, textures and emotions. Certainly, the relationship between vision and touch has been particularly prominent in the discussions of some film theorists.

MacDougall emphasises the relationship between touching and seeing as particularly relevant to filmic representations. He writes that 'touch and vision do not become interchangeable but share an experiential field. Each refers to a more general faculty. I can touch with my eyes because my experience of surfaces includes both touching and seeing, each deriving qualities from the other' (1998: 51). The film theorist Laura Marks also emphasises the connection between touch and vision in that 'if vision can be understood to be embodied, touch and other senses necessarily play a part in vision' (2000: 22). Applying this to film she argues that 'since memory functions multisensorially, a work of cinema, though it only directly engages two senses, activates a memory that necessarily involves all the senses' (2000: 22). Marks' comments similarly have relevance to the process of a sensory ethnography since they imply a point of connection between the idea of sensory memory as outlined in Chapter 2, and the evocation of such memories through audiovisual media. Although Marks' analysis (like MacDougall's) refers to completed films, her ideas are significant for the sensory ethnographer because they can inform our understanding of how the embodied and emplaced nature of ethnographic encounters and knowledge that might be neither visual nor verbal might be invested in video recordings or photographs produced as part of a sensory ethnography. Indeed, Hahn's discussion of how she analysed the video recordings she made of Japanese dance confirms that ethnographers have already begun to attend to this potential of video as a research material. Hahn describes how:

> Analysis of my video documentation of [Japanese dance] lessons enabled me to focus on very small units of transmission and analyze the gradual embodiment of the artistic practice. From personal experience, I 'knew' how Iemoto taught dance. My body had been through the methodical repetitions of movements. Curiously, kinaesthetic sensations (the sense of motion and orientation) often fell over me when I observed the videotapes, and somehow guided me through the analysis. It seemed that the field tapes were reinforcing my physical understanding of movement/sound while my body also informed the analytical process. (2007: 78)

Hahn's experiences highlight the interconnectedness of corporeal experiences with the analytical process. Embodied and sensory memories of fieldwork likewise informed my own analysis of domestic video tours (see Pink, 2004, 2006) and community garden tours. However, in contrast to the 'kinaesthetic sensations' Hahn (2007: 8) describes, my capacity to imagine myself into the corporeality represented by the video tapes was more specifically connected to my own research experiences. Whereas over an extended period of time Hahn had learned the movements that she was viewing on video, my own tours of homes and gardens were more concerned with understanding research participants' verbal and embodied commentary about and corporeal experience of particular physical environments. This nevertheless does not mean that my analytical process was any less corporeally informed, but that it was informed by a different type of corporeal engagement with the practices and environment inhabited by the research participants. In each of my video tours of the sensory home, I accompanied and video recorded the research participant around her or his home and while engaging in a cleaning task. When I came to analyse these materials I found myself concerned with the question of 'how to interpret these existing representations of my fieldwork experiences anthropologically'. In reflecting on this in *Home Truths* I noted how 'I *had* been there and to a certain extent the videos along with my more general fieldnotes were evocative of that experience' (2004: 38; and see Pink, 2006, Chapters 3 and 4). When in other projects I have viewed videos made by colleagues in a shared research process in which we followed the same style of video recording, I have used an empathetic viewing stance to seek to connect with their corporeal positioning when working with these materials. When re-viewing the garden tours undertaken as part of my research into the Cittàslow movement (2005–7) I was reminded of the importance of the sensations of being there in the garden, for example of the ground underfoot, the weather. This embodied, sensorial and emotional engagement with the materials was crucial to my analysis. It helped me to imagine and feel my way back into the research encounter. This can be understood likewise as a route into reconsidering the embodied knowing that was part of that research experience. I suggest that using video in this way can offer ethnographers ways to re-connect with those non-verbalised ways of experiencing and knowing that form an integral part of the research encounter, and use these as part of the analysis. On one level this process of re-visiting the research encounter through prompting the memory and imagination in such a way provides a way of contextualising the systematic analysis of what is said, done and enacted on video. On another however, it offers the ethnographer a corporeal route to the sensorial and emotional affects of that research encounter, which themselves are ways of ethnographic knowing. It also significantly provides the ethnographer with opportunities to self-consciously reflect on those experiences, and as such arrive at a new level of awareness about them.

The above discussion of how audiovisual materials might be used to make the research encounter present in the analysis are also suggestive of how other research materials might be used similarly. Indeed, it is not only visual images that might be memorable or evocative of the multisensoriality of a research encounter and of the researcher's emplacement. Thus MacDougall has suggested that 'voices have textures as though perceived tactilely and visually' (1998: 52) and within his notion of an 'acoustemology' Steven Feld has proposed that 'hearing and voicing link the felt sensations of sound and balance to those of physical and emotional presence' (2005: 184), arguing that 'the experience of place can always be potentially grounded in an acoustic dimension' (2005: 185). Desjarlais' work provides some insights into how audio recorded materials and audio memories can create strong connections to the research encounter. For example, reflecting on the death of the elderly Kisang Omu whose commentaries were central to his audio recorded biographical research, Desjarlais writes how 'A life is impermanent. And yet I hear the tones of her voice still' (2003: 351). In discussing an interview with Mheme, with whom he often used an intermediary to help 'mediate the spatial, linguistic and cultural divides that separated us now and then', Desjarlais reflects on a moment when their communication became more direct. He writes: 'Mheme asked me directly when I would be returning to Nepal. When I listen to the section of the tape that registered the exchange that followed, I hear Mheme's voice and can recall seeing in his eyes a tone of relaxed amicableness' (2003: 337). The type of linguistic encounter that this conversation involved, Desjarlais tells us, 'usually coincides with a sustained "eye encounter"' which, as on that occasion, 'often hints at a wished for co-substantiality of thought and feeling among speakers' (2003: 337–8). Although his interviews were audio recorded rather than video recorded, Desjarlais emphasises the enduring importance of the visual aspects of this encounter. Significantly he writes: 'This, then, is how I recall Mheme's "face," in dialogue with my own during my last visit to his home that year. It is the record of our engagement' (2003: 338). Likewise, the work of Lyon and Back discussed in Chapter 5 focuses on the importance of sound recordings of the busier context of a London fish market – these recordings brought to the fore for them a perspective that they were able to review after being there at the market. They note how 'the recordings highlight the presence of distinct layers of sound – that are hard to distinguish between when hearing them in real time' (Lyon and Back, 2012: 2.4). They also emphasise how these materials were used to create meaning in their research process, in that:

> the photographs and sounds we selected and sometimes put together in sequences or montages help us to focus on the embodied and sensuous character of work. Taking and reviewing photographs and sounds helped us to establish what might count as relevant data and to identify directions for analysis, enabling us to see and hear what we could not quite comprehend in the moment, and alerted us to connections that escaped us when in the field. (Lyon and Back, 2012: 8.1)

Understanding research materials and memories in this way brings to the fore the sensory and emotional affects of the research encounter, and the role of these aspects of experience in the making of memories, knowledge and, ultimately, academic meanings. The examples provide important examples of how acknowledging this can allow the analysis of the materials to be understood as inextricable from the processes through which they are produced and made meaningful.

As these examples illustrate, the process of analysis is both embedded in the research encounter itself and involves forms of memory work and imagination that link the researcher in the present to moments in the past. These connections can be thought of as involving sensory and embodied memories, of perhaps a look, a feeling, a sound, a taste, or any combination of these.

WORKING WITH SENSORY CATEGORIES

Ethnographers focusing on the senses have both emphasised the interconnectedness of the senses and stressed the importance of seeking to understand other people's sensoria. Indeed, sensory ethnographers have often been interested in identifying the specific culturally constituted sensory modalities that people associate with their physiologies and the categories that they use to express sensory experience.

One way to do this involves determining the different linguistic categories that the people one is doing research with use to describe sensory experience. The limitation of this approach is that if it is not appropriately combined with other forms of collaboration and experiential participation, it can give preference to spoken and written language above other ways of knowing and communicating. Nevertheless, it certainly offers important routes into understanding how other people's sensoria are constructed. This approach might be used to understand both the way sensory categories are used by people in the ethnographer's own culture and to elucidate the sensorium of people in other cultures. Both of these exercises might involve forms of comparison, although the latter would entail a more obvious form of cross-cultural comparison.

Doing research in my own culture, when interviewing research participants for a project about domestic laundry I was interested in how these participants used different sensory categories to refer to specific aspects of their laundry experiences and practices. I was also concerned with their ways of corporeal and sensory knowing and how they related these ways of knowing to specific sensory modalities. In the interview transcript discussed in Chapter 4, Jane, the research participant, was using established modern western sensory categories to describe how she *knew* that something was clean or dirty. She discussed visual stains, the tactile sense of pressed clothes and the smell of dirty clothes. It became clear through her deliberations however that she could not rely on just one of these sensory modalities to determine if a laundry item was clean, since the visual evidence of a stain would not be enough to give a dirty classification. Rather, the feel and smell of an item were also to be used to evaluate laundry. Jane and I were working with the same modern western sensorium, and it was a straightforward step for me to then undertake an analysis of her and the other research participants' interviews and video tapes that examined how they understood their laundry in terms of vision, touch and smell. In developing my analysis I therefore opted to use the standard modern western sensorium to structure my understanding of 'the sensory home'. My analysis remains rooted in the idea that phenomenologically the senses are inextricably interconnected. Yet to understand how people's self-identities and homes are mutually constituted in terms of social and cultural practices it is appropriate to separate the senses analytically. However, as I set out in my book *Home Truths* (2004), this false separation had another analytical objective. I was not simply interested in how the home was discussed in terms of the senses, but in how different individuals used their references to the sensory qualities of their experiences of home and their domestic practices, as ways of commenting on their own identities. Moreover, I was interested in how the actual living out of sensory domestic practices and engagements with the forms of sensory knowing embedded in them became in itself a way of constituting specific gendered and generational self-identities through practice. The analysis revealed that different individuals would both refer verbally and demonstrate performatively how they would use different sensory modalities to evaluate the same areas of their homes, types of 'dirt' or the urgency of doing similar domestic tasks. In doing so some participants used 'alternative' sensory categories to those used in what they understood as a housewifely approach to housework as ways of departing from 'conventional' housework practices and the identities that they implied.

Thus, the modern western five-sense sensorium can offer useful analytical categories that might lead us to understand embodied knowledge and practice. Several other scholars whose work is discussed in earlier chapters have similarly organised their discussions in sections or chapters focusing on various combinations of sight, sound, smell, taste and texture. For example, Tilley's discussion of gardening in Britain and Sweden (2006), Hockey's auto-ethnography of long distance running in Britain (2006), and Edvardsson and Street's exploration of the nurse as ethnographer (2007), all based in modern western contexts, make use of these categories. In these works the sensory categories used are of specific relevance in the context of the research and relate to the understanding of the world expressed by research participants as well as serving as analytical categories. As the following examples demonstrate, the process of creating a relationship between the way sensory experience is categorised by research participants and the use of sensory categories in the analysis and subsequent representation of other people's experience and understanding leads to different project-specific forms of presentation.

Gediminas Lankauskas (2006) compares the ways that sight and taste are implicated in how people experience and remember socialism at Grūtas Statue Park in Lithuania. In his discussion of the way the Park is experienced Lankauskas distinguishes between how sight and taste are activated 'as a means for memorializing socialism' (2006: 30). He describes how the 'park-museum' includes both exhibits and a café reached by a trail through the grounds (2006: 39). Through a discussion of a tour of the Park and comments made by people experiencing it he proposes that 'seeing socialism at Grūtas is not the same as savouring it' (2006: 45). Here the visual and the gustatory are associated with different types of memories, so that he writes:

> While for most of my informants beholding the dejected socialist icons constituted a distancing and hence dis-identifying experience, partaking of the recuperated 'Soviet' dishes and drinks at the café typically invoked sentiments of nostalgic longing and yearning – not for socialism as an oppressive system but for the quotidian sociability centred around kin and friends that that system inadvertently produced and perpetuated. (Lankauskas, 2006: 45)

Here, using sight and taste as analytical categories provides a useful contrast of the ways that memory is differentially bound up with specific ways of experiencing the materiality of the statues and cuisine of socialism. By focusing on visual and gustatory practices Lankauskas provides an insightful analysis that goes beyond simply considering visual and gustatory meanings. Rather, this emphasis leads him to a more complex analysis of remembering in a post-socialist context.

Whereas some research brings to the fore existing modern western sensory categories and thus allows researchers to make the straightforward connection of presenting these as equally useful analytical categories, other ethnographic contexts demand that researchers seek new categories. Edvardsson and Street's (2007) discussion of an embodied and sensory approach to nursing studies, discussed in Chapter 4, is a good example. Edvardsson and Street divided their discussion of the experiences of the 'nurse as embodied ethnographer' into a set of sub-sections, each of which is referred to as an 'epiphany'. Each epiphany stands for one of the moments at which the researcher realised that using his senses in the care environment impacted on his research practice – his 'sudden intuitive realizations that the use of his senses in these environments was gradually changing the way that he asked questions and conducted observations' (2007: 26). While sub-sections two to five refer to epiphanies that are concerned respectively with 'Sound', 'Smell', 'Taste', 'Touch' and 'Sight', the first sub-section is entitled 'Epiphany 1: Movement' (2007: 26). Thus, even when working in a modern western culture, the five-sense sensorium is not always sufficient to describe how we experience our social and material environments.

The ethnographies discussed above all involved the use of a selection of established modern western sensory categories (and in one case the addition of another category) as ways of classifying sets of embodied experiences. These examples also show that these categories might not be established at a post-fieldwork stage called 'analysis', but rather they begin to emerge through the researcher's culturally specific engagements as part of the research process. For the studies discussed above the use of these modern western sensory categories seems appropriate. Yet the five-sense sensorium is not universal across all cultures. There is thus no reason why it should dictate the sensory categories used by ethnographers to structure their analyses. Indeed, Geurts' (2003) analysis of the Anlo Ewe sensorium has revealed the complexities that might be faced by ethnographers working in cultures where people understand sensory experience through categories quite different from their own. On finding that the Anlo Ewe did not have an explicit verbally articulated sensorium she drew on a linguistic approach to construct what she calls a 'kind of (provisional) inventory of [Anlo Ewe] sensory fields' (Geurts, 2003: 40). This involved creating correspondences between the rather different ways of understanding experience in modern western and Anlo Ewe epistemologies. In the absence of explicit categories and in a context where 'there are no ancient (written or recorded) texts that we could pursue for epistemological clues about their sensorium', she investigated the question through 'combing through dictionaries, by listening to proverbs, and by scrutinizing conversations and notes from my observations of habitual forms of body practices' (2003: 39), as well as interviews. Geurts' 'inventory' is an excellent example of how under these circumstances a researcher might render complex indigenous sensory knowledge – in a way that is as loyal as possible to local epistemologies – accessible within the linguistic and conceptual categories that an academic readership will find meaningful.

Ethnographic analysis is never straightforward – whether or not it concerns the senses. It involves making connections between, on the one hand, complex phenomenological realities and the specificities of other people's ways of understanding these, and on the other, scholarly categories and debates. This inevitably involves processes of condensing and translating, as well as those of constructing a narrative and argument. As the examples above indicate, one option for the sensory ethnographer is to use modern western sensory categories, appropriately added to or perhaps embellished as a means of structuring an analysis. In cases where correspondences between the indigenous and western cultural categories used to classify multisensory experience are not obvious then the ethnographer's task may be to seek to construct sets of categories, and ways of comprehending phenomenological realities, that both represent indigenous meanings and are accessible to an intended audience. In this entire process, attention to the experiential elements I discuss in earlier sections of this chapter as well as cultural/discursive elements should be maintained. Indeed, the cultural categories that might become part of the focus and structure of analysis are produced only in relation to the multisensoriality of human perception.

AUDIO RECORDINGS AND TRANSCRIPTIONS IN THE ANALYTICAL PROCESS

Above and in earlier chapters I have emphasised with equal weight the role of visual, audio and material objects in the research process. However, we also need to recognise that much of what sensory ethnographers do involves listening and conversing with others; as such this often includes, as in the case of the classic ethnographic interview, the use of audio recordings and transcriptions. Transcription has been little discussed in the sensory ethnography literature that has been growing over the last years. Indeed, it has mostly been debated in the domain of fields dominated by linguistic approaches (O'Dell and Willim, 2013: 329). However, transcription has had a prominent place in ethnographic practice for many years, and, as the discussion in this section reveals, the complexity and significance of the role it plays in the making of sensory ethnographic knowing, deserves more attention, and has recently been brought to the fore in the work of Tom O'Dell and Robert Willim, discussed below.

Transcription is a time-consuming process and many researchers contract professional transcription services to undertake this task. There are various types of transcription, which involve different degrees of detail, some of which are required for specific analysis techniques such as conversation and discourse analysis. Here however I will refer to standard verbatim transcriptions, which would involve the transcriber documenting what the speakers have said. The use of professional transcriptions services is beneficial when the quantity of the transcriptions is large and would be time consuming. However, outsourcing transcription also has some disadvantages which sensory ethnographers may wish to balance against the benefits it brings. This is because, as I have discussed in relation to the work of researchers above (e.g. Lyon and Back, 2012), the recording itself becomes evocative of the environment in which the interview took place. In my own work I have found that listening to recordings enables me to recall the situation of the interviews and the affective and sensory dimensions of that experience, thereby renewing my feeling of connection to the research context. For example, in my research into Spanish Slow Cities (Pink and Servon, 2013) Lisa Servon and I interviewed several Spanish Slow City leaders, we audio recorded the interviews and in my own analytical work I listened to, took notes from and transcribed and translated into English the most significant quotations. The analytical process in this case happened alongside listening and transcribing. Whereas when the transcription is undertaken separately from the analysis and arrives printed for the researcher to analyse, there is inevitably a different relationship between the analysis and the research materials. In this case the process I used did not separate the sensory experience and evocative elements of listening to the recordings from the ways in which I interpreted the materials. This closeness to the materials was important for me as I focused in on how participants expressed their relationships to the

Slow City movement, using their voices, and sounds as part of this process. An example of the outcomes of this type of analysis is in how, in our published work, we were able to discuss the ways in which participants found it hard to put into words the sensory and embodied ways they experienced the town. For instance, at one point we were discussing with the mayor of a town their decision to feature a photograph of the rain in the town's brochure. As we describe the situation there:

> He explained that the photographs of rain represented Lekeitio at its best, that is, when one can experience the 'strongest sensations'. In the summer, José told us, the experience of going to the beach is good, but he said: 'if you come in February, when the sea is enormous, one of those periods when you can see the waves from there ... and there are these waves that are 25 metres high, and you are here. And I ask you "how was the view", and you will say "well look it was marvellous, there were waves 25 metres high". If you come in February at night and you hear the sea, which goes [he imitates its roar], and there is no one else. It's as if there was a giant'. (Pink and Servon, 2013: 460–1)

As we go on to describe, this was not the only way we made sense of the materials; we also accounted for our experiences of walking around the town with our participants and visiting a maritime heritage centre with them. However, in the analytical process listening to and transcribing the recording of this interview was very important as it enabled me to gain a sense of the ways this and similar experiences came alive in our conversations.

In Chapter 6 I discussed the video tour method. When working with recordings of the video tours, I am interested in engaging with the video recording through the relationship between tacit, embodied and performed ways of knowing, and the ways that participants describe and verbalise these, or talk about their lives, environments and activities *in relation to* these actions. This approach does involve directly transcribing specific and pertinent comments made by participants, however these are contextualised in relation to activities and environments, which enables a different approach to that which would be focused on the verbal talk of transcripts. However, this is not to say that a more conventional sociological or conversation analysis of transcribed audio would not be useful alongside this and I would consider such routes to be interesting to explore in future teamwork.

A key contribution to the discussion about transcription has been proposed by Tom O'Dell and Robert Willim in their article 'Transcription and the senses: cultural analysis when it entails more than words' (2013). O'Dell and Willim 'view ethnography as a compositional practice' and 'a process consisting of multimodal and sensuous practices, leaving room for possible connections between ethnography and creative practices like art and design' (2013: 316). Arguing for a greater focus on analysis in ethnography they focus in on the question of how 'transcriptions can be rethought as sensory experiences geared to move and engage different audiences' (2013: 317). They discuss different forms of transcription, one of which is 'ethnopoetic transcription' which, because it contains so much detail and is designed to reveal the relations that are part of what has been transcribed, they suggest is hard to simply read and is rather enacted so that it 'prompts new forms of performativity from the bodies of the transcript's reader' (2013: 318). Building on this and other examples they suggest a shift in the way we think about transcriptions, to regard them as 'compositional pieces' (2013: 319) and towards a more sensory approach. Their article also offers a very useful review of the ways in which transcription has been introduced in novel forms, such as through cartoons, sketching practices, and through a discussion of how scores are used in music. They urge us to attend to the roles played by the technologies and software that we use for transcription, and thus to be mindful of the 'sensory ecology of hidden code and algorithms that text, sound, and image will interplay, mutate, and thrive in the future' (2013: 326).

Reflections on the place of transcription in sensory ethnography practice are therefore nascent, yet as I have highlighted in this section they are significant to pursue. They might form part of the reflexive practice of the sensory ethnographer as she or he interrogates the ways in which ethnographic ways of knowing are produced, not simply through fieldwork but in the analytical process.

INTERPRETING AND SHARING SENSORY ETHNOGRAPHY IN RESEARCH TEAMS

As I have discussed above and elsewhere (Pink, 2013), doing ethnography in teams, and particularly interdisciplinary (and applied) research teams, creates fieldwork, analytical and dissemination processes and activities that can be different from those that would be practised by the more conventional figure of the lone academic ethnographer. In this section I outline two examples, which I have developed in my work with colleagues Jennifer Morgan and Andrew Dainty (Pink and Morgan, 2013) and Kerstin Leder Mackley (Leder Mackley and Pink, 2013) as part of two different projects which have in common that they were multi-team and interdisciplinary, but which have showed up different sensory ethnography research practices due to the different contexts we worked in and the different types of research materials that we generated.

Between 2012 and 2015 Morgan, Dainty and I collaborated on two projects related to occupational safety and health (OSH) across a number of different workplace environments in the UK. We formed a small team within a larger project, in which we undertook the ethnographic part of the project, which was connected to a larger qualitative study undertaken by our colleagues. We have developed a series of articles from this work (e.g. Pink et al., 2014) in one of which Morgan and I discuss how we developed a research process in which an ethnographic–theoretical dialogue played a central role in the ways in which we wrote, interpreted and performed the ethnographic research process (Pink and Morgan, 2013). During this process, as we outline in our article (Pink and Morgan, 2013), Morgan, based in the UK, undertook intensive short-term fieldwork with home visits to workers based at a Healthcare Trust, nevertheless working closely with me while I was in Australia. The short-term ethnography we undertook as part of this project was characterised by an explicit dialogue between the ethnographic findings as they emerged and their relationship to theoretical debates and arguments. The dialogue was made explicit precisely because it was laid out in written form, as Morgan wrote up her fieldnotes on a regular basis and sent these to Dainty and myself by email. Morgan's fieldwork was intensive in ways that differentiate it from long-term fieldwork. It was not characterised by the sense of hanging around, waiting to see life unfold, but rather by a need to engage with health care workers, to ask to accompany them on home visits and to rapidly develop as deep as possible an understanding of how they experienced and performed OSH in their working lives. During the fieldwork process we were ongoingly developing empathetic and analytical correspondences both with experiences from other contexts and with texts – for example, noting how:

> The embodied residues of sensory memory form a key element of this approach. For example, in the healthcare context, JM drew on her experience of using touch in her prior work as a museum curator to make correspondences with how nurses also use their hands in skilled and sensory ways. Although carried from a very different professional context, this experience enabled JM to recognize and ask participants to reflect on practices that were unspoken and would have been otherwise invisible, such as the removal of a fingertip from a pair of gloves to allow for the sensation of touch to be used when taking a blood sample. (Pink and Morgan, 2013: 356)

The other way we achieved this was through an ethnographic–theoretical dialogue, which involved 'continually bringing theoretical questions into dialogue with the ethnography' (Pink and Morgan, 2013: 357). As we explain, 'There are ways in which the lone researcher can do this, for instance by taking time away from fieldwork, and presenting preliminary work to peers'; in our teamwork context however, we 'developed this through an actual dialogue between JM, SP and AD. SP, located in Melbourne, Australia and AD located in Loughborough, UK followed the process through fieldnotes, commentaries and photographs. We corresponded nearly every day throughout the fieldwork and at one review meeting' (Pink and Morgan, 2013: 357). By standing both inside and outside the fieldwork context, and working in different time zones, we were able to focus in on Morgan's fieldnotes from different perspectives and at different times. When Morgan sent notes at night after writing up her fieldwork on a late shift, I would be able to look at these during the Australian day, so that my comments could feed into the next day's fieldwork. Through this process we were able to make an analytical process, which is so often part of fieldwork, very clearly at the core of our fieldwork. For example, this meant keeping questions about sensory and tacit ways of knowing about OSH to the fore, using knowledge of theories of the senses to inform our discussions and bringing to bear my own and Dainty's different knowledges of other examples and literatures.

A second example of analytical process being highlighted is discussed in my work with Kerstin Leder Mackley (Leder Mackley and Pink, 2013). Here, as part of the LEEDR project, Leder Mackley was often called on to communicate our ethnographic findings to our Design and Engineering colleagues. In our article we explore how, in this interdisciplinary context, through our sensory video ethnography materials we 'engaged analytically with verbal and nonverbal forms of knowing and representation' during the project (Leder Mackley and Pink, 2013: 336). Moreover, as we point out, as our work was part of an interdisciplinary and applied project it was part of a wider, and increasingly established, context in which 'Our responsibilities as ethnographers require us to be accountable to each other, to scholars outside our discipline, to participants, and, increasingly, to industry stakeholders and the wider public, to be able to demonstrate how we know' (2013: 337). I discuss issues of representation and dissemination further in Chapter 8; here however this stands as a reminder that the analytical process and the categories that we create during this process are integral to these ways of knowing, and ultimately to the recommendations that we might make to external stakeholders, and that therefore a level of reflexivity about how they are created is informative. Using the video tour methodology I have described in Chapter 5 (and see Pink and Leder Mackley, 2012), the materials we worked with were video tours of homes, focusing on the ways in which homes 'feel' and are made to feel that way, and observations and re-enactments (Pink and Leder Mackley, 2014) of activities through which participants consume energy. Our Design and Engineering colleagues produced interview and mapping data and energy monitoring data respectively. Our first task was to understand the ways in which our colleagues understood their data and the ideas underpinning these understandings. As we describe, given that behaviour change models originating from psychology tend to dominate in these fields, one of our tasks was to offer alternative ways of understanding how and why people consume energy in their homes, and to use our sensory ethnography materials to create alternative categories through which our colleagues might understand the 'social' elements of energy demand. One aspect of this was to use the materials to bring colleagues closer to participants, which had some success:

> as a design colleague who only recently joined the team put it:
>
> As a researcher who probably won't get an opportunity to meet the ... households prior to designing for them, such source material affords a level of *empathic understanding* and realistic contextual *texture* that is otherwise missing from thematic analysis and other written reports. (Personal communication; our emphasis)
>
> (Leder Mackley and Pink, 2013: 343)

However, our analytical work went beyond creating more tacit and sensory understandings within our team, in that we worked with our research materials to create what we saw as novel routes through which our colleagues (and other audiences for our work) might consider what people actually *do* in their homes. Rather than imposing the existing analytical categories on these activities that are usually used in psychological and sociological energy research (such as behaviours and practices) we took the stance of more anthropological ethnographers, to consider what we could learn from our materials about how energy use was woven into the ongoingness or 'flow' of everyday life. We were interested in how tacit ways of being and *doing* in the home were actually enacted by participants and in working out ways to define these through concepts that would be meaningful to our colleagues, and additionally that could be used to inform the making of design interventions. Therefore, our analysis took two directions. First, 'A series of theoretical–ethnographic relationships began to emerge as our video tours progressed, and continued through our practice studies. These included notions of flow, movement, invisible architectures, material agency, and everyday change' (Leder Mackley and Pink, 2013: 345). Second, we undertook a more thematic analysis across our sample of 20 households. This analysis used the concepts that had emerged from the first stage, and followed them across the sample, but 'was more formal and involved working through the materials to respond to our core research questions concerning how people "needed" to use energy to create and maintain a particular sensory aesthetic of home, to make their homes "feel right"' (Leder Mackley and Pink, 2013: 345). While on the one hand this analytical process enabled us to produce 'findings' relating to how and why people consume energy in their homes, and to develop a critical perspective on other social science approaches in this field, on the other, it offered a set of analytical concepts that we could see as 'building bridges' (Leder Mackley and Pink, 2013: 350) to our colleagues from other disciplines.

In this section I have focused in on analysis as part of the sensory ethnography research process, with specific reference to the relationships we might generate between theory, concepts and ethnography. As I have shown, this relationship is usually embedded in the research process as well as emerging from and going beyond the actual encounters we have with participants. I have also emphasised how doing teamwork, whether with colleagues from the same discipline or approach or from quite different disciplines, can shape the analytical process and enable us to reflect in new ways on how analytical categories are made and the implications these might have for the ways in which our research can be relevant to others.

INTERPRETING AND CONNECTING RESEARCH EXPERIENCES, MATERIALS AND TEXTS

As I have pointed out above, ethnographers who attend to the senses infrequently reveal the detail of how they have gone about their analysis. In some cases this process is represented in the ways their texts are constructed – for example, in the interweaving of description, theory, images and more. I discuss this question further in the next chapter. In my own experience, analysis in sensory ethnography usually involves a process that moves between different registers of engagement with research materials and between different materials. As I noted in the previous section this can involve analysing the same materials in different ways. Analysis is moreover, as I pointed out at the beginning of this chapter, a continuous and incremental process rather than simply a stage in a research process. Above I have discussed these issues in relation to research projects that have involved shorter-term and more intensive one-to-one encounters with research participants. To demonstrate how these continuities might develop in a different ethnographic context, which was more informally structured and stretched over a different period of time, I now discuss an example from my ethnography of the Cittàslow movement in one of the several British towns where I have done sensory ethnography research – Aylsham in Norfolk, UK.

In Aylsham I researched events that take place annually in the town, including the town's carnival. I was especially interested in the sensoriality of this event and my research involved a combination of attending committee meetings and taking written notes, audio interviewing key people involved in the production and attending the events themselves at which I participated by eating, drinking, socialising and generally 'being there' with others, photographing and video recording. These mixed qualitative methods provided me with a set of diverse research materials – written notes, committee papers, audio recorded and transcribed interviews, photographs and video footage including some video interviews. In terms of how these materials reconnected me to the research encounter(s) several elements come to the fore. For example, the material culture of committees in the form of the committee agendas and other papers I kept, became memory objects that aided me in remembering the sensoriality and sociality of committees and the importance of these qualities for my understandings of the way the carnival was produced. The video footage represented the social encounters that I experienced with local people keen to comment on a photographic exhibition, the soundscape of the hall where tea and cakes were also served, and the visual content of the photographic exhibition. This footage allowed me to engage reflexively with elements of the sociality of the exhibition and my own role in this. Outside in the square and streets where the stalls and processions were located, another soundscape and series of interviews and images are represented. One of my interests was in interpreting the town's carnival as an alternative sensescape that might be seen as offering sensory experiences that, following the principles of the Slow City movement, contrasted to those that formed part of global corporate capitalist consumption.

I took as a starting point for my analysis the idea of the town as a multisensory environment that I could interpret through the prism of a modern western sensorium. I was interested in analysing how the sensescape of the carnival had been imagined, planned or mapped out by the organisers, its materiality, sociality and sensoriality and its relationship to the principles of the Slow movement. To undertake this analysis involved my moving between different sets of research materials to make connections between the way the carnival was organised, the way it linked to the principles of Cittàslow and different ways it might be experienced. In contrast to the domestic laundry research I discussed earlier in this chapter I was not so much interested in determining how local people used specific linguistic categories to define different aspects of the carnival, but in understanding the carnival as a modern western sensescape.

I first began to consider the way the carnival was interwoven with the existing physical environment of the town, and how different sensations – for example, the tastes of locally produced foods offered on various stalls, the sounds of local musicians, the visual and material exhibition of photographs from past carnivals, and the corporeality of the carnival processions – were implicated in this. Having attended the carnival during the first year of my research I viewed my video recordings and associated memories of how the event was played out in the square and streets of the town. I began to remember my own routes through the carnival and the culinary, aural, visual and social experiences and encounters they entailed. I began to interpret these experiences as ways in which the sensescape of the carnival might immerse its participants in alternative sensory realities that represented the principles of Cittàslow. This in turn involved an analysis of the Cittàslow criteria and literature and attention to the global and national discourses and power relations these are interwoven within. However, these materials did not answer all my questions about this multisensory event.

The following year I had opportunities to sit in on some of the committee meetings where the carnival was planned. Here I began to understand not only the sociality and sensoriality of committees (Pink, 2008d) but also the ways in which people used their experience-based knowledge of the town to inform decisions about how the carnival should be created in it. Not once at these meetings did I see anyone pull out a map and begin to plot where the carnival displays, culinary stalls, music and other elements should be located. Rather, committee members appeared to employ forms of knowing derived from their own embodied, emplaced experiences of what it felt like to be in the town. They *knew* what it would sound and feel like if a particular sort of music was played at a particular location in the town and this tacit knowledge was crucial to the organisation of the event. By interpreting the carnival as a temporary alternative sensory environment I had been able to start thinking about how the event linked to the principles of the Slow movement which, in its literature, puts significant emphasis on the sensorial qualities of localities and produce. However, by considering how the actual constitution of this alternative sensescape was produced through local people's tacit, sensory emplaced knowing I could interpret the carnival as what Ingold calls a 'meshwork' (2008) of local and global elements.

Ethnographic research thus often entails long-term processes, perhaps through return visits, as was the case in the project described above. The research events and techniques used involve sensory engagements in different ways and on different levels. For the analytical process this might mean that interpreting one set of research materials will depend on the analysis of another set. In the above example from my own work, analysis entailed moving between different sets of research materials and memories to piece together abstractions of events and processes in such a way that they related the phenomenology of the research process to written academic debates.

Summing up

Processes or methods for analysing sensory ethnography materials are as yet under-represented in existing literature. This is perhaps unsurprising since processes for analysing ethnographic materials are generally infrequently formally defined. A potential way forward would be an engagement with existing methods of analysis, involving ethnographers re-thinking these methods in ways that are attentive to the senses.

The cases discussed above indicate that there are certain issues that need to be accounted for when considering other people's sensoria, whether in one's own culture or in other cultures. First, ethnographers need to develop an awareness of how different types of research materials might facilitate ways of being close to the non-verbal, tacit, emplaced knowledge that a sensory analysis seeks to identify. Second, it is crucial to recognise the constructedness of the modern western sensorium and the importance of understanding other people's worlds through their sensory categories. To understand the sensory categories that other people use involves both being aware of one's own sensory categories and the moralities and values one attaches to these and seeking to identify how, when and why others both construct and employ these categories in culturally specific and idiosyncratic and personal ways. Third, a sensory analysis will usually begin from the assumption that people inhabit multisensory environments, places which themselves are constantly being re-made. To understand how such places are made, experienced and understood by others ethnographers might need to employ mixed qualitative methods, analyse different sorts of research materials in different ways and make connections between the different levels of analysis and knowledge involved. Finally, reflexivity is a central element of sensory ethnography research and while it is usually discussed in relation to the actual fieldwork process, it is equally important to the ways in which we organise and analyse our research materials. As I have shown, attention to the ways in which and reasons why we approach our experiences and materials in particular ways, and to the categories we engage in analytical processes is important for understanding the nature, qualities and utility of the ways of knowing that our analyses can offer both us and other audiences for, stakeholders in and users of our work.

Recommended further reading

- Desjarlais, R. (2003) *Sensory Biographies: lives and death among Nepal's Yolmo Buddhists.* London: University of California Press.
- Geurts, K.L. (2003) *Culture and the Senses: bodily ways of knowing in an African community.* Berkeley, Los Angeles, London: University of California Press.
- Leder Mackley, K. and S. Pink (2013) 'From emplaced knowing to interdisciplinary knowledge: sensory ethnography in energy research', *The Senses and Society*, 8(3): 335–53.
- O'Dell, T. and R. Willim (2013) 'Transcription and the senses: cultural analysis when it entails more than words', *The Senses and Society*, 8(3): 314–34.
- Pink, S. and J. Morgan (2013) 'Short term ethnography: intense routes to knowing', *Symbolic Interaction*, 36(3): 351–61.

EIGHT

Representing sensory ethnography

Communicating, arguing and the non-representational

In the preceding chapters I have discussed how sensory ethnographers have developed novel ways to research and interpret their work, that often go beyond conventional verbal description. In this chapter I discuss the question of representing the non-representational. That is, I am concerned with how sensory ethnography research might be communicated both within and beyond academic audiences in ways that remain loyal to its ambition to go beyond conventional textual formats in both the ways of knowing it generates and the meanings its authors seek to convey. Developing further the notion of the ethnographic place as a site for sharing sensory ethnography, I focus on questions including the generation of intimacy and empathy and discuss how different media, technologies and types of practice have been engaged for sensory dissemination.

INTRODUCTION: APPROACHES TO REPRESENTING SENSORY ETHNOGRAPHY

Scholarly writing remains a central medium in which ethnographic research through and about the senses is described, evoked and theoretically debated. Yet conventional scholarly practice is limited in its capacity to communicate about the directness of the sensory and affective elements of emplaced experience. Alternative routes to representing sensory knowing have been developed in arts and media practice and there are opportunities for these practices to both inform and be developed collaboratively with sensory approaches to ethnographic representation.

Connections between artistic, scholarly and applied work are already made by a number of scholars in the social sciences. For example, the sociologist and cultural criminologist Maggie O'Neill, whose work involves collaborations with participants and different types of artists (2008: 4; and see O'Neill, 2012), argues that 'the role of the sociologist and artist as interpreters producing knowledge through interdisciplinary phenomenological research and artistic re-presentations of lived experience can help to counter identity thinking, make critical interventions, and help us to get in touch with our social worlds' (O'Neill, 2008: 53). O'Neill's points are relevant across the ethnographic disciplines. The anthropologist Arnd Schneider has specifically called for a further 'dialogue with the arts', to benefit both anthropologists and arts practitioners (2008: 172; see also Schneider and Wright, 2006). Such engagements have been developed in the work of anthropologists/artists (e.g. Ravetz, 2007, 2011) and in appropriations of arts practice techniques in geography (e.g. Butler, 2006) and archaeology (e.g. Witmore, 2004), and theory and practice in this field continues to develop (e.g. Ingold, 2011; Schneider and Wright, 2013). Yet meeting points between ethnography, scholarship, intervention and art also raise questions such as whether researchers harness arts practice for the production of scholarship and theoretically informed applied interventions *or* forsake the conventions of scholarship and established ethnographic epistemologies to produce ways of knowing that are more accessible through arts practice (see Ravetz, 2007). While in reality such binaries might not be so clear cut it is important to reflect on how or why different balances between these fields might develop in different projects with varied objectives.

The relationship between sensory ethnography and media practice is also a site where interesting projects are developing, through digital video and audio projects, and web-based media. Ethnographic filmmaking is often now re-framed as a sensory rather than simply visual practice. Moreover, given the increasing use of digital media and technologies in sensory ethnography research it is not surprising that there is corresponding interest in using digital and web-based methods to disseminate sensory ethnography in ways that attempt to evoke the corporeal and experiential feelings of *being there* from which academic understandings are produced, and indeed with which they are entangled. One question explored in this chapter is how sensory ethnographers might communicate and disseminate those aspects of their work that are tacit, unspoken, embodied and not easily or even possibly expressed in spoken or written words.

Sensory ethnographers developing academic or applied interventions, who wish to situate their work within the existing trajectories of their discipline, are faced with two challenges. The first is to seek appropriate (perhaps new) ways to communicate about their own and other people's sensory knowing, emplacement and mobilisations of cultural categories, and more. The second entails involving these more experiential engagements in the production of work that is at once theoretical (in that they can make a contribution to scholarship and discussion) *and* substantive (in that they contribute to a body of academic knowledge about a particular theme), as well as possibly informing or serving as social interventions.

THINKING ABOUT SENSORY DISSEMINATION: INTIMACY, MEDIA AND PLACE

In what follows I review pertinent existing works to suggest how the task of representing sensory knowing has been approached in ethnography and arts practice. Rather than proposing a template for creating sensory ethnographic representations, I draw from the theoretical approach proposed in Chapter 2 to examine the following themes: the production of a sense of intimacy; relationships between techniques and media in ethnographic and scholarly communication; and the idea of representation as ethnographic place. These themes and approaches, I suggest, might guide the production of sensory ethnography representations.

The possibility that bringing together ethnographic, artistic and media representations might create a sense of intimacy sufficiently powerful to invite empathetic understandings and communicate experiential knowing to audiences has been suggested across practices and media. The visual anthropologist Peter Biella has proposed that 'Ethnographic films that depict the intimate confidences between anthropologists and informants, and show intimacies among informants, offer viewers the vicarious experience and discovery of close personal revelations and vulnerabilities by people in other cultural worlds'. He suggests film offers a 'sense of *virtual intimacy*', which, because it does not require immediate reciprocation, 'is a safe first step into a world of increased awareness and compassion' (Biella, 2008). Similar possibilities have been attributed to written text. Stoller has proposed that 'Using sensuous ethnography to bear witness to ... forms of social trauma, abuse, and repression ... has the potential to shock readers into newfound awareness, enabling them ... to think new thoughts or feel new feelings' (2004: 832). Likewise, particular capacities to produce new forms of awareness and of intimacy have been claimed for sound (e.g. Feld and Brenneis, 2004) and smell (e.g. Arning, 2006). In Chapter 6 I have also written about the ways in which the association of smartphones and mobile media with 'co-presence' and their tactile, visual and audio qualities and affordances, come together to make these intimate technologies (see Richardson, 2011). Moreover, the rapid rise in popularity of the 'selfie' practice of photographing oneself with a smartphone, indicates the closeness that these technologies have to the ways people view and represent their own identities, thus suggesting that the personalisation, closeness and affective qualities of the smartphone create the potential to similarly create empathetic and corporeal connections with audiences through sensory ethnography media. These methods and media may provide routes through which ethnographers can communicate the sensory emplaced knowing of the research encounter and of participants to their audiences. However, this is not the only task of the sensory ethnographer.

While some have suggested that text-based scholarship might be challenged through alternative representations (e.g. MacDougall, 1997), my own approach focuses more on seeking ways that writing and other methods might work together (see Pink, 2006). Writing has already developed and maintained a central role and set of purposes in sensory ethnography representation. Significantly, it facilitates the contribution to existing scholarship that might be made through the kind of emplaced knowing that the sensory ethnographer is concerned with. Yet, while Stoller (2004) suggests written texts might propel readers to new levels of compassionate awareness, they cannot achieve the impression of a direct connection to experiential realities that is implied by sound or video recordings or scents. The use of alternative practices and media of representation to create a sense of intimacy and awareness however can also be developed in relation to more established forms of scholarship.

A number of the practitioners and scholars discussed below seek to represent the sensoriality and meanings of place. They are concerned with communicating aspects of how particular place-events are experienced. Here I suggest conceptualising such sensory representations as ethnographic places. Ethnographic places are abstractions. Using various narrative and technological practices and processes, they create routes to and bring together selected sensations, emotions, meanings, reflexivity, descriptions, arguments and theories. Ultimately, these components become involved in new place-events as they become interwoven with the trajectories of audiences and readers.

PRINTED TEXT: SENSUAL WORDS AND IMAGES

Many of the contributions to sensory sub-field(s) (for instance, in anthropology, geography and sociology) are written monographs, book chapters and journal articles. Some critics have suggested that ethnographic writing distracts us from the sensorial and experiential. For instance, MacDougall points to the 'potential incommensurability of sensory experience and anthropological writing' (2005: 60) and Schneider and Wright have suggested that most 'sensual experiences involved in fieldwork normally disappear from anthropological writing' (2006: 13). Yet, existing literature demonstrates how that writing plays the important role of connecting sensory experience and theory in dialogue (see also Howes, 2005b: 4).

There are good reasons for writing. The written word is the most embedded and developed form of ethnographic representation, and underpins sophisticated techniques for scholarly debate. It remains the dominant method of relating the findings, methodologies and theoretical implications of ethnographic studies. Written scholarship enables ethnographers to participate in theoretical debates. In doing so it is a medium through which we can harness the sensory knowing of ethnographic experience to contribute to existing scholarship.

Yet there is also a need to define what for and why we use text in relation to opportunities to use other media. For instance, the design scholar Alison Barnes has pointed out how although the shift in cultural geography towards using 'creative methods such as filmmaking or sound recording as ways to understand

and represent place' is enriching, 'In some ways, nonrepresentational theory has rendered the page and the printed word no longer productive tools or spaces to engage with place' (2013: 164). Barnes offers a new way to think about the book, and by bringing together geography and graphic design suggests that 'Rather than turning to other nontextual forms in order to "move beyond" the representational in a geographical engagement with the ongoing making of worlds, ... textual forms have the potential to be modes of that engagement that are more than representational artifacts' (2013: 164).

Thus ethnographers need to account for the role of written narratives in making crucial connections between on the one hand, alternative representations of knowing and arguments based on emplaced experience, and on the other, existing strands in scholarly and applied disciplines. Any call for greater attention to the senses in ethnographic writing should be accompanied by the need to develop relationships between sensual knowing description and evocation (whatever medium this is represented through) and theoretical discussion.

Writing sensory ethnography texts

The 'sensory ethnography' monograph, chapter or article does not constitute a genre in itself. While for the purposes of this book I have grouped a set of works together as sensory ethnographies, when viewed from the perspectives of other subdisciplines these books, articles or chapters equally belong to and share concerns with those of, for example, food studies (e.g. Sutton, 2001, 2006; Hayes-Conroy and Hayes-Conroy, 2008), urban geography (e.g. Law, 2005; Spinney, 2007), anthropology of the home (e.g. Pink, 2004, 2012), medical anthropology or sociology (e.g. Lammer, 2007, 2012; Rice, 2008), sociology of work (e.g. Lyon and Back, 2012; Lyon, 2013), media or energy research (Pink and Leder Mackley, 2013) and design research (Pink et al., 2013).

There are, however, some notable common concerns across sensory ethnography writing: the relationship or interweaving between descriptive and/or evocative text and theoretical and methodological discussion and argument; the question of how to work with sensory classifications and categories; and how to engage readers with the text in ways that are sensual, empathetic and reflexive. In addition to this sensory ethnography writing has often incorporated a level of reflexivity and acknowledgement of the processes through which knowing and knowledge are produced.

The idea of interweaving theoretical and experiential narratives in sensory ethnography was initially highlighted by Stoller through his monograph *Sensuous Scholarship*. Stoller describes the book as 'an attempt to reawaken profoundly the scholar's body by demonstrating how the fusion of the intelligible and the sensible can be applied to scholarly practices and representations' (Stoller, 1997: xv). Through six chapters he demonstrates how such essays might be composed to represent the embodied experiences of the ethnographer, of others and in the analysis of the sensorial evocation of film.

Words and images in sensory ethnography texts

Photographs are increasingly included in ethnographic publications, and sensory ethnography monographs and journal articles are no exception (e.g. Sutton, 2001; Geurts, 2003), although recent edited readers focusing on the senses (Bull and Back, 2003; Classen, 2005; Howes, 2005a; Drobnick, 2006) are curiously devoid of photographs. Sometimes there are good reasons for not including images – in my monograph *Home Truths* (Pink, 2004) for reasons relating to the image quality of video stills and confidentiality I restricted the representation to written words (see Pink, 2004). I have also written this second edition of *Doing Sensory Ethnography* with no images, as an experiment in text without images. However, a rich combination of written and visual representation can create possibilities for engaging them in mutual meaning making (see Pink, 2007a).

Images of hands offer an interesting example. In my work with Morgan and Dainty, we have sought to represent the sensory ways of knowing in how health care workers use their hands when applying disinfectant hand gel, by using video stills taken during our research, when we specifically asked participants to show and discuss with us these sensory ways of knowing through the hand (Pink et al., 2015). The hand is an important focus in sensory ethnography research, particularly for understanding touch and tactile ways of knowing. Other examples include Christina Lammer's writing about the interventional radiology (2007), and Dawn Lyon and Les Back's research into the experience of fishmongering (2012). Images of hands at work might be used to invite readers to encounter and comprehend the forms of intimacy and awareness of others' experiences by evoking touch and movement.

An example of the interweaving of writing and images to represent the sensoriality of ethnographic experience descriptively and analytically is demonstrated in Sutton's anthropological work on modern cooking practices (Sutton, 2006). Sutton's ethnography of cooking involved interviewing and filming research participants 'as they go about cooking "ordinary" and "special dishes"', which, he suggests, 'allows us to develop a profile and also a sort of culinary biography of some of the key experiences and values that have led people to their current cooking practices' (2006: 102). Before discussing the ethnography Sutton introduces a series of theoretical questions regarding skill and modernity. Thus he establishes that one of the tasks of his chapter is to respond to these issues. His presentation of the ethnographic detail is interesting in a number of ways. First, the analysis focuses on specific encounters that involved research participants engaging in activities on video and being interviewed. Sutton weaves together information about the participants, descriptions of their actual practices, quotations of participants' commentaries, discussions that link these to existing research and theory, and descriptively captioned video stills. The narrative moves between different registers (resonating to some extent with Stoller's call for ethnographic writing to move between the 'intelligible' and the 'sensible' (1997)). Sutton's chapter conforms to some principles of conventional academic writing and debate. Yet it simultaneously engages possibilities for empathetic engagement with participants' experiences through words and video stills. For example, Sutton's descriptions of one participant's cooking practices emphasise the visual and tactile aspects of her engagements with ingredients and tools. He writes:

> *In this recipe all but two ingredients were measured by sight. The two excluded from this were vinegar and an egg. Drawing her fingers together and pulling up slightly to create a cup of her right hand with her thumb forming the outer edge of the bowl by being crooked against her first finger, she poured the vinegar into her left hand to measure the correct amount.* (Sutton, 2006: 103–4, original italics)

These descriptions are italicised, and related directly to the video stills to represent aspects of the processes described. The images offer the reader a route through which to imagine the tactile and visual senses of pouring, measuring, rolling out and other skilled material engagements that cooking involves. Thus the text becomes an ethnographic place where theoretical debate, written description, visual evocation and more are intentionally brought together and interwoven. With the engagement of an audience these narratives become further entangled with other theoretical, biographical and imaginative threads brought by the reader/viewer.

Integrating action and experience in sensory ethnography writing

Reading experiences are themselves sensorial. The material and sensory environments in which paper or e-books are read, and readers' corporeal responses to their narratives, all contribute to the understandings that we gain from them. Another strategy shared by ethnographers who write about sensory experience entails inviting readers more directly to sensory engagements through exercises or activities. For example, in attempting to 'teach' her readers to be aware of their own sensory ways of knowing Hahn presents readers with a series of 'orientation' exercises. In the first of these she asks them to 'Imagine taking a drink of water from a glass *as* performance' (original italics), then to reflect on elements of this experience and describe it. Her point is that 'conveying lived experience is challenging, particularly if it is a performance practice you "know" in your own body but do not regularly transmit to someone else – either through demonstration or through writing' (2007: 19–21). Noting how anthropologists 'struggle with representing the dynamics of social life in static textual form, and work with various strategies – multivocality, evocation, indeterminacy – to subvert the limits of our genre' in his monograph *Remembrance of Repasts* (2001), Sutton invites readers to experience Greek cooking. However, providing two written recipes that might be followed he warns that it was unusual for research participants to give him recipes that could be transcribed and that there was part of one recipe that they 'could not articulate to me in written instructions' (2001: 156–7). Although the recipes Sutton relates were not initially presented to him in writing, in modern western cultures writing recipes down is a conventional practice. The recipes are not direct representations of tastes but offer routes to experience. Another non-textual experience that is nevertheless represented in written form is music. In the next section I discuss sound recording and composition in ethnography, yet written text can also be harnessed for sonic representation. For example, in an essay concerned with the atmosphere and soundscapes of football matches, Les Back uses musical scores to represent the tonal quality of the songs, along with their words printed underneath (2003). This invites readers to new and embodied engagements with texts and sounds should they seek to reproduce the sounds themselves by reading/playing/singing the tones – in ways informed by Back's written discussions. Thus readers might imagine themselves into the sensory or affective worlds of others by singing their songs, with the written knowledge about these 'others' situatedness already in mind. Such engagements do not guarantee that readers will reconstitute the printed music as performed song in the way it was sung in the research context, and indeed require some musical skills. They nevertheless suggest a route to another way of knowing.

The book beyond writing and images

Above I mentioned Barnes' argument for the book as a non-representational text. Barnes' own practice in this field has focused on creating a book, *Stuff*, which goes beyond the conventions of a written book. She describes the collaborative process of creating *Stuff*:

> I worked with the participants, closing the often-perceived gap between researcher and 'subject.' The book was inspired by participants' responses to the question, 'What makes your house a home?'. Many of the answers referred to items that related to memories and the process of one's life unfolding over time. For example, a respondent, whom I call 'CL,' said: 'All my "stuff" I suppose, of which there is a great deal'. (2013: 168)

The contents of *Stuff* are composed of 'four different texts: an essay; a life story; segments of conversations; and memories and photographs of items to which participants referred' (Barnes, 2013: 168). However, the material and sensory qualities and affordances of the book itself are also important in that

> Readers are able to develop a close physical relationship with the small form of 'Stuff' because the volume is easily held in their hands. The book's size reflects a close-up, intimate view of place. It does not, however, immediately reveal its contents or that it is anything other than 'traditional' in nature. The cover and binding are fairly straightforward, with the title embossed on buckram cloth ... The cover acts as a front door, a threshold between public and private space. On 'entering' the book, readers encounter end pages of brightly patterned wallpaper. (Barnes, 2013: 169)

Like the arguments about the intimacy and empathetic potentials of viewing film, video and using mobile media discussed above, Barnes' work shows how different media can participate in constituting these experiences in different ways.

Participation in the activities discussed in this section invites readers to their own experiences of elements of other people's worlds described in ethnographies. It creates routes to new levels of reflexive awareness of their own sensory subjectivities. The idea of the self-reflexive reader implies a reader whose awareness of her or his own subjectivity is constantly reconstituted. She or he is open to becoming aware of difference and uses her or his own experiences as routes to the appreciation of the emplacement, memories and imaginations of others. Facilitating such forms of readership can moreover support scholarship that hopes to create cross-cultural understanding by producing senses of intimacy with 'others'.

None of these methods of communicating about sensory knowing discussed above provide readers with the same sensory experiences of the ethnographer or research participants discussed in such texts. Yet they offer readers a basis from which to understand the experiences of both researcher and research participants and deeper reflexive understandings of their own sensory awareness.

AUDIOVISUAL MEDIA AND AESTHETIC EVOCATION

Visual ethnographers are increasingly developing audiovisual representations that are intended to invoke the sensorial, affective and aesthetic dimensions of the lives and environments of the participants in their research. Examples include MacDougall's Doon School documentary video project in which he focuses on the 'social aesthetics' of the school (see MacDougall, 2005: 94–119) and Lammer's *Making Contact* (2004), a video that represents the sensorial and affective world of interventional radiology: 'it engages all of the senses to tell a story: incorporating touch, taste and smell into a surreal, sterile yet fleshy audio-visual imagination' (Lammer, 2007: 99). MacDougall suggests that social aesthetics might be filmed 'through the events and material objects in which it played a variety of roles' (2005: 108) and Lammer's *Making Contact* uses observational, artistic and playful techniques (see Lammer, 2007: 98) to evoke the sensorial and experiential dimensions of interventional radiology.

The multisensoriality of video needs to be understood in relation to the ways in which it is viewed. This has long since been understood in film studies, for instance Marks has described the experience of viewing as embodied in that '[w]e take in many kinds of "extradiegetic" sensory information, information from outside a film's world, when we "watch" a film', inviting the comparison of different viewing contexts (2000: 211–12). If we think of viewing contexts as environments, through a theory of place, we might consider how these are already multisensory environments, evocative of sensory memories and imaginations and which combine different tastes, smells, proximities to others, types of seating, levels of comfort as well as being imbued with values, discourses, perhaps theoretical debate and more. Marks has also argued that 'the audiovisual image necessarily evokes other sense memories' happening 'through intersensory links: sounds may evoke textures; sights may evoke smells (rising steam or smoke evokes smells of fire, incense, or cooking)' (2000: 213) and that as 'a mimetic medium' cinema is 'capable of drawing us into sensory participation with its world' to an extent written language cannot (2000: 214). MacDougall has likewise proposed that the spectator's involvement in film is both psychological and corporal. He suggests that films 'provide us with a series of perceptual clues', creating 'spaces analogous to those we experience in everyday life, as we sample visual and other sensory information' (2005: 25). In both everyday life and as spectators of film we are urged to interpret and combine this information into a 'complete picture', thus, for the spectator there is an almost continuous impetus towards convergence with the objects and bodies on the screen' (2005: 25–6), as well as with the body of the filmmaker in that 'The viewer's response [to film] is ... one of double synchrony with the film subject and the filmmaker' (MacDougall, 1998: 53). These understandings combined with Biella's argument that films offer a 'sense of *virtual intimacy*' and a 'step into a world of increased awareness and compassion' (Biella, 2008) imply that film and video enable ethnographers to create a sense of sensory participation, intimacy and closeness for viewers. However we still need to know more about how viewers feel and sense when they are engaging with sensory ethnography video materials. To explore this further in practice, in an online article Kerstin Leder Mackley and I have included a set of video clips from our research with a participant in her home. There we have explicitly invited viewers to participate in the viewing experience and to reflect on their experiences (Pink and Leder Mackley, 2012). Our use of video in a sensory ethnography methodology in the LEEDR energy research project is also developed further in the *Energy and Digital Living* website, where our approach, research findings, design insights, part of the LEEDR design team's work and a video archive are presented, at www.energyanddigitalliving.com.

Therefore, we might think of the use of video as part of the ways in which the ethnographic place becomes one of sharing with audiences. MacDougall suggests films create '*spaces* analogous to those we experience in everyday life' (2005: 25, my italics). His use of 'space' might be refigured through a concept of place to conceptualise ethnographic documentary making as an intentional and/or serendipitous bringing together of a series of interconnected events involving encounters, objects, emotions, sensations, weather, persons and more, which together constitute place. These are edited/interwoven into a representation, a deliberate rendering of place, itself loaded with ideologies, theory and more. The viewing of the film however becomes another form of place – here through her or his 'sensory participation' (Marks, 2000) with the film and sense of 'virtual intimacy' (Biella, 2008) viewers become entangled corporeally, affectively and intellectually in an ethnographic place. This would engage the viewer's own cultural, biographical and scholarly experience and knowing, enabling her or him to participate in the constitution of a renewed ethnographic place, and to arrive at a particular form of multisensory knowing (see Pink, 2007d).

Thus film/video can be understood as a medium through which the specificity and experience of the ethnographic place-event might be opened out for audience participation. It may offer a sense of intimacy, a route to intercultural understandings and ways of knowing not available as directly through written words.

With the contemporary ubiquity of smartphones, tablets and other mobile screen devices, there are also additional issues to consider relating to the ways in which audiovisual media might generate feelings of intimacy and communicate about sensory experiences. The examples discussed above are concerned mainly with the screening of video through a projector or monitor. These are still widely used technologies for viewing video, which is why the discussion above is important to account for as part of the contemporary context, even if it has certain correspondences with the conventions of the era of analogue media. However, it is now becoming increasingly important for video to be produced and designed not just for conventional screens, but for smartphone and tablet technologies, to account for their sizes, shapes and mobility. The further issues raised by this shift to mobile technologies is, as I have suggested in Chapter 6, not simply their material forms, but the affective and sensory affordances and qualities that are associated with them, through their touch screens, images, video and audio, the very manipulability of the image that they offer. In addition, the sense of intimacy they can be used to generate through the possibilities for digital co-presence, connectivity and participation, mean that these technologies have emerged as being part of complex viewing arrangements, which will impact on how they can be engaged as sensory dissemination technologies.

THE SOUND OF ETHNOGRAPHY

In common with ethnographic writing and video/filmmaking, sound recording allows ethnographers and artists to create permanent edited recordings or compositions that might be disseminated to wide audiences. Scholars and artists working in this area frequently cite the World Soundscapes Project led by Murray Schafer in the 1970s as a key influence in the movement towards both sound ethnography and sound art. This project involved Shafer recording acoustic environments/ecologies in diverse geographical locations. Of particular relevance to discussions here, he often used the method of recording soundwalks (Adams and Bruce, 2008).

Soundscape composition and sensory intimacy

Sound ethnography involves recording as a research practice and composition as a representational practice. The acousmatic music and soundscape composition artist Drever has suggested a series of congruences between ethnography and soundscape composition and proposed that 'soundscape composition practice perhaps can offer ethnographic practice alternative models of cultural poetics: that of the analytical and creative tools for grasping at the sound world'. Going further he suggests 'soundscape composition [could be] ... a pertinent substitute to writing an academic ethnographic report and *vice versa*' (2002: 25). While such direct substitutions across any ethnographic dissemination media are difficult to achieve, as the work discussed below shows, sound composition has unique qualities that can contribute to communicating ethnography sensorially in ways writing cannot.

As an example, Drever discusses Feld's writing and sound art which is informed by (and informs) ethnographic and theoretical scholarship. Feld's practice is guided by the concept of 'acoustemology', which he defines as 'an exploration of sonic sensibilities, specifically of ways in which sound is central to making sense, to knowing, to experiential truth'. Theoretically and acoustemologically he focuses on place and suggests that 'the experience of place potentially can always be grounded in an acoustic dimension' (Feld, 1996: 97). In Chapter 5 I discussed Feld's audio recordings as a sonic elicitation method. His practice extends beyond this to include the production of sound ethnographies.

In an interview with Donald Brenneis (Feld and Brenneis, 2004) Feld has discussed his two earlier LPs – *Music of the Kaluli* (1982) and *Kaluli Weeping and Song* (1985) – that accompanied his monograph *Sound and Sentiment* (1990). The themes of *Music of the Kaluli*, as Feld describes them, are inextricable from central questions in the social sciences: 'the whole first side of the LP was about sociality in sound, acoustic co-presence and interaction – the relationship between the people, the forest, voice and sound' (Feld and Brenneis, 2004: 464); and in this and his later CD, *Voices of the Rainforest* (Feld, 1991), 'the idea was ... to have sound raise the question about the indexicality of voice and place, to provoke you to hear sound as place making'. Comparing the publication of a sound ethnography with written text he proposes that 'when you hear the way birds overlap in the forest and you hear the way voices overlap in the forest, all of a sudden you can grasp something at a sensuous level that is considerably more abstract and difficult to convey in a written ethnography' (Feld and Brenneis, 2004: 465).

The idea that sound recordings can represent a sense of intimacy is also suggested by Feld's work. He describes how his *Voices of the Rainforest* (1991) CD is 'a 30-minute soundscape of 24 hours of sounds, a day in the forest with Kaluli people' which was edited using a 'compositional technique ... layering and overlapping different recordings from the 24-hour cycle' (Feld and Brenneis, 2004: 465). He reflects on how when recording, 'the tape recorder was always something I wore. I just went where people went. And the editing involved techniques that heightened and marked that sense of intimacy and spontaneity and contact between recorder and recorded, between listener and sounds' (Feld and Brenneis, 2004: 465). Feld's concern with bringing this sense of intimacy to the forefront of the edited composition is also emphasised when he suggests that 'The recording takes you there, into that place, and you can have a very sensuous, affective, feeling relationship with voice and place by listening' (2004: 468). Returning to Biella's (2008) suggestion that the production of a sense of intimacy in ethnographic representation can contribute to a moral project of increasing intercultural awareness, this implies that sound ethnographies might likewise work towards such goals.

If we understand soundscape compositions not simply as ways of representing what 'places' sound like, but as invitations to listen in particular embodied ways, we can better understand what might be learnt from listening to what Feld calls the 'sonic everyday' of others. Discussing his later work *Rainforest Soundwalks* (2001a) he relates: 'It is through and on the attentive listening to this world that Bosavi people built their songs and musical lives' (Palombini, n.d.). Ethnographic soundscape representations might thus be designed to offer listeners a route through which to hear as others might. Yet listeners might also need guidance on how to hear. Indeed, Feld's work is not intended solely for academic audiences (see Palombini, n.d.), but is situated as scholarship through his written work (e.g. Feld, 1996) which theorises experience, intimacy and sound as place-making practice.

Soundscape composition as ethnographic representation is a complex process and requires specialist skills and sensitivities. Some of these are technical, while others relate to ethnographic experience. Paul Moore highlights some of the challenges through a consideration of his research about different (protestant and catholic) soundscapes in Northern Ireland. Some issues are unique to specific projects, thus to understand the challenges Moore discusses requires some knowledge of sound in the context of Northern Irish politics. He describes how 'the historical representations of the loyalist and nationalist communities resonate with opposing sounds and patterns' (2003: 268). Comparing protestant and catholic linguistic sounds, drumming and religious services he suggests these 'conflicting sectarian sounds ... dominate the aural soundscape in Northern Ireland'. Yet, simultaneously Moore points out that both groups share a soundscape of 'violence' which includes gunfire, bombings, riots, sirens and the silence of funerals (2003: 274). He analyses these sounds as 'purveyors and indicators of cultural memory', which are: 'echoes of the sacred, passed without words from generation to generation, underpinning the notion that for communities united under a perceived threat, hearing as well as seeing is believing' (2003: 274).

How might this auditory knowledge be represented to an audience unfamiliar with such ways of experiencing and knowing? Moore discusses the complexities of how an artificial soundscape composed from recorded sound might be produced for this purpose. He outlines how achieving this would require a self-conscious and reflexive composer who 'constantly interrogates the soundscape composition'. This would involve addressing a set of issues, to include: ensuring that visual props do not distract attention from sound in installations; attending to the 'active listening position' of soundscape listeners; questions of perspective; the listeners' 'point of listening' and understanding; and the potential cacophony of an edited soundscape that might lead it to become 'a meaningless jumble of indecipherable noise' (2003: 274–6). These are real concerns, which as Moore presents them, represent the beginnings of a checklist for ethnographers working in this area. More generally however they indicate that there would be a need for the education of both composers and listeners to facilitate means of communicating about sonic knowing that can accommodate both scholarly and experiential understandings.

Audio in mixed media sensory ethnography

Recent uses of sound in ethnographic representation include Dawn Lyon and Les Back's inclusion of sound recordings in their online essay (Lyon and Back, 2012). I discussed their work in Chapter 5 and above I have noted their effective use of photography to invoke the work of fishmongering. Some of their images are also accompanied by audio recordings made at the market, enabling the reader/viewer/listener to engage with that very sonic sensoriality of place that would otherwise be difficult to describe verbally. Back has also used background sound in his e-book *Academic Diary* (www.academic-diary.co.uk/), and there are an increasing number of online dissemination projects which include innovative uses of audio. I have also discussed Andrew Irving's work in Chapter 6. His projects are also disseminated online, through video recordings, which are accompanied by the sound recordings of his participants speaking about their interior thoughts (http://blog.wennergren.org/2013/06/interview-dr-andrew-irving-new-york-stories/). Here we are invited to view and listen, the spoken narratives bringing to the fore what we cannot see or know when we see a person walking down the street. As Irving puts it, 'the person remains a social being and is required to act accordingly but their inner dialogues and lifeworlds are not necessarily made apparent to the wider world', and he reminds us that such inner thoughts are not usually the subject matter of anthropological research.

Sound is inevitable in ethnography and even silences are laden with meanings. Making sounds and silences explicit in the representation of ethnographic places and experiences can be an evocative route to multisensory ways of knowing. However, this also requires some degree of educating listeners in how to hear and as such how to engage in the aural ways of knowing of others, and of making embodied aural knowing meaningful in relation to scholarly understandings.

OLFACTION, ART AND POTENTIAL LESSONS FOR ETHNOGRAPHERS

It is perhaps more difficult to imagine how an ethnographer might represent olfactory experiences, let alone reproduce these. Writing in the catalogue for an exhibition entitled *Sensorium* Bill Arning comments that 'To attempt to include smell-based work in a catalogue like this is to experience the inadequacy of both reproductive media and language', noting how 'In distributed smell technologies, the olfactory equivalent of a photographically illustrated text is barely on the horizon today' (Arning, 2006: 98). Yet some olfactory artists have attempted to 'put smell to paper'. While I was writing the first edition of *Doing Sensory Ethnography* a colleague forwarded to me a postcard announcing an event entitled *If There Ever Was: an exhibition of extinct and impossible smells* at the Reg Vardy Gallery (University of Sunderland, UK, 2008). As I handled the textured card I noticed a faint and unfamiliar smell; holding it closer to inhale confirmed that the card was scented and drew my attention to its written text which ended with the words 'This is what the sun smells like'. The back of the card acknowledged the creator of the odour (Geza Schön, International Flavours and Fragrances). The smell of the card was crucial in determining my relationship to its materiality, my experience of it, and its sensory agency as a reminder about the exhibition, as at odd moments I was drawn to it as I caught a whiff of its smell while writing at my desk.

Olfactory experience and cinema

The use of scents in arts and documentary practice is not new (and as I noted in Chapter 1 has some parallels in business and marketing contexts). For instance, Marks describes how since the early twentieth century filmmakers have used smell to create part of a 'cinematic experience'. This has included burning incense during film screenings, scratch and sniff cards coordinated to correspond to the film narrative, the diffusion of smells into rooms during films, and following film screenings with 'recreations of the meals in the films at local restaurants' (see Marks, 2000: 212 for details). However, Marks points out that while 'Such extradiegetic sense experience amplifies the multisensory appeal of a movie' there are also limits and possible problems associated with such practices. Indeed, one of the examples she cites led to a 'public panic'. This, she suggests, is because 'Associations with actual smells are so haphazard and individual that even the commonest odors incite reactions from relaxation to arousal, disgust or horror' (2000: 212; and see Hinton et al., 2006). While Marks' comments imply that there might be little certainty in how one might use scent to communicate with others and in particular across cultures these characteristics are also part of its appeal. Indeed, Drobnick and Fisher suggest that in a contemporary context artists who are 'seeking to redefine aesthetic experience' tend to be attracted to 'the distinctive qualities of scent – such as its ephemerality, evocativeness, intimacy, variability, intensity' (2008: 350).

Scent and art: lessons from olfactory arts practice

The olfactory artist Sissel Tolaas researches and then recreates smells from a variety of lived contexts. Ceri Hand's description of a project Tolaas undertook in Liverpool, UK, outlines how: 'For her project OUSIDEIN Tolaas walked with Liverpudlians from the north, west, south and east of the city. Together they paced the city, using high-end technology to collect smells from streets and neighbourhoods and recording perceptions and feelings in response to their sense of smell' (Hand, 2007: 41). Tolaas then recreates these scents chemically in her laboratory for public exhibition in gallery spaces. This short description of Tolaas' practices already begins to strike resonance with some of the sensory ethnography practices discussed in earlier chapters. Her practice of pacing the city with local people to 'collect smells' and record 'perceptions and feelings' corresponds with the ethnographic methods involving 'walking with' research participants discussed in Chapter 5. How, and what, then might smells communicate to audiences in gallery contexts? Arning, noting the impossibility of communicating about smell verbally, suggests that the audience for Tolaas' work is limited because 'scents cannot be conveyed beyond the first person sniffer'. He identifies a further limitation in that 'many exhibition visitors' are unwilling 'to put their noses on the line and sniff'. Smell can signify an intense form of intimacy with a person or object. Arning suggests that some 'refuse Tolaas's open invitation to conceptually dense olfactory experiences, as if to accept would forever compromise their personal security' (2006: 98), thus indicating indeed that opening oneself up to the intimacy of smell in a gallery context might invite a challenging way of knowing.

Our experiences of other people and places, including the home, inevitably involve smell. While domestic odours often escape the control of human agents, the intentional addition of scents, and production and concealment of smells (e.g. of cooking, cleaning and more) is equally important to the constitution of place. My research about domestic life demonstrated how people engage in everyday practices aimed at creating specific olfactory environments in their homes, which are attached to identities, moralities and more. These involve considerations about the relationship between 'natural' outdoor smells, domestic cleaning or other products, cooking smells, and olfactory 'decoration' through the use of, for example, scented oils or candles (e.g. Pink, 2004). In a review of an olfactory exhibition Drobnick and Fisher discuss the work of artist Oswaldo Maciá which represents domestic spaces vis à vis their odours. Maciá's installation *1 Woodchurch Road, London NW6 3PL*, draws on a building in which the artist once lived along with other people of diverse generations, nationalities and household compositions. The installation, consisting of five garbage cans, is described as presenting 'a selection of smells that Maciá found most typical of the building's occupants' which were 'naftalin (mothballs), olive oil, Listerine, eucalyptus, and baby powder' (Drobnick and Fisher, 2008: 350). Visitors to the exhibition lifted the lids of the garbage cans to inhale their scents. Drobnick and Fisher suggest that one of the effects of this is that 'Each sniff of the contents of the containers inspires reflection upon how a sense of community can develop from a heterogeneous mix of identities' (2008: 350–2). While I imagine the reflections actually inspired amongst diverse sniffers of the scents would vary, the connection that Drobnick and Fisher make between scents and identities is significant. These insights also have implications for academic sensory ethnography. For instance, although the sensory home is much more than its odours (see also Pink, 2004) Maciá's discussion invites us to consider how olfactory installations might be mobilised to communicate about the relationship between on the one hand the materiality and multisensoriality of domestic (and other) practices and environments and on the other the identities and moralities that are lived and constituted through these.

Olfaction and text: the scented book

In existing practice scents are not only 'exhibited' but disseminated as part of printed texts. This might be hard to achieve in the context of academic publishing, however one example demonstrates some of the possibilities of such experimentation. Robert Blackson's (2008) *If There Ever Was: a book of extinct and impossible smells* was published in connection with *If There Ever Was: an exhibition of extinct and impossible smells* (also 2008). The book provides an interesting example of the intimacies, empathies and challenges scents might invite. The scents commissioned for this exhibition were 'inspired by absence'. They represent historical 'stories' referring to things that in most cases no longer exist in material forms. Blackson describes each scent as 'a harmonious composition blending multiple notes and, like a story, have a beginning, middle and end' (Blackson, 2008: 6). In the book each scent, which is represented on a piece of card that the reader must rub to release the smell, is guided by one of Blackson's written narratives printed on the facing page. 'These words' he writes, 'are not intended to direct interpretation, but to set a stage for the scent to fill' (2008: 6–7). The book provides an example of how text and scent together offer readers/smellers seductive resources through which to create routes into empathetic imaginaries about the material, sensorial and affective elements of other people's emplacement. These are not all comforting experiences, for instance Steven Pearce's scent represents the last meal of a man who was executed in the United States. Here in particular the written text frames the scent through a story that potentially creates sympathy between the reader and the representation of the executed man: Blackson tells how his conviction would probably have been overturned had evidence that became available later been forthcoming earlier. The prospect of smelling this meal invites the reader to imagine a level of intimacy and empathy that goes beyond the sympathetic engagement invoked through the written text. This makes it a difficult level of engagement since it offers the reader an olfactory route into imagining *his* emplacement and the material and affective aspects of this. Other scents represent collective experiences, for example two scents by Christophe Laudamiel are inspired by 'the vibration of Hiroshima's atomic blast' (Blackson, 2008: 16) and air of the middle ages (2008: 32), and Sissel Tolaas created what is described as 'the smell of communism' characterised as 'the stale air of imposed uniformity' (Blackson, 2008: 36). Rather differently, another text describes how in East Berlin the Stasi took samples of suspects' body odour on pieces of fabric, through the story of a young woman who was tried and cautioned by the Stasi (Blackson, 2008: 20). Whether or not the accompanying scent by Maki Udea included on the page facing the narrative reproduces the sweat of this particular woman, the sense of it being a personal odour produced under particular circumstances is what makes it compelling.

If There Ever Was affords a series of insights that are useful for considering the roles scent might play in sensory ethnography representation, that are broadly coherent with the themes of intimacy, place and the text/sense relationship explored in this chapter. The idea of sharing a scent that was experienced by other individuals or collectivities, historically or biographically, can be highly evocative of feelings of empathy and intimacy. Such scents do not necessarily allow us to share *the same* scents as others – positioned historically, socially or culturally differently to us. Moreover, the multisensoriality of the specific environments in which individual users of the book experience the scents means their sensing always takes 'place' in a new environment. Indeed, whether or not the chemically reproduced smells are identical to those experienced by others historically is less important than the point that they offer us sensory routes into imagining other people's material and emotional emplacement. Thus using scent to create such routes, connections, intimacies and empathies offers sensory ethnographers a way to invite their audiences to sense the places occupied by others. As Blackson notes, 'To know something by its scent alone, as a pure "olfactory image" is a rare event' (2008: 7), and indeed for those who read the texts in his volume before rubbing and smelling the scents on their opposite pages, the olfactory experience is already set in relation to a series of other biographical and cultural frames that contribute to the sense that is made from it. Thus the written narratives play an important role in framing olfactory arts practice and making it accessible to its audience. Such combinations would be equally important in ethnographic representations that work with scent.

Olfactory reproduction on cards and in books, as exhibition installations, through emplaced practices, and more, hold exciting potential for sensory ethnography representation. Scents alone could not contribute to scholarly debates or make theoretical arguments. However, their introduction into ethnographic representations could produce forms of intimacy and senses of place that draw audiences into new relationships to ethnographers and research participants.

THE PARTICIPATING AUDIENCE: WALKING ETHNOGRAPHIC REPRESENTATION

Several experimental approaches that combine ethnography and performance – including theatre anthropology (Hastrup, 1998; and see also Barba, 1995), ethnomimesis (O'Neill, 2008) and the film genre of ethno-fiction (originating in the work of the anthropological filmmaker Jean Rouch) – have been developed. More recently, and with specific attention to the senses there has been a growing interest in walking as a way of communicating about academic work. Such approaches include elements of documentary and performance, often through video and audio recordings. In earlier chapters I discussed the research methods of walking with others and walking with video. Building on these approaches and practices the idea of walking as ethnographic representation offers a potential route to communicating about the emplaced knowing of ethnographers and of research participants, using technologies designed to engage audiences through the senses.

The soundwalk method is well established in arts practice and increasingly so in ethnographic practice. A number of examples of soundwalks and their documentation can be found online. Above I have discussed Feld's audio recorded *Rainforest Soundwalks* (2001a) as a method of representing other people's emplacement through sound. Another approach to the soundwalk invites audiences to engage not only by listening but also by simultaneously walking themselves. This method, which is becoming increasingly established in arts practice, usually involves the participant wearing headphones through which she or he listens to and is guided by an audio narrative while walking predetermined routes designed by the artist. The work of the soundwalk artist Janet Cardiff, which follows this principle, is generating significant interest amongst scholars interested in the senses (e.g. Witmore, 2004; Butler, 2006; Rawes, 2008). The multisensoriality of the experience of Cardiff's work has been characterised by Marjory Jacobson as follows:

> Instead of hearing the standard audioguide tape, the listener is immediately plunged into a discordant world where reality, reverie, and fiction coexist. Before long, 'Janet's' memories seem implanted into our consciousness. Our proprioceptive sense heightened, we're thinking, touching, and smelling in unison with our guide. (2006: 58)

Jacobson goes on to suggest that this feeling of unison can be disturbing in that 'As the synaesthetic aura becomes unbearably intense, the very notion of the self is called into question' (2006: 58). While the experiences Jacobson describes do not necessarily represent *the* universal experience of Cardiff's work, they resonate with ideas discussed earlier in this book: that we might come to share other people's emplacement as a route to understanding how they experience their worlds; and that as one engages in new emplaced forms of knowing, the self is transformed. Thus the soundwalk presents a medium and practice that might offer ethnographic audiences routes to understanding the emplacement of both researcher and research participants.

Scholars/practitioners have already begun to make these connections. For example, Toby Butler has suggested that 'experiments in combining walking, sound, memory and artistic practice could be useful tools for the geographer to research, apply and present site-specific cultural geography' (2006: 890). His work suggests that the soundwalk might be connected to both the sensoriality and sociality of place in that: walks in which participants listen to the artist's guiding narrative through headphones can be understood as multisensorial experiences of place (with all the implications for invoking memories and imagination this holds); and soundwalks may create relationships between their participants and other elements of the environment – rather than isolating them through the dominance of the headphone audio track (2006: 298). Butler's oral history research involved recording 'experiences and memories of people at riverside locations' along the River Thames in London (2006: 901). From these materials he produced 'a carefully constructed three mile walk with 12 different sound points along the route, containing a total of an hour of memories from 14 people' (2006: 903). While soundwalks require their users to actually participate through walking, the presence of the ethnographer her- or himself is represented through the audio recording, which can be disseminated digitally. In 2006 Butler reported that during a five-month period his soundwalk had been downloaded digitally (from the website www.memoryscape.org.uk/) or purchased on CD by 600 people and at least 350 had participated in the walks (2006: 906). Butler's comments concerning how people experienced these walks are especially pertinent:

> The recordings slowed walkers down, gave people time to consider their surroundings and experience other people's memories in a more sensitised way. Hearing authentic voices from other people also seemed to make people empathise towards the community that they listened to, despite their prior assumptions or even antipathy towards, say, houseboat dwellers or West London bungalow owners. (Butler, 2006: 904)

As I suggested above, alternative forms of representation might engender a sense of intimacy and a route to other people's experiences. Butler's work, along with his emphasis on the multisensoriality and sociality implied by the soundwalk, continues this theme.

In Chapter 6 I introduced the idea of walking with video (see also Pink, 2007d), already an established technique in ethnographic film and visual ethnography practice. The associations between video, walking and place and their capacity to invoke imaginations and memories that make this technique so effective in visual ethnography research are also relevant to other emergent uses of walking with video which draw from arts practice. Christopher Witmore develops similar themes to explore the relationship between art and archaeology. Witmore is particularly concerned with place (a central concept in archaeology) and with sensory embodied experience (2004: 59). In seeking ways to communicate about place that go beyond 'documentation and inscription' (2004: 59–60) he proposes a process of 'mediation'. This 'mode of engagement' that goes beyond scholarly narrative (2004: 60) would permit ethnographers to, as Witmore puts it, 'attain richer and fuller translations of bodily experience and materiality that are located, multi-textured, reflexive, sensory and polysemous' (2004: 60).

Witmore also draws on Janet Cardiff's practice, which, like Jacobson (2006) he suggests 'explores sensory evocation by creating moments of intimacy with the participant' (2004: 61). While Butler's (2006) developments built on Cardiff's audio recorded soundwalk practice, Witmore draws on her video walks – whereby participants walk while viewing a pre-recorded walk on the screen of a digital video camera and listening with headphones. Witmore points out how 'Cardiff asks participants to synchronize their movements through the same locale with her prerecorded journey by maintaining the same pace' (2004: 61). Thus the participant's body becomes engaged in the work of evoking Cardiff's experience. The potential of this practice for bringing audiences closer to elements of the emplacement of ethnographers and research participants is clear. Indeed, Witmore suggests that thus 'Throughout the walk the body of the participant (the listener-viewer) and the artist occupy the same space and perform the same movements' (2004: 61). For Witmore such 'peripatetic video infuses aural and visual mediation into the corporeal activities of movement and interaction' (2004: 62). He proposes that when applied to the task of communicating about experience in archaeology 'this form of media overlay constitutes a more fulfilling means of interposing the lived experience of the archaeologist with that of the participant' (2004: 63–4). Through a discussion of a series of experiments with peripatetic video in archaeological field sites Witmore's conclusions include two points that resonate strongly with the themes identified at the beginning of this chapter. He suggests that 'this form of mediation brings us to new levels of intimacy between archaeologists and their audience' and that 'disparities between different individuals' negotiations and interpretations of place are set in high relief when they themselves surrender to the experience of another' (2004: 68). Walking with 'peripatetic video' cannot reproduce exactly the past emplacement of others. Nevertheless, Witmore's discussion indicates how it might enable users to feel in some ways *similarly* emplaced and evoke a sense of another's 'being there'.

While the walks discussed above rely on pre-produced audio/visual digital media, other recent arts practice has engaged audiences/participants in different activities. In March 2008 as part of ROAM, a walking arts event developed by Loughborough University, UK, I participated in one of the artist Tim Brennan's walks. Brennan describes his walks as 'manoeuvres' that 'exist in a region between traditions of performance art, the historical tour, loco-descriptive poetry, pilgrimage, expanded notions of sculpture, curating and plain old pedestrianism' (www.arts.lboro.ac.uk/radar/project/roam_a_weekend_of_walking_spring_2008/tim_brennan/).The walk was based on careful planning and research. It was described as follows:

> Tim Brennan's new walk for Loughborough retraces the route taken by the town's Luddites on an infamous evening in June 1816. The route drops into a number of the pubs in which the Luddites drank, shoring up their nerve prior to their notorious night of machine wrecking.
>
> Using a broad range of quotations, which revisit or undermine historical facts, Tim Brennan's guided walks encourage new takes on historical events. (ROAM programme, Loughborough University, 2008, online at www.arts.lboro.ac.uk/radar/project/roam_a_weekend_of_walking_spring_2008/tim_brennan/)

Describing the process by which he creates the walks Brennan told me:

> There are two main aspects to each manoeuvre coming into being: the route and the quotations. I begin by walking around the area to which I have been invited and thinking through fields of cultural interest. ... Through this 'scouting' I try and focus down on what it is that I want to hold as a primary object of study (so from the outset the manoeuvre is never encyclopaedic or random). (Brennan, personal communication, 2008)

In Loughborough, he 'discovered that the Luddites went on their own journey (a pub crawl/drinking spree) before raiding the mill and developed a spatialised/geographic relationship through a walking practice'. Once Brennan has determined a rough annotated route (which covers different types of pathways and terrains) he then works through an 'iterative method', in his words:

> I go back and forth between route planning and sourcing texts. I treat this stage as if the work (the montage of quotes and sites) was a concrete poem. This leads to an editing of quotes which end up pasted into a journal/study book which is used on the walk. Sometimes quotes are placed in envelopes to be distributed or exist as a published guidebook. (Brennan, personal communication, 2008)

Brennan's manoeuvres offer an example of how an experiential performance-based way of making, and knowing, a place might be constituted and communicated through a form of audience engagement. During the walk I participated in, Brennan's readings were largely historical as his route through Loughborough focused, amongst other things, on the town's Luddite history. I shared the Luddite's route through the town, traversed different terrains under foot, listened to Brennan's readings, gazed on sculptures, houses, etc. The performance included a stop at a Loughborough pub where we bought drinks and socialised. In this sense the engagements that this walk offered were multisensory and multimedia. They included sensing the town underfoot, through the rainy weather, through the tastes of the drinks in the pub, listening to and interacting with the readings, making a wish as I touched the toe of the statue in the marketplace, having been told by a fellow participant that this was a local practice. It also involved different sorts of engagement, from the intellectual task of thinking about the issues and debates that were raised by the readings and articulating questions about these verbally, to picking my way through the rubble surrounding a site where buildings had recently been demolished. The walk communicated effectively because it involved a process of learning through participation, and shared experience, thus offering participants an embodied way of knowing that went beyond what we were told verbally. It inspired me to think about how a multimedia, multisensorial academic presentation might be created.

Ethnographers now recognise the significance of walking as a practice of everyday life (e.g. Ingold and Lee-Vergunst, 2008) and walking with others as a research method (see Chapter 4). This, combined with the developments in scholarly and arts practice discussed above in this section, suggests that walking offers a potentially rich medium for sensory ethnographic representation. Ethnographic filmmakers have already, for many years, represented their own walks with others (including walking with processions) in documentary film (see Pink, 2007d, for a discussion of this). The experienced walk of course only happens once. Therefore, walking as ethnographic representation would have a similar temporality to that of a performed conference paper, but it would differ in that it would entail a more participatory performance. If it was to be written up then it would inevitably be flattened. If it were filmed then it would create a new type of academic film genre which would offer its audience new possibilities for imagining (as outlined above with reference to ethnographic filmmaking). Scholarly discussions of walking in common have established the idea of walking as a form of place-making (e.g. de Certeau, 1984; Gray, 2003; Lee and Ingold, 2006). Walking as sensory ethnography representation can be understood in the same way. It offers walkers an opportunity to experience place in ways that are informed by the experiences of ethnographers and participants in their research. It might include walking over different terrains, consuming food or drink, sound- and smellscapes, visual displays, sculptures, verbal lectures, distributing leaflets – a whole range of possible strategies that might be developed as ways of encouraging participants to engage with different ways of knowing about and feeling a sense of intimacy with the ethnographers' and research participants' experience of place. However, such a representation would simultaneously invite walkers to create their own places in relation to these representations. It is thus emblematic of the idea of a 'sensory ethnographic place' – that is constituted through the practices of, and occupied by, the consumers of the ethnography.

THINKING ABOUT SENSORY AUDIENCES

At the beginning of this chapter I highlighted the inevitable falsity of separating out the senses in ethnographic representation. Yet as in the discussion above, the practices of representation developing in arts and ethnographic practice – at least amongst that reported on in Europe and the United States – follow the classifications set out by a modern western five-sense sensorium. They moreover often focus on one sensory modality as a route to knowing – as in, for example, the *sound*walk or *olfactory* art. The use of these categories is not surprising given that these works are largely developed for and presented in modern western cultures. A cross-cultural tour to review the sensory strategies and categories used in other arts cultures would surely reveal different practices and categories. Nevertheless, the existing practices of, for instance, soundscape composition (e.g. Drever, 2002; Feld and Brenneis, 2004), olfactory art works (e.g. Blackson, 2008; Drobnick and Fisher, 2008), not to mention audiovisual art, immediately invite at the least a qualification through the prism of multisensoriality, and at the most a critique.

Most scholars who practise or write about sensory representation are aware that no one sense can truly be isolated from others. Moreover, often their practice is directed at the evocation of fuller embodied multisensory experience through a focus on one sensory modality.

How then might we understand audience encounters with these sensory representations? How might the audiences of a sensory ethnography 'make sense' of soundwalks or -scapes, olfactory installations, audiovisual performances and more? Or, to put it another way, how are understandings of ethnographic representations bound up with human perception, the precise nature of our engagements and the power relations through which audiences are situated? In Chapter 2 I introduced a series of principles for a sensory ethnography through a focus on perception, place, knowing, memory and imagination. These ideas have informed my discussions of sensory ethnographic practice throughout this book and are equally relevant to an understanding of ethnographic representation. Thus, audience engagements with representations are, whether they are with an olfactory installations or a soundwalk, always multisensorial. For instance, olfactory installations or scratch and sniff books are not experienced simply through the nose. The smells that are released as audiences engage with the material guardians of such scents become, and are perceived as, part of a total environment, through sensing bodies. Indeed, a scratch and sniff book already implies the tactile experience of contact with the page and the visual experience of reading its pages. In such contexts scents might be seen as the manufactured 'drivers' in the experience of a representation, in as far as they stand for the intentionality of the ethnographer/artist. However, a scent in isolation is neither the complete nor direct medium of communication, nor is it registered directly on the perceiving body as such. Likewise, our experiences of viewing films are not simply audiovisual and when we eat we do not simply taste, but engage with textures, visual impressions and smells. These are nevertheless the categories through which the experience is presented by the ethnographer/artist. They can thus be understood as categories and routes through which embodied ways of knowing are created.

Thus we might understand the potential for ethnographic representation to harness existing culturally specific sensory categories as contexts through which to produce meanings, imaginaries and memories. In doing so, as I have outlined above, there are a good number of techniques through which ethnographers might go about inviting audiences to engage in the empathies, intimacies, self-reflexivity and intellectual/scholarly engagements that we would hope could bring them closer to imagining and comprehending the lives of others. We cannot know what audiences themselves will come to know through their encounters with representations. Nevertheless, a consideration of audience practices should also involve accounting for the memories, knowing, theoretical commitments and more that audiences bring to any ethnographic representation.

Summing up

Ethnographic representation is a complex craft. It involves the creation of media through which the ethnographer seeks to lend audiences a sense of knowing as she or he and others have. It is moreover a strategic practice – the ethnographer's task is not simply to *represent*, but to convince. She or he seeks to invite empathetic engagements and in doing so to invoke a sense of intimacy and sympathy in the viewer/reader/user. This task involves not only engaging audiences in ways that enable their sense of knowing, in some embodied way, about what it was like to be with – or even to be – the person(s) who participated in the research. It also involves a theoretical narrative through which this knowing informs a scholarly knowledge and that convinces an audience through an established form or method of intellectual argumentation.

A sensory ethnography invites new forms of ethnographic knowing and routes into other people's experiences. It provides us with ways of responding to research questions that involve focusing on forms of intimacy, sociality and emplacement which ethnographers who are not sensitive to the multisensoriality of our experiences and environments would not engage with. The results are inspiring new layers of knowing, which when interrogated theoretically can challenge, contribute to and shift understandings conventional to written scholarship. Yet our exposure to and engagement with the multisensoriality of the places we encounter, share and make as ethnographers simultaneously complicate our task. It leads us to doubt the adequacy of the existing methods and genres of ethnographic representation for the task of communicating about these ways of knowing. As the examples and arguments discussed in this chapter demonstrate, this urge to seek forms of representation that can go beyond ethnographic writing has produced a series of recent innovations (as well as the established work of ethnographic filmmakers such as David MacDougall and sound artists such as Steven Feld). These doubts and the explorations and innovations they are leading to are of themselves an outcome of the 'sensory turn' in the social sciences and humanities. Accompanied by a strong interest in the senses amongst contemporary artists, this mix of more established and emergent ethnographic genres and styles and sensory arts practice offers ethnographers a series of inspiring models.

Recommended further reading

- Barnes, A. (2013) 'Geo/graphic design: the liminal space of the page', *The Geographical Review*, 103(2): 164–76.
- Butler, T. (n.d.) *Memoryscape audiowalks: voices from the hidden history of the Thames.* Available online: www.memoryscape.org.uk/ (accessed 12 May 2008).
- Butler, T. (2006) 'A walk of art: the potential of the sound walk as practice in cultural geography', *Social and Cultural Geography*, 7(6): 889–908.
- Lyon, D. and L. Back (2012) 'Fishmongers in a global economy: craft and social relations on a London market', *Sociological Research Online*, 17(2): 23. Available online: www.socresonline.org.uk/17/2/23.html.

AFTERWORD

Imagining sensory futures

Ethnography, design and future studies

To close this second edition of *Doing Sensory Ethnography* I make a set of observations relating to the potential and role of sensory ethnography as a field of research practice in an emergent context. In doing so I pull together some of the insights that have emerged from the preceding chapters. As I have stressed throughout this book in both my arguments and through the examples I have used, sensory ethnography does not belong to any scholar or any discipline, but is always redeveloped and enacted in its use. There seem to me to be some pointers to where it might develop in the next years and here I acknowledge these as possible ways forward. There will no doubt, along with the ongoing improvisation in scholarship practice and the emergence of new issues and technologies, be other future shifts. Some of these will follow on from the kinds of improvisations in research and technology I have already discussed in the preceding chapters, but others will be unexpected and will surprise us.

SENSORY ETHNOGRAPHY AND FUTURE-ORIENTED RESEARCH

There is increasingly an urge for scholars and researchers involved in the scholarly disciplines I have discussed in this book to become involved in research that seeks to intervene in the world, to make change and to have 'impact'. Such approaches are oriented towards the future, and need in this sense to consider how a sensory approach can enable us to understand this unknown and uncertain domain. In more practical terms in this context there has been an emergent development in the relationship between sensory scholarship and applied research practice, which I have highlighted in Chapter 1 of this book. Also, in a context where approaches and methods from design practice and scholarship are increasingly integral to the ways in which researchers from across disciplines seek to make interventions in the world, the relationship between sensory research and design practice is likewise growing with the emergence of design anthropology. These growing connections between sensory research and impact, intervention and design, traverse the fields for which I have discussed the emergence of sensory ethnography practice, albeit in different ways – for example, in human geography and anthropology there has been analysis of how futures are imagined in human computer interaction (HCI) fields (e.g. Dourish and Bell, 2011; Kinsley, 2011), and the development of design anthropology, and its attention to sensory experience connects with the idea of a sensory ethnography (e.g. Gunn and Donovan, 2012). There is also an emerging relationship between sociology and design, at its most interesting edge, as developed in the work of Mike Michael on an 'idiotic methodology' (Michael, 2012). Design practice can be involved in the processes through which sensory understandings are brought to bear in interventions towards change – what we might call future-making processes – for instance, in the ways in which climate change and sustainability are being addressed through research and design around activities such as everyday showering (e.g. Kuijer et al., 2013; Pink et al., 2013; Pink and Leder Mackley, forthcoming). The connections between sensory ethnography and these contexts are starting to be made in some areas, especially as earlier and more recent sensory approaches to design (Malnar and Vodvarka, 2004; Pink et al., 2013; Pink, 2014) are increasingly established.

The trend towards research which is increasingly seeking to make an impact in the world though the making of interventions is also connecting these fields, in anthropology, geography and sociology, theoretically, methodologically and empirically, increasingly to the study of the future. In common with this move, design and planning research has always engaged with the future, in ways that have been less problematised than they are in the social science literatures. Yet this creates a meeting point where academic and applied ethnographic scholarship and design research meet. This encounter has been increasingly central to my own work for the last five years, as the emphasis has moved from the development of an applied sensory–visual ethnography to what I have recently called a digital–visual–sensory-design ethnography approach (Pink, 2014).

ETHNOGRAPHIC SENSIBILITY AND MORAL RESPONSIBILITY

What role then might a sensory ethnography approach have in the making of the future? We might begin to see sensory ethnography as an approach that takes seriously what scholars from across the disciplines in which it is used, refer to as our moral responsibility to engage with the future. For example, writing of the sociology of the future Barbara Adam and Chris Groves argue that we have a responsibility to attend to this issue and

> to understand processes and events in the wider scheme of things, to recognise connections and implications, to appreciate things in their continuity and emergence, to know the future as embodied in things and events, embedded in processes and as carrying forth the deeds of the past. (Adam and Groves, 2007: 14)

This responsibility is emphasised further in a later article by Adam, where taking as a starting point the idea that 'futurity is inescapably endemic to the scientific methodology' she writes that:

> This makes investigators responsible for the effects of their choices and knowledge practices conducted from the standpoint of present futures. Social scientists taking responsibility for their actions from the standpoint of future present, in contrast, accompany their knowledge practices (as well as their complicit silences on certain subject matters) to their (un)known, (un)certain and (in)determinate time-space distantiated impacts and effects. Like their economic and political counterparts, they are required to know themselves to be responsible for that which they cannot know empirically, that is, for the invisible process reality of their making. (Adam, 2011: 594)

Writing of the anthropology of the future Samuel Collins (2008) likewise suggests that the discipline holds some responsibility for the future. In Chapter 3 I discussed the critical moralities that are embedded in research projects and the moral dimension of sensory investigation as creating an involved caring (Porteous, 1990) and humble (Stoller, 1997) appreciation. These both lead to the notion of working towards a better world and again the question of our responsibility as researchers. These arguments and questions might be debated, and I am sure they will be: *Is* it our responsibility as researchers to seek to bring about change in the world, do we even have the right to assume that we ought to be involved in such processes, and is our role as analysts of what is already happening in the world enough?

HOW MIGHT WE THINK OF THE FUTURE?

In the growing interdisciplinary literature about futures, there are different treatments of the ways in which we might engage with the future, for instance as part of the present, as temporally near or far, as imagined, as the possible and in other ways. Given the difficulties in pinning down the future as a single concept or set of understandings, the ways it is encountered in sensory ethnography practice are also likely to be variable. It will both vary in the sense of how and why we are interested in how participants engage with, imagine, project into and work on their future, and in terms of how interdisciplinary collaborators envisage future possibilities, scenarios and issues.

Drawing together some of the key themes that are emerging in the recent waves of literature that address the future, three themes offer us a way to consider the types of questions sensory ethnographers might encounter when engaging with this field. For instance, the sociology of expectations, as discussed by Nik Brown and Mike Michael involves a focus on 'the future as an analytical object, and not simply a neutral temporal space into which objective expectations can be projected' (2003: 4). They, like other scholars in this field (e.g. Galloway, 2010), focus thus away from the future as predicted to see it as a zone of expectations. Geographers have emphasised the anticipatory logics and imaginations that are part of the way the future is thought of and of how forms of governance are applied to it. For example, in the work of Ben Anderson the politics of anticipatory action are discussed in terms of the way that future uncertainties are problematised in liberal democracies (Anderson, 2010). In the design anthropology literature a more ethnographic stance has been taken to understanding the future as imagined through 'ethnographies of the possible' (Halse, 2013). Futures, however they are defined, are nonetheless not simply cerebral imaginings but embodied and sensory ways of perceiving what is not known. Uncertainty, anticipation and expectation are often considered to be feelings, as much as a verbal articulations of what has not yet happened. We imagine not only with our minds, but also with our bodies.

The ethnographic encounter is, as I have argued in Chapter 2, also an encounter with our own imaginations as ethnographers, as we seek to empathise with, remember and understand what it is like to be someone other than oneself. It might equally be an imaginative encounter with the ways in which futures are part of the present.

SENSORY ETHNOGRAPHY FOR FUTURE-MAKING

Since my writing of the first edition of this book there has been an interesting uptake of sensory ethnography approaches and methods in applied research leading to change. Examples of how sensory ethnography approaches are being developed in applied research fields that have typically been more conventional in their methods are now emerging in contemporary literatures. For instance, Sunderland et al. (2012) discuss how they used a sensory ethnography approach in an applied project about social determinants of health (SDOH) to research the relationship between place and health. Here they saw sensory ethnography as 'an innovative methodology for studying the lived experience of place based SDOH' (2012: 1056) in a pilot study carried out in Queensland, Australia, in 2010–11. Using methods including observation, walking and video, they suggest they were able to produce new findings. Particularly interesting for the discussion here however is the ways in which the sensory ethnography approach led them to be able to address change processes and engage with stakeholders in new ways. They propose that '*While we cannot claim that the reported outcomes of the SELB are wholly related to the sensory ethnographic methodology, audience members consistently reported that they had not experienced this level of rich "grass roots" lived experience data previously*' (2012: 1064, original italics). Moreover, one of the applied outcomes of the project involved introducing sensory learning into the school curriculum. They write that

> Teachers in the children's documentaries project have incorporated sensory ethnography and associated documentary making into the Grade 5 curriculum for 2012. Students will undertake sensory observation of their local environments and filming and editing on a weekly basis throughout one term of the school year. (2012: 1064)

These and other changes that came about as outcomes of their work therefore show how sensory ethnography can play a key, and moreover convincing, role in change-making processes.

My own practice as an applied researcher has also continued to develop with attention to sensory ethnography. An example is the LEEDR (Lower Effort Energy Demand Reduction) project discussed earlier in this book. In LEEDR I have worked with a team of what has been up to 17 researchers at its height, from a range of social science, design, engineering and computer science disciplines. In this project, as discussed in some of the examples in earlier chapters (see especially Chapter 8), we had similar experiences to those discussed by Sunderland et al., of using the materials to communicate across our team (Leder Mackley and Pink, 2013) and we also used the findings of our ethnography to develop alternative concepts through which designers might understand what people actually do in their homes when they are using energy (Pink et al., 2013, and see also our *Energy and Digital Living* website at www.energyanddigitalliving.com). Further work in this area is being developed as part of the Design+Ethnography+Futures research programme which I have developed at RMIT University with Yoko Akama. Design+Ethnography+Futures can be followed online at http://d-e-futures.com/.

A design-focused and future-oriented sensory ethnography approach has a key role to play in change processes and in what I would call future-making, precisely because it promises to bring to the fore the tacit, normally unspoken (about) ways of knowing and doing that are part of everyday life. These activities underpin much of what we do and what it means to us; they are often mundane and feel so 'normal' to our participants that they might not even think they are worth mentioning, but they are also part of the way we feel and sense our futures. They are part of the ways we imagine, plan and hope. The everyday ways of knowing, being and experiencing that I have focused on throughout this book are not just related to the past and present, but rather they are part of the ways in which the future is present in our lives as we live them, and as we ongoingly slip over the edge of the present into the immediate future. This applies equally to us as researchers as it does to the people who participate in our projects.

THE FUTURE OF SENSORY ETHNOGRAPHY

It has never been my intention in *Doing Sensory Ethnography* to call on readers to follow any one particular agenda, and even less to follow one that I would set. Rather, my invitation is for readers to use their own practice and the examples discussed in this book to reflect on how attention to the senses might be harnessed in their ethnographic work. This means not only considering their uses for the traditional forms of scholarship in the social science and humanities that lead us to study the world and/with people, but also to consider how engaging with other people's sensory perception, activities and environments might become the basis for understandings that might inspire, direct or be part of processes of intervention and change.

I end this book with the openness that I believe we should always take with us as sensory ethnographers. That is, an openness to an uncertain future, and to contemplating sensorially the uncertainty of what we cannot yet know.

References

Adam, B. (2011) 'Wendell Bell and the sociology of the future: challenges past, present and future', *Futures*, 43: 590–5.

Adam, B. and C. Groves (2007) *Future Matters: action, knowledge, ethics*. Leiden: Brill Academic Publishing.

Adams, M. and N. Bruce (2008) 'Soundwalking as methodology for understanding soundscapes', *Proceedings of the Institute of Acoustics*, 30(2): 552–8.

Amin, A. (2008) 'Collective culture and urban public space', *City*, 12(1): 5–24.

Anderson, B. (2010) 'Preemption, precaution, preparedness: anticipatory action and future geographies', *Progress in Human Geography*, 34(6): 777–98.

Appadurai, A. (1996) *Modernity at Large*. Minneapolis: University of Minnesota Press.

Ardévol, E. (2012) 'Virtual/visual ethnography: methodological crossroads at the intersection of visual and internet research', in S. Pink (ed.) *Advances in Visual Methodology*. London: Sage.

Arning, B. (2006) 'Sissel Tolaas', in C.A. Jones (ed.) *Sensorium: embodied experience, technology, and contemporary art*. London: MIT Press.

Atkinson, P. and A. Coffey (2003) 'Revisiting the relationship between participant observation and interviewing', in J.F. Gubrium and J.A. Holstein (eds) *Postmodern Interviewing*. London: Sage.

Atkinson, P., S. Delamont and W. Housley (2007) *Contours of Culture: Complex Ethnography and the Ethnography of Complexity*. Lanham, MD: Altamira Press.

Back, L. (2009) 'Researching community and its moral projects', *Twenty-First Century Society*, 4(2): 201–14.

Back, L. (2012) 'Live sociology: social research and its futures', *Live Methods*. A Sociological Review Monograph. Oxford: Blackwell. pp. 18–39.

Back, L. and N. Puwar (2012) 'A manifesto for live methods: provocations and capacities', in L. Back and N. Puwar (eds) *Live Methods*. Oxford: Blackwell.

Baldwin, T. (2004) 'Introduction', in M. Merleau-Ponty *The World of Perception*. Oxford: Routledge.

Banks, M. (2001) *Visual Methods in Social Research*. London: Sage.

Barba, E. (1995) *The Paper Canoe: a guide to theatre anthropology*. London: Routledge.

Barnes, A. (2013) 'Geo/graphic design: the liminal space of the page', *The Geographical Review*, 103(2): 164–76.

Basso, K.H. (1996) 'Wisdom sits in places: notes on a Western Apache landscape', in S. Feld and K.H. Basso (eds) *Senses of Place*. Santa Fe, NM: School of American Research Press.

Beaulieu, A. (2010) 'From co-location to co-presence: shifts in the use of ethnography for the study of knowledge', *Social Studies of Science*, 40(3): 453–70.

Bell, D., P. Caplan and W. Jahan Karim (1993) *Gendered Fields: Women, Men and Ethnography*. London: Routledge.

Bendix, R. (2000) 'The pleasures of the ear: toward an ethnography of listening', *Cultural Analysis*, 1: 33–50.

Bendix, R. (2006) 'Introduction: ear to ear, nose to nose, skin to skin – the senses in comparative ethnographic perspective', in R. Bendix and D. Brenneis (Guest Editors) 'The Senses', *Etnofoor: Anthropological Journal*, 18(1): 3–14.

Bendix, R. and Brenneis, D. (eds) (2006) 'The Senses', a guest-edited issue of *Etnofoor: Anthropological Journal*, 18(1).

Berger, J. (1972) *Ways of Seeing: A Book*. London: British Broadcasting Corporation.

Biella, P. (2008) 'Visual anthropology in a time of war', in M. Strong and L. Wilder (eds) *Viewpoints: visual anthropologists at work*. Austin: University of Texas Press.

Blackson, R. (2008) *If There Ever Was: a book of extinct and impossible smells*. Sunderland: Arts Editions North, School of Art and Design, University of Sunderland.

Blasco Ibáñez, V. (1908) *Sangre y Arena*. Valencia, Spain: Prometeo.

Blasco Ibáñez, V. (2005) *Blood and Sand* (trans.). Whitefish, MT: Kessinger Publishing. W. A. Gillespie.

Boellstorf, T., B. Nardi, C. Pearce and T.L. Taylor (2012) *Ethnography and Virtual Worlds: a handbook of method*. Foreword by George Marcus. Princeton: Princeton University Press.

Bonapace, L. (2002) 'Linking product properties to pleasure: the sensorial quality assessment method', in W.S. Green and P.W. Jordan (eds) *Pleasure with Products: beyond usability*. London: Taylor & Francis.

Brown, N. and M. Michael (2003) 'A sociology of expectations: retrospecting prospects and prospecting retrospects', *Technology Analysis & Strategic Management*, 15(1): 3–18.

Buckingham, S. and M. Degen (2012) 'Sensing our way: using yoga as a research method', *The Senses and Society*, 7(3): 329–44.

Bull, M. (2000) *Sounding out the City: personal stereos and the management of everyday life*. Oxford: Berg.

Bull, M. (2001) 'The world according to sound: investigating the world of Walkman users', *New Media and Society*, 3: 179–97.

Bull, M. and L. Back (eds) (2003) *The Auditory Culture Reader*. Oxford: Berg.

Bust, P.D., A.G.F. Gibb and S. Pink (2007) 'Managing construction health and safety: migrant workers and communicating safety messages', *Safety Science*, 46(4): 585–602.

Butler, T. (2006) 'A walk of art: the potential of the sound walk as practice in cultural geography', *Social and Cultural Geography*, 7(6): 889–908.

Casey, E. (1996) 'How to get from space to place in a fairly short stretch of time', in S. Feld and K. Basso (eds) *Senses of Place*. Santa Fe, NM: School of American Research Press, pp. 13–52.

Casey, E. (2001) 'Between geography and philosophy: what does it mean to be in the place-world?' *Annals of the Association of American Geographers*, 91(4): 683–93.

Chandola, T. (2013) 'Listening in to water routes: soundscapes as cultural systems', *International Journal of Cultural Studies*, 16(1): 55–69.

Classen, C. (1993) *Worlds of Sense: exploring the senses in history and across cultures*. London: Routledge.

Classen, C. (1998) *The Colour of Angels: of cosmology, gender and the aesthetic imagination.* London: Routledge.

Classen, C. (ed.) (2005) *The Book of Touch.* Oxford: Berg.

Classen, C., D. Howes and A. Synnott (1994) *Aroma: the cultural history of smell.* London: Routledge.

Clifford, J. (1986) 'Introduction: partial truths', in J. Clifford and G. Marcus (eds) *Writing Culture: the poetics and politics of ethnography.* Berkeley, CA: University of California Press.

Clifford, J. and G. Marcus (1986) *Writing Culture: the poetics and politics of ethnography.* Berkeley: University of California Press.

Coffey, A. (1999) *The Ethnographic Self: fieldwork and the representation of identity.* London: Sage.

Cohen, A. and N. Rapport (1995) 'Introduction: consciousness in anthropology', in A. Cohen and N. Rapport (eds) *Questions of Consciousness.* London: Routledge.

Cohen, E. (2006 [1988]) 'The broken cycle: smell in a Bangkok lane', in J. Drobnik (ed.) *The Smell Culture Reader.* Oxford: Berg.

Coleman, S. and P. Collins (2006) '"Being ... where?": performing fields on shifting grounds', in S. Coleman and P. Collins (eds) *Locating the Field: Space, Place and Context in Anthropology.* Oxford: Berg.

Collier, J. (1967) *Visual Anthropology: photography as a research method.* Albuquerque: University of New Mexico Press.

Collins, S.G. (2008) *All Tomorrow's Cultures: anthropological engagements with the future.* Oxford: Berghahn.

Connerton, P. (1989) *How Societies Remember.* Cambridge: Cambridge University Press.

Couldry, N. (2004) 'Theorising media as practice', *Social Semiotics*, 14(2): 115–32.

Cowan, A. and J. Steward (2007) *The City and the Senses: urban culture since 1500.* Aldershot, UK: Ashgate.

Coy, M. (1989) 'From theory', in M.W. Coy (ed.) *Apprenticeship: from theory to method and back again.* Albany: State University of New York Press, pp. 1–11.

Crapanzano, V. (2004) *Imaginative Horizons.* London: University of Chicago Press.

Crouch, D. and L. Desforges (2003) 'The sensuous in the tourist encounter: introduction: the power of the body in tourist studies', *Tourist Studies*, 3: 5–22.

Csordas, T.J. (1990) 'Embodiment as a paradigm for anthropology', Ethos, 18: 5–47.

Degen, M.M. and G. Rose (2012) 'The sensory experiencing of urban design: the role of walking and perceptual memory', *Urban Studies*, 49(15): 3271–87.

Delamont, S. (2004) 'Ethnography and participant observation', in C. Seale and G. Downey (eds) *Learning Capoeira: lessons in cunning from an Afro-Brazilian art.* Oxford: Oxford University Press.

Desjarlais, R. (2003) *Sensory Biographies: lives and death among Nepal's Yolmo Buddhists.* London: University of California Press.

Desjarlais, R. (2005) 'Movement, stillness: on the sensory world of a shelter for the "homeless mentally ill"', in D. Howes (ed.) *Empire of the Senses: the sensory culture reader.* Oxford: Berg.

Dicks, B., B. Soyinka and A. Coffey (2006) 'Multimodal ethnography', *Qualitative Research*, 6(1): 77–96.

Dourish, P. and G. Bell (2011) *Divining a Digital Future: mess and mythology in ubiquitous computing.* Cambridge, MA: MIT Press.

Downey, G. (2005) *Learning Capoeira: lessons in cunning from an Afro-Brazilian art.* Oxford: Oxford University Press.

Downey, G. (2007) 'Seeing with a "sideways glance": visuomotor "knowing" and the plasticity of perception', in M. Harris (ed.) *Ways of Knowing: new approaches in the anthropology of experience and learning*. Oxford: Berghahn.

Drever, J.L. (2002) 'Soundscape composition: the convergence of ethnography and acousmatic music', *Organised Sound: An International Journal of Music Technology*, 7(1): 21–7.

Drobnick, J. (ed.) (2006) *The Smell Culture Reader*. Oxford: Berg.

Drobnick, J. and J. Fisher (2008) 'Odor limits', *The Senses and Society*, 3(3): 349–58.

Duffy, M. and G. Waitt (2013) 'Home sounds: experiential practices and performativities of hearing and listening', *Social & Cultural Geography*, 14(4): 466–81.

Edensor, T. (2007) 'Sensing the ruin', *The Senses and Society*, 2(2): 217–32.

Edensor, T. (2013) 'Reconnecting with darkness: gloomy landscapes, lightless places', *Social & Cultural Geography*, 14(4): 446–65.

Edgar, I. (2004) 'Imagework in ethnographic research', in S. Pink, L. Kürti and A. Afonso (eds) *Working Images*. London: Routledge.

Edvardsson, D. and A. Street (2007) 'Sense or no-sense: the nurse as embodied ethnographer', *International Journal of Nursing Practice*, 13: 24–32.

Edwards, E. and K. Bhaumik (eds) (2008) *Visual Sense: a cultural reader*. Oxford: Berg.

Fabian, J. (1983) *Time and the Other: how anthropology makes its object*. New York: Columbia University Press.

Fahy, S. (2012) 'Recalling what was unspeakable: hunger in North Korea', in J. Skinner (ed.) *The Interview: an ethnography approach*. Oxford: Bloomsbury.

Feld, S. (1990) *Sound and Sentiment*. Philadelphia: University of Pennsylvania Press.

Feld, S. (1991) *Voices of the Rainforest* (CD). Salem, MA: Rykodisc.

Feld, S. (1996) 'Waterfalls of song: an acoustemology of place resounding in Bosavi, Papua New Guinea', in S. Feld and K. Basso (eds) *Senses of Place*. Santa Fe, NM: School of American Research Press.

Feld, S. (2001a) *Rainforest Soundwalks* (CD). Santa Fe, NM: EarthEar.

Feld, S. (2001b) 'Dialogic editing: interpreting how Kaluli read sound and sentiment', in A. Robben and J.A. Sluka (eds) *Ethnographic Fieldwork*. Oxford: Blackwell Publishing.

Feld, S. (2003) 'A rainforest acoustemology', in M. Bull and L. Back (eds) *The Auditory Culture Reader*. Oxford: Berg.

Feld, S. (2005) 'Places sensed, senses placed: towards a sensuous epistemology of environments', in D. Howes (ed.) *Empire of the Senses: the sensory culture reader*. Oxford: Berg.

Feld, S. and K. Basso (eds) (1996a) *Senses of Place*. Santa Fe, NM: School of American Research Press.

Feld, S. and K. Basso (1996b) 'Senses of place', in S. Feld and K. Basso (eds) *Senses of Place*. Santa Fe, NM: School of American Research Press.

Feld, S. and D. Brenneis (2004) 'Doing anthropology in sound', *American Ethnologist*, 13(4): 461–74.

Finnegan, R. (2002) *Communicating: the multiple modes of human connectedness*. London: Routledge.

Fors, V. (2013) 'Teenagers' multisensory routes for learning in the museum: pedagogical affordances and constraints for dwelling in the museum', *The Senses and Society*, 8(3): 268–89.

Fors, V., A. Backstrom and S. Pink (2013) 'Multisensory emplaced learning: resituating situated learning in a moving world', *Mind, Culture, and Activity: An International Journal*, 20(2): 170–83, published online first at www.tandfonline.com/doi/abs/10.1080/10749039.2012.719991.

Gallagher, M. and J. Prior (2014) 'Sonic geographies: exploring phonographic methods', *Progress in Human Geography*, 38(2): 267–84.

Galloway, A. (2010) 'Locating media futures in the present: or how to map emergent associations and expectations', *Aether: the Journal of Media Geography*, 5a: 27–36.

Geertz, C. (1973) *The Interpretation of Cultures: selected essays*. New York: Basic.

Geurts, K.L. (2002) *Culture and the Senses: bodily ways of knowing in an African community*. Berkeley, CA: University of California Press.

Geurts, K.L. (2003) 'On embodied consciousness in Anlo-Ewe worlds: a cultural phenomenology of the fetal position', *Ethnography*, 4(3): 363–95.

Gibson, J. (1966) *The Senses Considered as Perceptual Systems*. Boston, MA: Houghton Mifflin.

Gibson, J. (1979) *The Ecological Approach to Visual Perception*. Boston, MA: Houghton Mifflin.

Gobo, G., J.F. Gubrium and D. Silverman (eds) *Qualitative Research Practice*. London: Sage.

Goodwin, C. (2001) 'Practices of seeing visual analysis: an ethnomethodological approach', in T. van Leeuwen and C. Jewitt (eds) *Handbook of Visual Analysis*. London: Sage.

Goody, E.N. (1989) 'Learning, apprenticeship and the division of labour', in M.W. Coy (ed.) *Apprenticeship: from theory to method and back again*. Albany: State University of New York Press, pp. 233–56.

Grasseni, C. (2004a) 'Video and ethnographic knowledge: skilled vision and the practice of breeding', in S. Pink, L. Kürti and A.I. Afonso (eds) *Working Images*. London: Routledge.

Grasseni, C. (2004b) 'Skilled visions: an apprenticeship in breeding aesthetics', *Social Anthropology*, 12: 41–55.

Grasseni, C. (2007a) 'Introduction', in C. Grasseni (ed.) *Skilled Visions*. Oxford: Berghahn.

Grasseni, C. (2007b) 'Good looking: learning to be a cattle breeder', in C. Grasseni (ed.) *Skilled Visions*. Oxford: Berghahn.

Grasseni, C. (2007c) 'Communities of practice and forms of life: towards a rehabilitation of vision', in M. Harris (ed.) *Ways of Knowing: new approaches in the anthropology of experience and learning*. Oxford: Berghahn.

Grasseni, C. (2011) 'Skilled visions: toward an ecology of visual inscriptions', in M. Banks and J. Ruby (eds) *Made to Be Seen: perspectives on the history of visual anthropology*. Chicago: University of Chicago Press.

Gray, J. (2003) 'Open spaces and dwelling places: being at home on hill farms in the Scottish Borders', in S.M. Low and D. Lawrence-Zuniga (eds) *The Anthropology of Space and Place: locating culture*. Oxford: Blackwell.

Grimshaw, A. and A. Ravetz (eds) (2005) *Visualizing Anthropology*. Bristol: Intellect.

Gunn, W. and J. Donovan (2012) 'Design anthropology: an introduction', in W. Gunn and J. Donovan (eds) *Design and Anthropology*. Farnham, UK: Ashgate.

Gunn, W., T. Otto and R.C. Smith (eds) (2013) *Design Anthropology: theory and practice*. Oxford: Bloomsbury Publishing.

Gupta, A. and J. Ferguson (1997) *Culture, Power, Place: explorations in critical anthropology*. Durham, NC: Duke University Press.

Hahn, T. (2006) '"It's the RUSH ... that's what drives you to do it": sites of the sensually extreme', *The Drama Review: the Journal of Performance Studies*, 50(2): 87–97.

Hahn, T. (2007) *Sensational Knowledge: embodying culture through Japanese dance*. Middletown, CT: Wesleyan University Press.

Halse, J. (2013) 'Ethnographies of the possible', in W. Gunn, T. Otto and R.C. Smith (eds) *Design Anthropology: theory and practice*. London: Bloomsbury.

Hand, C. (2007) 'OUTSIDEIN', in P. Domela (ed.) *Liverpool Biennial Exhibition Catalogue*. Liverpool: Liverpool Biennial of Contemporary Art Ltd.

Harper, D. (2002) 'Talking about pictures: a case for photo-elicitation', *Visual Studies*, 17(1): 13–26.

Harris, A. and M. Guillemin (2011) 'Developing sensory awareness in qualitative interviewing: a portal into the otherwise unexplored', *Qualitative Health Research*, 22(5): 689–99.

Harris, M. (2007) 'Introduction: ways of knowing', in M. Harris (ed.) *Ways of Knowing: new approaches in the anthropology of experience and learning*. Oxford: Berghahn.

Hastrup, K. (1998) 'Theatre as a site of passage: some reflections on the magic of acting', in F. Hughes Freeland (ed.) *Ritual, Performance, Media*. London: Routledge.

Hayes-Conroy, A. (2010) 'Feeling Slow Food: visceral fieldwork and empathetic research relations in the alternative food movement', *Geoforum*, 41: 734–42.

Hayes-Conroy, A. and J. Hayes-Conroy (2008) 'Taking back taste: feminism, food and visceral politics', *Gender, Place & Culture: a Journal of Feminist Geography*, 15(5): 461–73.

Hayes-Conroy, A. and J. Hayes-Conroy (2010) 'Visceral geographies: mattering, relating, and defying', *Geography Compass*, 4(9): 1273–83.

Herzfeld, M. (2001) 'Senses', in A. Robben and J.A. Sluka (eds) *Ethnographic Fieldwork*. Oxford: Blackwell Publishing.

Hindmarsh, J. and C. Heath (2003) 'Transcending the object in embodied interaction', in J. Coupland and R. Gwyn (eds) *Discourse, the Body and Identity*. London: Palgrave.

Hindmarsh, J. and A. Pilnick (2007) 'Knowing bodies at work: embodiment and ephemeral teamwork in anaesthesia', *Organization Studies*, 28(9): 1395–416.

Hine, C. (2000) *Virtual Ethnography*. London: Sage.

Hinton, D.E., V. Pich, D. Chhean and M.H. Pollard (2006) 'Olfactory-triggered panic attacks among Khmer refugees', in J. Drobnik (ed.) *The Smell Culture Reader*. Oxford: Berg.

Hjorth, L. and S. Pink (2014) 'New visualities and the digital wayfarer: reconceptualizing camera phone photography and locative media', *Mobile Media and Communication*, 2: 40–57. doi: 10.1177/2050157913505257.

Hockey, J. (2006) 'Sensing the run: the senses and distance running', *The Senses and Society*, 1(2): 183–202.

Hockey, J. and J. Allen-Collinson (2006) 'Seeing the way: visual sociology and the distance runner's perspective', *Visual Studies*, 21(1): 71–81.

Hockey, J. and J. Allen-Collinson (2009) 'The sensorium at work: the sensory phenomenology of the working body', *The Sociological Review*, 5(2): 218–39.

Hockey, J. and M. Forsey (2012) 'Ethnography is not participant observation: reflections on the interview as participatory qualitative research', in J. Skinner (ed.) *The Interview: an ethnography approach*. Oxford: Bloomsbury.

hooks, b. (1989) *Talking Back: thinking feminist, thinking black*. Boston, MA: South End Press.

Hoskins, J. (1998) *Biographical Objects: how things tell the stories of people's lives*. London: Routledge.

Howes, D. (ed.) (1991a) *The Varieties of Sensory Experience: a sourcebook in the anthropology of the senses*. Toronto, Buffalo, London: University of Toronto Press.

Howes, D. (1991b) 'Introduction: "To summon all the senses"', in D. Howes (ed.) *The Varieties of Sensory Experience: a sourcebook in the anthropology of the senses*. Toronto, Buffalo, London: University of Toronto Press, pp. 3–21.

Howes, D. (2003) *Sensing Culture: engaging the senses in culture and social theory*. Ann Arbor: University of Michigan Press.

Howes, D. (ed.) (2005a) *Empire of the Senses: the sensual culture reader*. Oxford: Berg.

Howes, D. (2005b) 'Introduction', in D. Howes (ed.) *Empire of the Senses: the sensual culture reader*. Oxford: Berg.

Howes, D. (2005c) 'HYPERESTHESIA, or, the sensual logic of late capitalism', in D. Howes (ed.) *Empire of the Senses: the sensual culture reader*. Oxford: Berg.

Howes, D. (2010a) 'Response to Sarah Pink', *Social Anthropology*, 18: 333–6.

Howes, D. (2010b) 'Response to Sarah Pink', *Social Anthropology*, 18: 338–40.

Howes, D. (2011a) 'Reply to Tim Ingold', *Social Anthropology*, 19: 318–22.

Howes, D. (2011b) 'Reply to Tim Ingold', *Social Anthropology*, 19: 328–31.

Howes, D. and C. Classen (1991) 'Conclusion: sounding sensory profiles', in D. Howes (ed.) *The Varieties of Sensory Experience: a sourcebook in the anthropology of the senses*. Toronto: University of Toronto Press, pp. 257–88.

Howes, D. and C. Classen (2014) *Ways of Sensing: understanding the senses in society*. London: Routledge.

Hurdley, R. and B. Dicks (2011) 'In-between practice: working in the "thirdspace" of sensory and multimodal methodology', *Qualitative Research*, 11(3): 277–92.

Imai, H. (2008) 'Senses on the move: multisensory encounters with street vendors in the Japanese urban alleyway roji', *The Senses and Society*, 3(3): 329–38.

Ingold, T. (2000) *The Perception of the Environment*. London: Routledge.

Ingold, T. (2007) *Lines: A Brief History*. London: Routledge.

Ingold, T. (2010) *Being Human*. London: Routledge.

Ingold, T. (2011a) 'Worlds of sense and sensing the world: a response to Sarah Pink and David Howes', *Social Anthropology*, 19: 313–17.

Ingold, T. (2011b) 'Reply to David Howes', *Social Anthropology/Anthropologie Sociale*, 19(3): 323–7.

Irving, A. (2010) 'Dangerous substances and visible evidence: tears, blood, alcohol, pills', *Visual Studies*, 25(1): 24–35.

Irving, A. (2013) 'Bridges: a new sense of scale', *The Senses and Society*, 8(3): 290–313.

Jacobson, M. (2006) 'Janet Cardiff and George Bures Miller', in C.A. Jones (ed.) *Sensorium: embodied experience, technology, and contemporary art*. London: MIT Press.

James, A., J. Hockey and A. Dawson (1997) *After Writing Culture: epistemology and praxis in contemporary anthropology*. London: Routledge.

Jhala, J. (2007) 'Emergency agents: a birthing of incipient applied visual anthropology in the "media invisible" villages of western India', in S. Pink (ed.) *Visual Interventions: applied visual anthropology*. Oxford: Berghahn.

Jones, C.A. (ed.) (2006a) *Sensorium: embodied experience, technology, and contemporary art*. London: MIT Press.

Jones, C.A. (2006b) 'Introduction', in C.A. Jones (ed.) *Sensorium: embodied experience, technology, and contemporary art*. London: MIT Press.

Jones, C.A. (2006c) 'The mediated sensorium', in C.A. Jones (ed.) *Sensorium: embodied experience, technology, and contemporary art*. London: MIT Press.

Kinsley, S. (2011) 'Anticipating ubiquitous computing: logics to forecast technological futures', *Geoforum*, 42(2): 231–40.

Korsmeyer, C. (ed.) (2005) *The Taste Culture Reader: experiencing food and drink*. Oxford: Berg.

Kozinets, R. (2010) *Netnography: doing ethnographic research online*. London: Sage.

Kress, G. and T. van Leeuwen (2001) *Multimodal Discourse: the modes and media of contemporary communication*. London: Hodder Arnold.

Kuijer, L., A. de Jong and D. van Wijk (2013) 'Practices as a unit of design: an Exploration of theoretical guidelines in a study on bathing', *Transactions on Computer–Human Interaction*, 20(4): Article no. 21.

Kulick, D. and M. Willson (eds) (1995) *Taboo: sex, identity and erotic subjectivity in anthropological fieldwork*. London: Routledge.

Lammer, C. (2004) *Making Contact* (video). Christina Lammer, MedArt/somafilm (Vienna, Austria) 20 mins. Available online: www.corporealities.org.

Lammer, C. (2007) 'Bodywork: social somatic interventions in the operating theatres of invasive radiology', in S. Pink (ed.) *Visual Interventions: applied visual anthropology*. Oxford: Berghahn.

Lammer, C. (2012) 'Healing mirrors: body arts and ethnographic methodologies', in S. Pink (ed.) *Advances in Visual Methodology*. London: Sage.

Lammer, C. (n.d.) *CORPOrealities* website: www.corporealities.org.

Lankauskas, G. (2006) 'Sensuous (re)collections: the sight and taste of socialism at Grūtas Statue Park, Lithuania', *The Senses and Society*, 1(1): 27–52.

Lapenta, F. (2011) 'Some theoretical and methodological views on photo-elicitation', in L. Pauwels and E. Margolis (eds) *The Sage Handbook of Visual Research Methods*. London: Sage, pp. 201–13.

Largey, G. and R. Watson (2006 [1972]) 'The sociology of odors', in J. Drobnick (ed.) *The Smell Culture Reader*. Oxford: Berg.

Law, L. (2005) 'Home cooking: Filipino women and geographies of the senses in Hong Kong', in D. Howes (ed.) *Empire of the Senses: the sensual culture reader*. Oxford: Berg.

Leder Mackley, K. and S. Pink (2013) 'From emplaced knowing to interdisciplinary knowledge: sensory ethnography in energy research', *The Senses and Society*, 8(3): 335–53.

Lee, J. and T. Ingold (2006) 'Fieldwork on foot: perceiving, routing, socializing', in S. Coleman and P. Collins (eds) *Locating the Field: space, place and context in anthropology*. Oxford: Berg, pp. 67–86.

Lengen, C. and T. Kistemann (2012) 'Sense of place and place identity: review of neuroscientific evidence', *Health and Place*, 18: 1162–71.

Levy, R.M., P.C. Dawson and C. Arnold (2004) 'Reconstructing traditional Inuit house forms using three-dimensional interactive computer modelling', *Visual Studies*, 19(1): 26–36.

Lindstrom, M. (2005) *Brand Sense*. London: Kogan Page.

Low, K. (2005) 'Ruminations on smell as a socio-cultural phenomenon', *Current Sociology*, 53(3): 397–417.

Lucas, R. and O. Romice (2008) 'Representing sensory experience in urban design', *Design Principles and Practices*, 2(4): 83–94.

Lund, K. (2006) 'Seeing in motion and the touching eye: walking over Scotland's mountains', in R. Bendix and D. Brenneis (Guest Editors) 'The Senses', *Etnofoor: Anthropological Journal*, 18(1): 27–42.

Lund, K. (2008) 'Listen to the sound of time: walking with saints in an Andalusian village', in T. Ingold and J. Lee Vergunst (eds) *Ways of Walking: ethnography and practice on foot* Aldershot, UK: Ashgate.

Lyon, D. (2013) 'The labour of refurbishment: the building of the body in space and time', in S. Pink, D. Tutt and A. Dainty (eds) *Ethnographic Research in the Construction Industry*. Oxford: Routledge.

Lyon, D. and L. Back (2012) 'Fishmongers in a global economy: craft and social relations on a London market', *Sociological Research Online*, 17(2): 23. Available online: www.socresonline.org.uk/17/2/23.html.

MacDougall, D. (1998) *Transcultural Cinema*. Princeton, NJ: Princeton University Press.

MacDougall, D. (2005) *The Corporeal Image: film, ethnography, and the senses*. Princeton, NJ: Princeton University Press.

MacDougall, D. and J. MacDougall (1977) *Lorang's Way* (film). Watertown, MA: Documentary Educational Resources.

Malinowski, B. (1915) *The Natives of Mailu: preliminary results of the Robert Mond research work in British New Guinea*. Adelaide: Royal Society of South Australia.

Malnar, J. and F. Vodvarka (2004) *Sensory Design*. Minneapolis: University of Minnesota Press.

Manalansan IV, M.F. (2006) 'Immigrant lives and the politics of olfaction in the global city', in J. Drobnik (ed.) *The Smell Culture Reader*. Oxford: Berg.

Marchand, T.H. (2010) 'Making knowledge: explorations of the indissoluble relation between minds, bodies, and environment', *Journal of the Royal Anthropological Institute*, 16: S1–S21.

Marks, L. (2000) *The Skin of the Film*. Durham, NC and London: Duke University Press.

Massey, D. (2005) *For Space*. London: Sage.

McLuhan, M. (2005 [1964]) *Understanding Media: the extensions of man*. New York: McGraw Hill.

McQuire, S., M. Martin and S. Niederer (2009) *Urban Screens Reader*. Amsterdam: Institute of Network Cultures.

McQuire, S., S. Pedell, M. Gibbs, F. Veter, N. Papastergiadis and J. Downs (2012) 'Public screens: from display to interaction', *International Journal of E-Planning Research*, 1(2): 23–43.

Merleau-Ponty, M. (2002 [1962]) *The Phenomenology of Perception*. London: Routledge.

Michael, M. (2012) 'De-signing the object of sociology: toward an "idiotic" methodology', *The Sociological Review*, 60(S1): 166–83.

Miller, J. (2014) 'The fourth screen: mediatization and the smartphone', *Mobile Media & Communication*, 2(2): 209–26.

Moore, P. (2003) 'Sectarian sound and cultural identity in Northern Ireland', in M. Bull and L. Back (eds) *The Auditory Culture Reader*. Oxford: Berg.

Newell, F. and L. Shams (2007) 'New insights into multisensory perception', Guest editorial in *Perception*, special issue on 'Advances in multisensory research', 36: 1415–18.

Nicolini, D., S. Gherardi and D. Yanow (eds) (2003) *Knowing in Organizations*. New York: M.E. Sharpe Inc.

Oakley, A. (2000) *Experiments in Knowing: gender and method in the social sciences*. Cambridge: Polity Press.

O'Dell, T. and R. Willim (2013) 'Transcription and the senses: cultural analysis when it entails more than words', *The Senses and Society*, 8(3): 314–34.

Okely, J. (1994) 'Vicarious and sensory knowledge of chronology and change: ageing in rural France', in K. Hastrup and P. Hervik (eds) *Social Experience and Anthropological Knowledge*. London: Routledge.

Okely, J. (1996) *Own or Other Culture*. London: Routledge.

Orobitg, G. (2004) 'Photography in the field: word and image in ethnographic research', in S. Pink, L. Kürti and A. Afonso (eds) *Working Images*. London: Routledge.

O'Neill, M. (2008) 'Transnational refugees: the transformative role of art?', *Forum Qualitative Sozialforschung/Forum: Qualitative Social Research*, 9(2). Available online: www.qualitative-research.net/index.php/fqs/article/view/403/873 (accessed 14 November 2008).

O'Neill, M. (2012) 'Ethnomimesis and participatory art', in S. Pink (ed.) *Advances in Visual Methodology*' London: Sage.

O'Reilly, K. (2005) *Ethnographic Methods*. London: Routledge.

Pallasmaa, J. (2005 [1999]) 'Lived space: embodied experience and sensory thought', in *Encounters: Architectural Essays*. Hämeenlinna, Finland: Rakennustieto Oy.

Palombini, C. (n.d.) 'Steven Feld on *Rainforest Soundwalks*'. Available online: http://cec.sonus.ca/econtact/Soundwalk/Feld.html (accessed 9 October 2014).

Petrini, C. (2001) *Slow Food: the case for taste*. New York: Columbia University Press.

Petrini, C. (2007) *Slow Food Nation: why our food should be good, clean and fair*. New York: Rizzoli Ex Libris.

Pickering, M. (2008) 'Experience and the social world', in M. Pickering (ed.) *Research Methods in Cultural Studies*. Edinburgh: Edinburgh University Press.

Pink, S. (2004) *Home Truths: gender, domestic objects and everyday life*. Oxford: Berg.

Pink, S. (2005a) 'Applications of anthropology', in S. Pink (ed.) *Applications of Anthropology: professional anthropology in the twenty-first century*. Oxford: Berghahn.

Pink, S. (2005b) 'Dirty laundry: everyday practice, sensory engagement and the constitution of identity', *Social Anthropology*, 13(3): 275–90.

Pink, S. (2006) *The Future of Visual Anthropology: engaging the senses*. Oxford: Routledge.

Pink, S. (2007a) *Doing Visual Ethnography*, second edition. London: Sage.

Pink, S. (2007b) 'Sensing Cittàslow: slow living and the constitution of the sensory city', *The Senses and Society*, 2(1): 59–77.

Pink, S. (2007c) 'The sensory home as a site of consumption: everyday laundry practices and the production of gender', in E. Casey and L. Martens (eds) *Gender and Consumption: material culture and the commercialisation of everyday life*. Aldershot: Ashgate.

Pink, S. (2007d) 'Walking with video', *Visual Studies*, 22(3): 240–52.

Pink, S. (2007e) 'Applied visual anthropology: social intervention and visual methodologies', in S. Pink (ed.) *Visual Interventions: applied visual anthropology*. Oxford: Berghahn.

Pink, S. (2008a) 'Sense and sustainability: the case of the Slow City movement', *Local Environment*, 13(2): 95–106.

Pink, S. (2008b) 'An urban tour: the sensory sociality of ethnographic place-making', *Ethnography*, 9(2): 175–96.

Pink, S. (2008c) 'Analysing visual experience', in M. Pickering (ed.) *Research Methods in Cultural Studies*. Edinburgh: Edinburgh University Press.

Pink, S. (2008d) 'Re-thinking contemporary activism: from community to emplaced sociality', *Ethnos*, 73(2): 163–88.

Pink, S. (2008e) 'Mobilising visual ethnography: making routes, making place and making images', *Forum Qualitative Sozialforschung/Forum: Qualitative Social Research*, 9(3). Available online: www.qualitative-research.net/index.php/fqs/article/view/1166 (accessed 11 November 2014).

Pink, S. (2010a) 'Response to David Howes', *Social Anthropology*, 18: 336–8.

Pink, S. (2010b) 'The future of sensory anthropology/the anthropology of the senses', *Social Anthropology*, 18: 331–3.

Pink, S. (2011a) 'From embodiment to emplacement: re-thinking bodies, senses and spatialities', *Sport, Education and Society (SES)*, special issue on 'New directions, new questions: social theory, education and embodiment', 16(34): 343–55.

Pink, S. (2011b) 'Sensory digital photography: re-thinking "moving" and the image', *Visual Studies*, 26(1): 4–13.

Pink, S. (2012) *Situating Everyday Life: practices and places*. London: Sage.

Pink, S. (2013) *Doing Visual Ethnography*, third edition. London: Sage.

Pink, S. (2014) 'Digital–visual–sensory-design anthropology: ethnography, imagination and intervention', *Arts and Humanities in Higher Education*, 13(4): 412–27.

Pink, S. (2015) 'Approaching media through the senses: between experience and representation', *Media International Australia*, 254.

Pink, S. and L. Hjorth (2012) 'Emplaced cartographies: reconceptualising camera phone practices in an age of locative media', *MIA (Media International Australia)*, no. 145.

Pink, S. and K. Leder Mackley (2013) 'Saturated and situated: rethinking media in everyday life', *Media, Culture and Society*, 35(6): 677–91. doi: 10.1177/0163443713491298.

Pink, S. and K. Leder Mackley (2014) 'Reenactment methodologies for everyday life research: art therapy insights for video ethnography', *Visual Studies*, 29(2): 146–54.

Pink, S. and T. Lewis (2014) 'Making resilience: everyday affect and global affiliation in Australian Slow Cities', *Cultural Geographies*, 21(4): 695–710.

Pink, S. and J. Morgan (2013) 'Short term ethnography: intense routes to knowing', *Symbolic Interaction*, 36(3): 351–61.

Pink, S. and L. Servon (2013) 'Sensory global towns: an experiential approach to the growth of the Slow City movement', *Environment and Planning A*, 45(2): 451–66.

Pink, S. Kürti, L. and A.I. Afonso (eds) (2004) *Working Images*. London: Psychology Press.

Pink, S., K. Leder Mackley, V. Mitchell, C. Escobar-Tello, M. Hanratty, T. Bhamra and R. Morosanu (2013) 'Applying the lens of sensory ethnography to sustainable HCI', *Transactions on Computer-Human Interaction* 20(4): Article no. 25. Available online: http://dl.acm.org/citation.cfm?doid=2494261.

Pink, S., J. Morgan and A. Dainty (2014) 'Safety in movement: mobile workers, mobile media', *Mobile Media and Communication*, 2(3): 335–51.

Plummer, K. (2001) 'The call of life stories in ethnographic research', in P. Atkinson, A. Coffey, S. Delamont, J. Lofland and L. Lofland (eds) *Handbook of Ethnography*. London: Sage.

Porcello, T., L. Meintjes, A.M. Ochoa and D. Samuels (2010) 'The reorganization of the sensory world', *Annual Review of Anthropology*, 39: 51–66.

Porteous, D. (1990) *Landscapes of the Mind: worlds of sense and metaphor*. Toronto: University of Toronto Press.

Postill, J. and S. Pink (2012) 'Social media ethnography: the digital researcher in a messy web', *MIA (Media International Australia)*, no. 145.

Rapley, T. (2004) 'Interviews', in C. Seale, G. Gobo, J.F. Gubrium and D. Silverman (eds) *Qualitative Research Practice*. London: Sage.

Rapport, N. (2012) 'The interview as a form of talking-partnership: dialectical, focused, ambiguous, special', in J. Skinner (ed.) *The Interview: an ethnography approach*. Oxford: Bloomsbury.

Ravetz, A. (2007) '"A weight of meaninglessness about which there is nothing insignificant": abjection and knowing in an art school and on a housing estate', in M. Harris (ed.) *Ways of Knowing? New anthropological approaches to method, learning and knowledge.* Oxford: Berghahn.

Ravetz, A. (2011) '"Both created and discovered": the case for reverie and play in a redrawn anthropology', in T. Ingold (ed.) *Redrawing Anthropology: materials, movements, lines.* Farnham, UK: Ashgate.

Rawes, P. (2008) 'Sonic envelopes', *The Senses and Society*, 3(1): 61–76.

Rice, T. (2005) 'Getting a sense of listening', *Critique of Anthropology*, 25(2): 199–206.

Rice, T. (2006) *Stethoscapes: listening to hearts in a London hospital.* PhD thesis, Goldsmiths College, University of London.

Rice, T. (2008) '"Beautiful murmurs": stethoscopic listening and acoustic objectification', *The Senses and Society*, 3(3): 293–306.

Richardson, I. (2010) 'Faces, interfaces, screens: relational ontologies of framing, attention and distraction', *Transformations*, Issue no. 18, 'The face and technology'. Available online: www.transformationsjournal.org/journal/issue_18/article_05.shtml.

Richardson, I. (2011) 'The hybrid ontology of mobile gaming', *Convergence: the International Journal of Research into New Media Technologies*, 17(4): 419–30.

Robben, A.C.G.M. (2007) 'Sensorial fieldwork', in A.C.G.M. Robben and J.A. Sluka (eds) *Ethnographic Fieldwork: an anthropological reader.* Oxford: Blackwell.

Rodaway, P. (1994) *Sensuous Geographies: body, sense and place.* London: Routledge.

Ronzon, F. (2007) 'Icons and transvestites: notes on irony, cognition and visual skill', in C. Grasseni (ed.) *Skilled Visions.* Oxford: Berghahn.

Roseman, M. (2005) 'Engaging the spirits of modernity: Teimar songs of a changing world', in D. Howes (ed.) *Empire of the Senses: the sensual culture reader.* Oxford: Berg.

Rubin, H.J. and I.S. Rubin (2005) *Qualitative Interviewing: the art of hearing data* (revised second edition). London: Sage.

Schneider, A. (2008) 'Three modes of experimentation with art and ethnography', *JRAI*, 14(1): 171–94.

Schneider, A. and C. Wright (2006) 'The culture of practice', in A. Schneider and C. Wright (eds) *Contemporary Art and Anthropology.* Oxford: Berg.

Schneider, A. and C. Wright (2013) *Anthropology and Art Practice.* Oxford: Bloomsbury.

Schweitzer, P.B. (2000) 'Introduction', in P.B. Schweitzer (ed.) *Dividends of Kinship.* London: Routledge.

Seale, C. (1998) 'Qualitative interviewing', in C. Seale (ed.) *Researching Society and Culture.* London: Sage.

Seremetakis, C.N. (1994) 'The memory of the senses: historical perception, commensal exchange, and modernity', in L. Taylor (ed.) *Visualizing Theory.* London: Routledge.

Sherman Heyl, B. (2001) 'Ethnographic interviewing', in P. Atkinson, A. Coffey, S. Delamont, J. Lofland and L. Lofland (eds) *Handbook of Ethnography.* London: Sage.

Shilling, C. (1991) *The Body and Social Theory.* London: Sage.

Shilling, C. (2003) *The Body and Social Theory*, second edition. London: Sage.

Shimojo, S. and L. Shams (2001) 'Sensory modalities are not separate modalities: plasticity and interactions', *Current Opinion in Neurobiology*, 11(4): 505–9.

Silberg, S. (2013) *Places in the Making: how placemaking builds places and communities.* MIT. Available online: http://dusp.mit.edu/cdd/project/placemaking.

Simmel, G. (1997 [1907]) D. Frisby and M. Featherstone (eds) *Simmel on Culture: selected writings.* London: Sage.

Skinner, J. (2012) *The Interview: an ethnographic approach*. Oxford: Bloomsbury.
Spinney, J. (2006) 'A place of sense: a kinaesthetic ethnography of cyclists on Mont Ventoux', *Environment and Planning D: Society and Space*, 24(5): 709–32.
Spinney, J. (2007) 'Cycling the city: non-place and the sensory construction of meaning in a mobile practice', in D. Horton, P. Cox and P. Rosen (eds) *Cycling and Society*. Aldershot: Ashgate.
Spinney, J. (2008) 'Cycling the city: meaning, movement and practice', PhD thesis, Royal Holloway College, University of London.
Stafford, B.M. (2006) *Echo Objects: the cognitive work of images*. Chicago, IL: University of Chicago Press.
Stevenson, A. (2013) 'Dog team walking: inter-corporeal identities, blindness and reciprocal guiding', *Disability & Society*, 28(8): 1162–7.
Stoller, P. (1989) *The Taste of Ethnographic Things: the senses in ethnography*. Philadelphia: University of Pennsylvania Press.
Stoller, P. (1994) '"Conscious" ain't consciousness: entering "the museum of sensory absence"', in N. Seremetakis (ed.) *The Senses Still: Perception and Memory as Material Culture in Modernity*. Boulder, CO: Westview Press.
Stoller, P. (1997) *Sensuous Scholarship*. Philadelphia: University of Pennsylvania Press.
Stoller, P. (2004) 'Sensuous ethnography, African persuasions, and social knowledge', *Qualitative Inquiry*, 10(6): 817–35.
Strang, V. (2005) 'Common senses: water, sensory experience and the generation of meaning', *Journal of Material Culture*, 10: 92–120.
Sunderland, N., H. Bristed, O. Gudes, J. Boddy and M. DaSilva (2012) 'What does it feel like to live here? Exploring sensory ethnography as a collaborative methodology for investigating social determinants of health in place', *Health and Place*, 18: 1056–67.
Sutton, D. (2001) *Remembrance of Repasts*. Oxford: Berg.
Sutton, D. (2006) 'Cooking skill, the senses, and memory: the fate of practical knowledge', in E. Edwards, C. Gosden and R.B. Phillips (eds) *Sensible Objects*. Oxford: Berg.
Sutton, D. (2010) 'Food and the senses', *Annual Review of Anthropology*, 39: 209–23.
Tolia-Kelly, D.P. (2007) 'Fear in paradise: the affective registers of the English Lake District landscape re-visited', *Senses and Society*, 2(3): 329–51.
Thrift, N. (2004) 'Movement-space: the changing domain of thinking resulting from the development of new kinds of spatial awareness', *Economy and Society*, 33(4): 582–604.
Thrift, N. (2006) 'Space', *Theory, Culture and Society*, 23(2–3): 139–55.
Throop, J. (2003) 'Articulating experience', *Anthropological Theory*, 3(2): 219–41.
Tilley, C. (2006) 'The sensory dimensions of gardening', *The Senses and Society*, 1(3): 311–30.
Tromp, N. and P. Hekkert (2012) 'Designing behaviour', in W. Gunn and J. Donovan (eds) *Design and Anthropology*. Farnham, UK: Ashgate.
Tuan, Yi-Fu (1977) *Space and Place: the perspective of experience*. Minneapolis: University of Minnesota Press.
Tuan, Yi-Fu (1993) *Passing Strange and Wonderful: aesthetics, nature, and culture*. Washington, DC: Island Press, Shearwater Books.
Turnbull, C. (1961) *The Forest People*. New York: Simon Schuster.
Turner, V. (1986) 'Dewey, Dilthey and drama: an essay in the anthropology of experience', in V. Turner and E. Brunner (eds) *The Anthropology of Experience*. Urbana: University of Illinois Press.

Tuzin, D. (2006) 'Base notes: odor, breath and moral contagion in Ilahita', in J. Drobnick (ed.) *The Smell Culture Reader*. Oxford: Berg.

Vannini, P., D. Waskul and S. Gottschalk (2012) *The Senses in Self, Society, and Culture: a sociology of the senses*. Oxford: Routledge.

Vergunst, J. (2008) 'Taking a trip and taking care in everyday life', in T. Ingold and J. Lee Vergunst (eds) *Ways of Walking: ethnography and practice on foot*. Aldershot: Ashgate.

Vokes, R. (2007) '(Re)constructing the field through sound: actor-networks, ethnographic representation and "radio elicitation" in south-western Uganda', in E. Hallam and T. Ingold (eds) *Creativity and Cultural Improvisation*. Oxford: Berg.

Walmsley, E. (2006) 'Race, place, taste: making identities through sensory experience', in R. Bendix and D. Brenneis (Guest Editors) 'The Senses', *Etnofoor: Anthropological Journal*, 18(1): 43–60.

Warren, S. (2008) 'Empirical challenges in organizational aesthetics research: towards a sensual methodology', *Organization Studies*, 29(4): 559–80.

Wenger, E. (1998) *Communities of Practice: learning, meaning, and identity*. Cambridge: Cambridge University Press.

Willerslev, R. (2007) '"To have the world at a distance": reconsidering the significance of vision for social anthropology', in C. Grasseni (ed.) *Skilled Visions*. Oxford: Berghahn.

Witmore, C. (2004) 'Four archaeological engagements with place: mediating bodily experience through peripatetic video', *Visual Anthropology Review*, 20(2): 57–71.

Wulff, H. (2012) 'Instances of inspiration: interviewing dancers and writers', in J. Skinner (ed.) *The Interview: an ethnography approach*. Oxford: Bloomsbury.

Young, D. and J. Goulet (eds) (1994) *Being Changed by Cross-cultural Encounters: the anthropology of extraordinary experiences*. Ontario, Canada: University of Toronto Press.

Zardini, M. (2005) *Sense of the City: an alternate approach to urbanism*. Baden, Switzerland: Lars Müller Publishers.

Zomerdijk, L.G. and C.A. Voss (2010) 'Service design for experience-centric services', *Journal of Service Research*, 13(1): 67–82.

Index

Bibliographical information in the 'Recommended further reading' sections is indicated by a page number followed by 'bib'.